Mobile DevOps Playbook

A practical guide for delivering high-quality mobile applications like a pro

Moataz Nabil

BIRMINGHAM—MUMBAI

Mobile DevOps Playbook

Group Product Manager: Preet Ahuja
Publishing Product Manager: Vidhi Vashisth
Book Project Manager: Ashwin Kharwa
Senior Editor: Divya Vijayan
Technical Editor: Arjun Varma
Copy Editor: Safis Editing
Proofreader: Safis Editing
Indexer: Subalakshmi Govindhan
Production Designer: Aparna Bhagat
DevRel Marketing Coordinator: Rohan Dobhal

First published: September 2023

Production reference: 2060923

Published by Packt Publishing Ltd.
Grosvenor House
11 St Paul's Square
Birmingham
B3 1RB

ISBN 978-1-80324-255-2

www.packtpub.com

I want to express my heartfelt gratitude to my wonderful wife, Basma, who has been by my side throughout this long journey. Her unwavering support has meant the world to me, especially during the challenging moments. I am also immensely grateful to my beloved daughter, Malak, whose presence has constantly motivated me to strive and set a positive example.

Additionally, I would like to sincerely thank my parents, Mr. Nabil and Mrs. Hadaya, sincerely. They have been a source of inspiration, always encouraging me to pursue greatness and never give up, regardless of the obstacles that may come my way.

To Basma, Malak, Mr. Nabil, and Mrs. Hadaya, your love, support, and encouragement have been invaluable to me. I deeply appreciate all you have done and continue to do for me.

– Moataz Nabil

Contributors

About the author

Moataz Nabil is a highly skilled Developer Advocate and Test Automation Consultant who excels in cultivating meaningful connections with developers and clients. With over 12 years of experience in software development and testing, Moataz has successfully led and managed test automation teams, focusing on designing, developing, and maintaining automated testing solutions for various software products. As a respected speaker, Moataz has shared his expertise at numerous global developer events and conferences.

In the past, Moataz has held positions at prominent companies such as Bitrise, Delivery Hero, and Zalando SE. In addition to his primary role, Moataz is an AWS Community Builder and a valued member of the DevNetwork and Packt Advisory Board.

About the reviewer

Eslam Mohammed Anwar is a distinguished Staff DevOps Engineer boasting over a decade of experience. A fervent advocate for efficient practices and cost-effective solutions, he has redefined the art of building native mobile CI/CD pipelines.

I'd like to thank my family, who understand the time and commitment it takes to research and test data that is constantly changing.

Sergey Akentev began his journey in development as a backend engineer in 2016. With a profound passion for automation and mobile, he shifted his focus to Mobile DevOps in 2020, mastering build and release engineering and mobile-specific CI/CD for both apps and SDKs. He evaluates the whole process on a large scale, always with a keen focus on the customer, whether they are a teammate or an end user. Sergey is determined to deliver results, driving the highest standards and diving deep to innovate. His solutions have automated the workflows of hundreds of engineers and currently serve millions of end users.

Table of Contents

Part 1: Introduction to Mobile DevOps

1

2

3

Mobile DevOps Fundamentals 49

Part 2: Implementing the Mobile DevOps Environment

4

Achieving Continuous Integration and Delivery with Mobile DevOps 67

Part 3: Monitoring, Optimizing, and Securing Mobile DevOps

7

8

9

Mobile DevOps Best Practices   293

Part 4: Moving Beyond Mobile DevOps and the Future of DevOps

10

Improving Productivity with Developer Experience and Platform Engineering   319

Preface

Hello there! *Mobile DevOps Playbook* is a practical guide to building, testing, releasing, monitoring, and managing mobile applications. As you learn how companies use Mobile DevOps methodologies to improve collaboration between development, testing, releasing, and operations teams, you can deliver features, bug fixes, and updates to mobile applications more quickly and efficiently.

It's a step-by-step guide to understanding mobile DevOps concepts, processes, and use cases from development to release, as well as predicting how mobile DevOps will evolve in the future, including new technologies and tools that are necessary.

This book is an invaluable resource for developers who want to stay up to date on the rapidly changing mobile app development landscape. This book provides a comprehensive overview of the mobile development process, covering the different architectures, platforms, and technologies available to developers. It also offers useful advice on how to manage the software development life cycle effectively and use DevOps to ensure successful, high-quality releases. Mobile DevOps is a must-have resource for developers looking to stay ahead of the curve.

By learning about mobile DevOps, developers can save time, reduce errors, and ensure applications are optimized for the best user experience. Additionally, understanding the principles of mobile DevOps can help developers create more efficient and effective mobile applications, as they will have greater insight into the process of developing, testing, and deploying applications.

The mobile DevOps book includes a comprehensive overview of mobile development and DevOps principles, an in-depth look at the tools and techniques used to manage mobile app development, practical advice on how to successfully deploy and maintain mobile applications, and tips for streamlining the mobile DevOps process. Additionally, the book includes a variety of case studies to illustrate best practices and provide real-world examples.

I will provide relevant information and guide you through some elements of mobile DevOps based on my experience and knowledge from the past few years in the mobile DevOps domain.

After reading this book, you will be able to implement mobile DevOps in your company and decide which tools or approaches are useful for your team. You will also learn how to use mobile DevOps to help your team when the business is scaling and growing.

Who this book is for

The book will focus on the stages of the mobile DevOps process and implementation and is intended for everyone involved in mobile development. The primary target audience is engineers and first-line engineering management who are interested in DevOps. Furthermore, the audience includes CTOs, DevOps engineers, mobile developers, IT enterprise architects, mobile release managers, mobile architects, mobile platform engineers, QA engineers, and release engineers at all levels who will be able to implement the prescribed solutions. A basic understanding of DevOps concepts and practices is necessary to gain maximum benefit from this book.

The reader of this book is likely to already have some familiarity with DevOps and mobile app challenges and know the pain of testing, releasing, and monitoring mobile apps, especially at scale.

What this book covers

Chapter 1, Resolving Challenges in Mobile DevOps, provides an introduction to mobile DevOps. We will delve into the world of mobile app development and explore how mobile-first features can contribute to the more efficient and faster testing, building, and releasing of mobile apps.

Chapter 2, Understanding the Mobile Ecosystem, explores the mobile ecosystem and its crucial role in developing successful mobile apps. It covers essential components such as hardware, software, operating systems, networks, and services. Topics include challenges, mobile DevOps, mobile OSes/frameworks/platforms, app functionalities, and mobile app architecture.

Chapter 3, Mobile DevOps Fundamentals, explores the fundamentals of Mobile DevOps and its role in enabling fast and effective mobile app development. Topics covered include Mobile DevOps principles, implementing mobile **continuous integration/continuous delivery (CI/CD)**, the stages of Mobile DevOps, choosing between self-hosted and cloud-based CI/CD, the Mobile Release Train concept, a checklist for app releases, and the need for a Mobile DevOps engineer.

Chapter 4, Achieving Continuous Integration and Delivery with Mobile DevOps, explores the implementation of CD for mobile apps using Mobile DevOps. It covers selecting a CI/CD provider, establishing a tailored CI/CD pipeline, and setting up effective build and unit tests for mobile apps.

Chapter 5, Implementing a Robust Mobile App Testing Strategy, examines the implementation of a robust mobile app testing strategy to ensure high-quality apps. Topics covered include mobile app testing introduction, test automation, creating a testing strategy, different types of mobile testing, continuous testing with Mobile DevOps, testing tools and frameworks, using AI for app quality, achieving test coverage, and improving mobile testing skills.

Chapter 6, Mobile App Release Management, focuses on the essential stage of mobile app release management, covering challenges, CI/CD implementation, compliance with app store guidelines, release and distribution, beta testing, app store submission, ASO, and monitoring progress.

Chapter 7, Establishing Mobile App Monitoring, Observability, and Analytics, explains the significance of monitoring and observability for mobile apps. It covers establishing effective practices, key metrics for app monitoring, choosing the right tool, and implementing continuous monitoring.

Chapter 8, Keeping Mobile Apps and DevOps Secure, discusses the significance of mobile app security in the DevOps context. It covers topics such as the importance of security in mobile development, introducing mobile DevSecOps, mobile app security threats, secure app architecture, mobile security testing methods and tools, starting the mobile DevSecOps journey, and tips for security automation in mobile DevOps.

Chapter 9, Mobile DevOps Best Practices, focuses on leveraging mobile DevOps for faster and higher-quality app development. Topics covered include CI/CD best practices, version and release management, **Infrastructure as Code** (**IaC**), configuration management, A/B testing, caching, parallel execution, fastlane automation, API mocking, and ChatOps collaboration.

Chapter 10, Improving Productivity with Developer Experience and Platform Engineering, explores the concepts of **Developer Experience** (**DX**) and **Internal Developer Productivity** (**IDP**) teams, emphasizing their importance in mobile development. It highlights the relationship between Mobile DevOps and DX teams, introduces platform engineering principles, and distinguishes it from DevOps and SRE engineering.

Chapter 11, Predicting the Future of Mobile DevOps, discusses future trends in mobile app development and mobile DevOps. It provides insights into upcoming advancements and recaps *Mobile DevOps Playbook*.

To get the most out of this book

It is essential to have an understanding of mobile app development, including the development life cycle, coding practices, and mobile platform considerations. Familiarity with agile methodologies and **CI/CD** principles is also crucial. Additionally, a working knowledge of mobile app testing and release management processes will be beneficial.

I assume readers have a basic understanding of mobile development concepts, DevOps principles, and the tools and technologies commonly used in the field.

The best way to ensure an understanding of the process and the steps required is to implement the mobile DevOps framework in your company or team after reading this book.

Software/hardware covered in the book	Operating system requirements
Java +8	Windows, macOS, or Linux (Ubuntu)
Node.js and npm	Windows. macOS and Linux
Xcode	macOS
Android Studio	Windows, MacOS and Linux

Software/hardware covered in the book	Operating system requirements
Git	Windows, MacOS and Linux
React Native	Windows, MacOS and Linux
Flutter	Windows, MacOS and Linux
Apple Developer account	MacOS
Google Play Store account	Windows, MacOS and Linux

If you are using the digital version of this book, we advise you to type the code yourself or access the code from the book's GitHub repository (a link is available in the next section). Doing so will help you avoid any potential errors related to the copying and pasting of code.

Download the example code files

You can download the example code files for this book from GitHub at `https://github.com/PacktPublishing/Mobile-DevOps-Playbook`. If there's an update to the code, it will be updated in the GitHub repository.

We also have other code bundles from our rich catalog of books and videos available at `https://github.com/PacktPublishing/`. Check them out!

Conventions used

There are a number of text conventions used throughout this book.

`Code in text`: Indicates code words in text, database table names, folder names, filenames, file extensions, pathnames, dummy URLs, user input, and Twitter handles. Here is an example: It is not necessary to call `sleep()` repeatedly in your tests. Maestro waits for the content to load automatically (but not too long) when this process takes a long time.

When we wish to draw your attention to a particular part of a code block, the relevant lines or items are set in bold:

```
[default]
exten => s,1,Dial(Zap/1|30)
exten => s,2,Voicemail(u100)
exten => s,102,Voicemail(b100)
exten => i,1,Voicemail(s0)
```

Any command-line input or output is written as follows:

```
wget --quiet https://github.com/TestArmada/flank/releases/download/
v22.05.0/flank.jar -O /usr/local/bin/flank.jar
java -jar /usr/local/bin/flank.jar firebase test android run
```

Bold: Indicates a new term, an important word, or words that you see onscreen. For instance, words in menus or dialog boxes appear in **bold**. Here is an example: "Select **System info** from the **Administration** panel."

> **Tips or important notes**
> Appear like this.

Get in touch

Feedback from our readers is always welcome.

General feedback: If you have questions about any aspect of this book, email us at customercare@ packtpub.com and mention the book title in the subject of your message.

Errata: Although we have taken every care to ensure the accuracy of our content, mistakes do happen. If you have found a mistake in this book, we would be grateful if you would report this to us. Please visit www.packtpub.com/support/errata and fill in the form.

Piracy: If you come across any illegal copies of our works in any form on the internet, we would be grateful if you would provide us with the location address or website name. Please contact us at copyright@packt.com with a link to the material.

If you are interested in becoming an author: If there is a topic that you have expertise in and you are interested in either writing or contributing to a book, please visit authors.packtpub.com.

Share Your Thoughts

Once you've read *Mobile DevOps Playbook*, we'd love to hear your thoughts! Scan the QR code below to go straight to the Amazon review page for this book and share your feedback.

https://packt.link/r/1803242558

Your review is important to us and the tech community and will help us make sure we're delivering excellent quality content.

Download a free PDF copy of this book

Thanks for purchasing this book!

Do you like to read on the go but are unable to carry your print books everywhere? Is your eBook purchase not compatible with the device of your choice?

Don't worry, now with every Packt book you get a DRM-free PDF version of that book at no cost.

Read anywhere, any place, on any device. Search, copy, and paste code from your favorite technical books directly into your application.

The perks don't stop there, you can get exclusive access to discounts, newsletters, and great free content in your inbox daily

Follow these simple steps to get the benefits:

1. Scan the QR code or visit the link below

https://packt.link/free-ebook/9781803242552

2. Submit your proof of purchase
1. That's it! We'll send your free PDF and other benefits to your email directly

Part 1: Introduction to Mobile DevOps

Building mobile apps at scale requires mobile-first features that help you build, test, and deploy apps faster and more efficiently. The challenges due to the nature of mobile, native iOS and Android development, cross-platform frameworks, and scaling architecture in large teams are numerous and can prolong the release process. In this part, we will learn about Mobile DevOps and why it's important, as well as understanding the mobile ecosystem and how to set up a successful Mobile DevOps environment.

This part has the following chapters:

- *Chapter 1, Resolving Challenges in Mobile DevOps*
- *Chapter 2, Understanding the Mobile Ecosystem*
- *Chapter 3, Mobile DevOps Fundamentals*

1

Resolving Challenges in Mobile DevOps

Release times for mobile apps can be extended due to their nature. Mobile-first features help you test, build, and release them more efficiently and quickly.

To ensure Mobile DevOps is successful, it is imperative for development, operations, and QA teams to collaborate closely. Establish clear lines of communication to ensure everyone is on the same page.

Due to this, in this chapter, we're going to cover the following main topics:

- The importance of mobile apps
- Understanding Mobile DevOps
- How does Agile work in Mobile DevOps?
- Transforming Mobile DevOps effectively
- How to accelerate Mobile DevOps in your organization
- Team roles and responsibilities for Mobile DevOps
- Large-scale mobile app development challenges

The importance of mobile apps

Every day, digital transformation gains traction. Consumers today demand better products and services and businesses need to adopt technologies to stay competitive. This will enable them to be more efficient and to make better decisions.

In addition, there is room for innovation that meets customer needs. All of this requires integration, continuous development, innovation, and deployment. It is all possible with Mobile DevOps.

In particular, mobile app development is becoming more challenging and complicated every day. Today, we rely on mobile apps to accomplish a number of tasks, including online shopping, online payments, money transfers, medical consultations, e-learning, social sharing, and so much more.

With all of these activities, customers expect mobile apps to perform better, have a friendly user interface, be customizable, and multilingual, and have more advanced features, with a small footprint.

When your mobile app launches with bugs, it is very difficult, if not impossible, to maintain and recover it. The process of finding the root cause, preparing a new release, testing it, and releasing the hotfix again requires a lot of effort on the part of the team. You may need to wait weeks or months for that to happen. As a result, your customers **will** leave negative reviews on the App Stores during this time.

"To maximize customer satisfaction and value, you must examine your processes and tooling and identify opportunities for improvement."

But the question is, can your current workflow or setup support your mobile app in the long run? What about the future? Is your team able to cope with the scale? What happens if the business and the team grow? Last but not least, is your team satisfied with the tasks they perform on a daily basis?

Mobile teams focus on handling increasingly challenging tasks. Because of this focus, it is all too easy to miss the process altogether. Mobile developers will spend less time fixing bugs if they stop and check their work regularly (a DevOps process).

Challenges lie ahead

Smartphone usage is growing worldwide. **In 2025, there are expected to be 7.49 billion smartphone users worldwide, up from 7.26 billion in 2022.** More details can be found at this link: `https://shorturl.at/vCQ13`.

By 2026, it is estimated that the worldwide spending on premium apps, in-app purchases, and subscriptions will reach $233 billion across Apple's App Store and Google Play, which is 77 percent above the $132 billion spent in 2021 by consumers.

Additionally, it is expected that over the next 5 years, the gross revenue on both app stores will continue to rise at a rate of 12 percent at a **compound annual growth rate (CAGR)** of 19 percent, reaching $233 billion in 2026. More details can be found at this link: `https://sensortower.com/blog/sensor-tower-app-market-forecast-2026`.

Wow, that's a lot! There is no doubt that all businesses need to prepare for the next wave, be aware of their challenges, put together a plan for the next wave, and not mention the opportunity to grow and improve.

In mobile development, every business has the following:

- Unique processes
- Unique investments and goals
- Unique people and culture

Here's an example

Fintech apps play a huge role in our everyday activities. Individuals can use these apps to manage their finances and make financial decisions, and they often offer personalized recommendations and insights using advanced technology such as artificial intelligence and machine learning.

Whether in e-commerce, food/groceries delivery, or digital banking, fintech is becoming an integral part of our personal and professional lives.

In the digital age, fintech has already made a significant impact, and these advanced technological tools for both private and marketable finance will only evolve further in their usage and effectiveness.

Mobile apps of this type require different processes from other apps. They need an effective test automation strategy including security testing since security is very important here, app performance is also important, and releasing frequently and quickly is a high priority due to competition or customer satisfaction.

On the other hand, if we are creating a social media app, the requirements and processes will differ.

Because of this, I believe that there is **no silver bullet** and each team or company should come up with its own solutions.

Let me tell you a story

In order to understand the importance of Mobile DevOps, let me share with you a real-world scenario that occurred before we had any processes, technologies, or stack in place for Mobile DevOps.

Suppose that we are working at XYZ, a fintech company, and the process of developing and releasing mobile apps could be faster and more efficient. Before an app can be released, the development team spends weeks or even months building and testing new features, and the QA team finds bugs that needed to be fixed manually because they don't have test automation scripts. Because of this, new versions of the app are rarely released, and when they are, they often have issues that need to be fixed later.

The current challenges can be summarized as follows:

- **Our new features are released every 3 months**: This is a huge factor because we have to keep up with competitors and release new features as quickly as possible.

- **Our deployment process is chaotic and painful** because we don't have a clear deployment process or release manager.

- **The Continuous Integration (CI) pipelines or workflows are inflexible and fragile** and our team spends a great deal of time and effort dealing with daily issues related to the CI server and configuration, as well as network issues and device issues.

- **There are a lot of problems associated with manual testing**, including them being time-consuming and effort-consuming. Additionally, UI tests as well as emulators may not work well if we have automated tests, which drives us to have flaky tests.
- **There are no security testing tools available to us** and we have no idea which tools to use for security testing.

It was frustrating for the management team to see the slow rate of app development and the many issues with it. Despite knowing it needed to improve the way it developed and released mobile apps, it didn't know where to begin. Previously, the team released every **3 months**, and the first goal was to reduce the release cycle to **1 month or 2 weeks (a weekly or bi-weekly release cadence)**.

In order to improve its mobile app development process, the company adopted **Mobile DevOps** practices. It started a collaboration process between its mobile development and QA teams on the principles of Mobile DevOps, including CI, continuous delivery, and continuous deployment.

Mobile DevOps = faster releases

With Mobile DevOps, the company was able to significantly improve the speed and reliability of its mobile app development process. The mobile development team was able to make small, frequent updates to the app, and the QA team was able to quickly identify and fix any issues that arose.

As a result, the company was able to release new versions of the app more frequently, with fewer issues.

The management team was pleased with the results of the Mobile DevOps implementation, and the more stable and frequently updated apps led to significant improvements in user satisfaction. As a result, the company was able to deliver high-quality apps to users more quickly and efficiently than before.

But was it easy? No, it required a change in the team's mindset and the involvement of all the team members to achieve success.

Is this something that takes a short amount of time? No, it's a journey that never ends, a process that's always evolving to address the challenges of developing mobile apps.

Considering my point of view, I believe the following:

"Mobile DevOps is a journey, not a destination."

Now that we have addressed most of the main challenges that mobile teams face on a daily basis, let's learn why we need to consider a process such as Mobile DevOps.

Why does Mobile DevOps matter?

Mobile DevOps enables teams to release new features, updates, and bug fixes at a faster pace. This agility helps meet evolving user demands and gain a competitive edge in the market. It ensures higher app quality with automated testing and continuous monitoring by reducing the number of bugs and issues reaching end users, which leads to improved user experience and customer satisfaction.

It also promotes collaboration and communication between developers, testers, and operations teams. This collaborative environment facilitates knowledge sharing, feedback exchange, and a culture of teamwork and collective ownership.

During the previous short story, we encountered different challenges that hindered our progress such as the following:

- Inflexible and fragile development environment
- The QA team takes a long time to approve the new release
- Releasing a new version of the app takes a long time
- We don't have a clear process or responsibilities for the releases

It then realized Mobile DevOps processes could help it resolve all of these issues because of the benefits of Mobile DevOps, including the following:

- Solving problems and delivering results faster
- Your business will be more agile as a result
- Building trust and collaboration
- Innovation results from automation
- Costs and risks are significantly reduced
- Focusing on customer satisfaction
- Faster feedback and time to market
- Improved ability to build the right solution
- Better product quality
- More reliable releases
- Improved productivity

Mobile DevOps processes can help businesses solve problems faster, become more agile, build trust and collaboration, reduce costs and risks, focus on customer satisfaction, and improve product quality, reliability, productivity, and the time to market.

This will be a quick introduction to Mobile DevOps since we will go into it further in *Chapter 3, Mobile DevOps Fundamentals*.

Understanding Mobile DevOps

Mobile DevOps is a set of practices that speeds up the development and delivery of mobile apps. The approach combines the principles of DevOps, which emphasize collaboration and automation in software development, with the specific challenges and considerations of developing mobile applications.

Mobile DevOps involves the following:

- **Collaboration and communication**: Mobile DevOps requires close collaboration and communication between development, operations, and QA teams. It is important to establish clear lines of communication and channels for feedback and collaboration to ensure that everyone is working together toward the same goals.

- **Continuous integration, deployment, and delivery**: Mobile DevOps relies on automated processes for the CI and delivery of mobile apps. This means that code changes are automatically built, tested, and deployed to staging and production environments, without the need for manual intervention.

- **Testing and quality assurance**: Testing and quality assurance are critical components of Mobile DevOps. Automated testing tools and processes should be integrated into the development workflow to ensure that new code changes do not introduce bugs or regressions.

- **Monitoring and feedback**: Mobile DevOps also involves monitoring the performance and usage of mobile apps in production environments, and using that data to provide feedback to development teams. This can help identify and resolve issues quickly and improve the overall user experience.

- **Tooling and technology**: To implement Mobile DevOps effectively, organizations need to invest in the right tools and technologies. This may include tools for CI and delivery, automated testing, monitoring, and feedback.

For the Mobile DevOps approach to be as effective as possible, you should also integrate security throughout the entire life cycle of the mobile app releases. The Mobile DevOps approach integrates security into the process from the start, with security becoming a shared responsibility. It is called "DevSecOps" because all DevOps initiatives must be based on a secure foundation.

DevOps versus Mobile DevOps

Almost every company now uses DevOps to build, test, and deliver their backend services (APIs), websites, or infrastructure.

In the context of mobile engineering, Mobile DevOps is a variant of DevOps that focuses on the ability to rapidly deliver high-quality apps to the market, through faster iteration cycles and improved collaboration between the mobile development, operation and QA teams. A key goal of Mobile DevOps and DevOps is to promote fast, high-quality software delivery by automating, collaborating, and communicating between teams.

During the Mobile DevOps life cycle, a slightly different approach is taken. There is a change made to the steps, but the continuity symbol remains the same to deliver value apps frequently to customers, maintain quality, and monitor the applications' health in real time. An updated mobile development life cycle would likely include **continuous integration/continuous delivery (CI/CD)** strategies, builds, tests, releases, monitoring, and measurement.

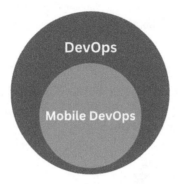

Figure 1.1 – Mobile DevOps versus DevOps

Mobile DevOps extends the principles of DevOps to mobile app development, emphasizing collaboration and automation throughout the development life cycle. Because of fostering collaboration between developers, testers, and operations teams, I'm using the preceding figure. It's the same practices but, for mobile, they're unique and include different challenges.

The focus

DevOps focuses on different types of software or applications such as websites, and backend services, but Mobile DevOps is specifically focused on mobile applications.

The complexity

The wide range of device types, OS versions, and network conditions that mobile applications must support often makes their deployment environments more complex and varied than those of traditional software or applications.

How does Agile work in Mobile DevOps?

Since we have already spent so much time describing the differences between the Waterfall model and Agile in different books, articles, and videos, I don't want to spend more time describing the Waterfall model. However, let me ask you a question: **can a Waterfall model be used with DevOps, or is Agile more appropriate?**

You can find the answer if you take the advantages of Mobile DevOps (listed previously) and the challenges in Mobile App Development (listed previously) and apply them to the Waterfall Model and Agile.

If you're still confused, remember the Agile Manifesto at the following link: `https://agilemanifesto.org/`.

What's the answer now? I can help you, but first, let's recall the Waterfall model and identify the problems.

The Waterfall model

The Waterfall model is a **linear** approach to software development that involves a sequential and linear flow from one phase to the next in a downward direction. Therefore, each phase must be completed in its entirety before the next phase can begin.

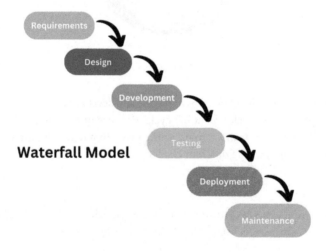

Figure 1.2 – The Waterfall model

The phases in the Waterfall model are as follows:

- **Gathering and analyzing requirements**: This phase involves identifying the problem that the software will solve, determining the requirements for the software, and creating a specification.

- **Design**: A detailed technical design of the software is created, as well as interfaces between various components, and a plan for implementing the software is constructed.

- **Implementation**: In this phase, the actual coding of the software takes place. The code is created based on the previous phase's design.

- **Testing**: In this phase, software testing is performed to ensure that the software meets the specifications in the specification document and performs as intended.

- **Deployment**: During this phase, the software is deployed to its target environments, such as production servers or mobile devices.

- **Maintenance**: As part of the maintenance phase, any bugs or issues found in the software are fixed, new features or functionality are added, and the software's performance is improved.

There are some drawbacks to the Waterfall model. It assumes that the requirements for the software can be gathered and analyzed upfront, which may not always be possible. Furthermore, it assumes that the software is designed correctly and completely, which may not always be the case. As a final note, once the development process has moved on, no changes can be made to the software.

Is Waterfall a viable model for Mobile DevOps? In practice, no, because Mobile DevOps involves CI, continuous testing, continuous deployment, and continuous monitoring changes are normal and phases are not silos or isolated islands. In Mobile DevOps, all the cross-functional teams work together in one process, with one goal and one objective, which is to deliver mobile apps quickly, frequently, and at a high level of quality in order to satisfy customers.

Agile

In contrast, the agile methodology is regarded as the direct successor to the waterfall methodology. It is a set of principles that emphasizes **collaboration, flexibility, and rapid iteration** in software development. This is a system that is built on the Agile Manifesto, which outlines a set of values and principles that are critical to delivering high-quality software within a short time frame.

Often, Agile is implemented using Agile methodologies such as **Scrum**, in which team members communicate and provide feedback to each other in short development cycles (called sprints).

In the Agile Principles (`https://agilemanifesto.org/principles.html`) behind the Agile Manifesto, we can find the **first** principle is as follows:

> *"Our highest priority is to satisfy the customer through early and continuous delivery of valuable software."*

Do you remember the benefits of Mobile DevOps? **Customer stratification** and **frequent delivery** of mobile apps. Due to this, the Agile Principle with Mobile DevOps aims to speed up the development and delivery of mobile apps using a CI, continuous delivery, and continuous deployment strategy, enabling teams to release mobile applications rapidly and reliably.

There is a strong emphasis in both Mobile DevOps and Agile on **collaboration and communication between teams,** and both emphasize the **importance of automating repetitive tasks** in order to generate high-quality software products as quickly and efficiently as possible. Both also emphasize the **importance of delivering high-quality software products as quickly and as efficiently as possible**.

Agile emphasizes short development cycles, while DevOps emphasizes continuous delivery.

Plan
Design
Code & Test
Release
Feedback

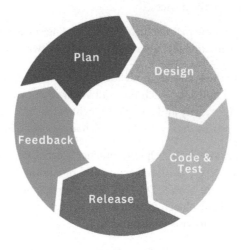

Figure 1.3 – Agile methodology

Achieving maximum velocity with minimal risks is the goal – you need to experiment, test, and turn every stone in order not to fall behind customer demands or crash your current structure in the process. It is not important to prevent failure, but rather to recover quickly. The only thing that matters is how fast you recover.

Mobile DevOps stages

Like DevOps, Mobile DevOps has different stages for mobile apps from planning to monitoring, including all the practices that help the mobile team to deliver qualitative mobile apps smoothly, quickly, and frequently.

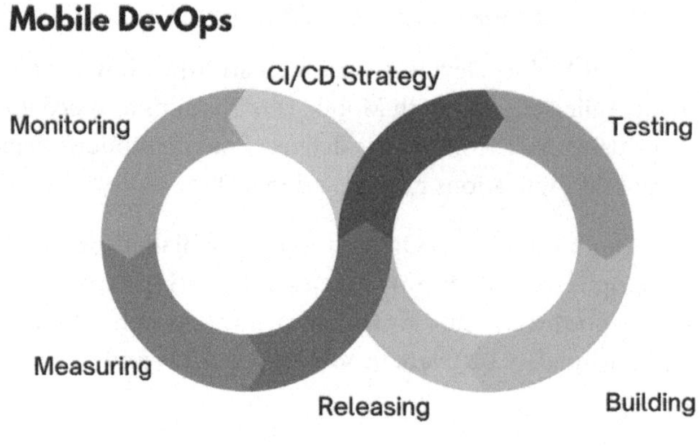

Mobile DevOps
CI/CD Strategy
Monitoring
Testing
Measuring
Releasing
Building

Figure 1.4 – Mobile DevOps stages

- **Strategy and planning**: This involves identifying the goals and objectives of the mobile app, as well as the target audience and any specific requirements or constraints.

- **Development**: In this stage, the mobile app is developed using agile methodologies and CI/CD practices. This includes writing code, building and testing the app, and integrating any required APIs or services.

- **Testing**: Mobile app testing is an important part of the DevOps process to ensure the app is stable and performs well on different devices and operating systems. This can include unit testing, integration testing, and user acceptance testing.

- **Releasing**: Once the app is tested and ready for release, it can be released to the appropriate app store or distribution platform.

- **Monitoring**: After the app is deployed, it is important to monitor its performance and address any issues that arise. This can include crash reporting, error tracking, network request analysis, memory leakage, and app performance.

This was a quick introduction to the stages but in *Chapter 3*, *Mobile DevOps Fundamentals*, we will deep dive into all of them, and in the rest of the chapters, we'll explore each one separately with real examples and use cases.

Having gained an understanding of the differences between DevOps and Mobile DevOps and the strong relationship between Agile and Mobile DevOps and seen the different stages of Mobile DevOps, let's see how we can transform our team or organization successfully and effectively to Mobile DevOps.

Transforming Mobile DevOps effectively

The success of a Mobile DevOps transformation and CI/CD implementation can be tracked using KPIs, which are measurable values. The effectiveness of your mobile CI/CD efforts can be tracked by setting specific, quantifiable KPIs and monitoring their progress regularly.

In order to drive a mobile CI/CD transformation, the following KPIs can be used:

- **The deployment frequency** determines how often new code changes are deployed to production. An efficient and successful CI/CD process involves a high deployment frequency.

- **Mean time to restore or recover (MTTR)** measures how quickly an organization can resume operations after an outage. CI/CD processes with a low MTTR show that they are robust and capable of detecting and resolving issues quickly. Mobile apps may have a few challenges because once our apps are released, they will be hard to measure, but in general, we can apply the measurement to other services mobile apps use.

- **Defect density**: How many bugs are being found in production? A low number of bugs indicates that the CI/CD process is thorough and effective at identifying and fixing issues.

- **User satisfaction**: Is the mobile app well received by users? A good indicator of app quality is user satisfaction. If your app is rated poorly or has negative feedback in the app stores, this can indicate that your quality and release processes need to be revisited.

- **Measure developer satisfaction** with the tools, processes, and support they receive while building and maintaining the company's products. To save money, companies often build their own tools, but developers may not be satisfied with them, and the company should know if developers are satisfied. This is an extremely important issue. On a scale from 0 to 10, companies ask their internal developers to rate the likelihood that they would recommend the company's development environment to a colleague. Based on this data, improvements can be made to the development environment to better support internal developers' needs.

We can also measure DevOps and Mobile DevOps performance and productivity using a variety of metrics, such as the MODAS survey (`https://shorturl.at/beAX1`) from Bitrise and the DORA metrics (`https://cloud.google.com/devops/`) from Google.

ROI of Mobile DevOps

Return on investment (**ROI**) is a measure of an investment's efficiency. The ROI from Mobile DevOps can be calculated by determining the costs of implementing the approach and comparing them to the benefits gained.

You would first need to determine the costs associated with implementing the Mobile DevOps approach for mobile app development, including any training or certification costs for your team, any tools or technologies that will be used, and any other associated costs. Using this information, you can calculate the total cost of implementing Mobile DevOps.

The next step is to determine the benefits of using Mobile DevOps, such as increased efficiency, improved collaboration and communication between team members, and faster deployment and release cycles. In order to measure these benefits, you can conduct surveys as we mentioned previously (developer satisfaction), analyze project performance data, and compare the results to those of similar projects that did not utilize DevOps.

In order to calculate the ROI of Mobile DevOps, you will need to determine the costs and benefits:

ROI = (Benefits - Costs) / Costs

How to accelerate Mobile DevOps in your organization

Mobile DevOps is a collaborative effort involving a team, mindset, and commitment as well as a process and toolset.

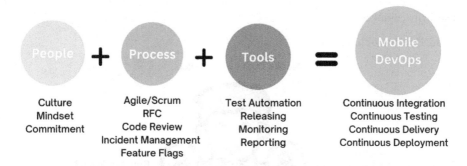

Figure 1.5 – Mobile DevOps considerations

In order to accelerate the Mobile DevOps process and success, the team should consider the following considerations and best practices:

- Ensure that version control is robust so that merging conflicts and lost work are minimized
- Build automation (CI/CD) so you can focus on creating rather than managing complex pipelines
- Test frequently and automate to respond to feedback (shift-left testing)
- Manage your mobile apps' artifacts to release them where they belong
- Be sure to keep your security in mind
- Make a small start and grow intelligently from there
- Creating is about designing and developing
- Perform app monitoring and status checking continuously

Team roles and responsibilities for Mobile DevOps

As we discussed previously, Mobile DevOps involves a cross-functional team, and each role has unique responsibilities, such as CI/CD pipelines, cloud architecture, security compliance, and on-call (incident management). Each of them completes the other. Assuming the team follows a squads-and-tribes approach, maybe a dedicated and centralized team can handle Mobile DevOps practices and processes as follows:

- A release manager
- Mobile engineering managers
- Quality assurance engineers
- A DevOps engineer
- Mobile engineers

- A security engineer
- Cloud/DevOps architecture

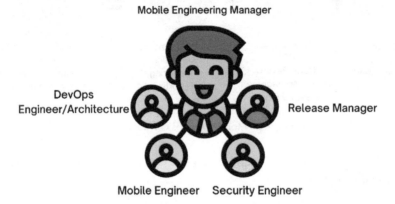

Figure 1.6 – Mobile DevOps team

This approach or setup can help enterprise companies scale their teams and business effectively.

In medium-sized or small teams, the mobile developers with the DevOps engineers can do the same job but this might require time and effort from them, so it always depends on the goal of Mobile DevOps.

Large-scale mobile app development challenges

Aside from the unique nature of mobile apps, there are many challenges to be faced when developing them. Among the most common challenges are the following:

- **Integrating multiple platforms to create a seamless user experience**: Mobile applications often need to be developed for multiple platforms, such as iOS and Android. This can create additional complexity in terms of testing, deployment, and maintenance.

- **Monorepos and multiple repositories**: When working on large-scale projects, coordination and version control become challenging.

- **Adapting the app to different devices and operating systems**: Emulators and simulators can be useful for testing, but they can't replicate the full range of experiences and issues that users may encounter on real devices. This can make it difficult to ensure the quality and reliability of mobile applications.

- **Assuring the app is secure and meets security and data privacy requirements**: Mobile applications often handle sensitive data, such as personal information and financial transactions. This requires careful management of the security and privacy risks.

- **Staying up to date with mobile app trends and technology**: In order to develop mobile apps, you need a unique toolset that is constantly evolving. With ever-growing market demands, there are always new technologies for building, deploying, and monitoring performance.

- **Ensuring continuous delivery and deployment**: Mobile applications need to be updated frequently to fix bugs, add new features, and improve performance. This requires a robust DevOps process that can handle multiple releases per day.

- **Integrating with APIs**: Mobile applications often rely on external APIs for features such as location tracking, and data storage. These APIs can be prone to change or downtime, which can impact the stability of the mobile application.

As we mentioned in the Mobile DevOps fundamentals previously, since every business has unique investments, goals, and processes, as well as unique processes and goals, developing mobile applications can be a challenge. Here are a few examples of different kinds of mobile apps that we have, and each needs to be explored briefly in order to better understand their purpose.

In light of all of these challenges, there are different kinds of mobile app companies that can develop.

Super apps

A super app is a mobile application that offers a wide variety of services. A few examples of these services include ride-hailing, food delivery, online shopping, and financial services. A super app provides users with a one-stop shop for all their needs, allowing them to access multiple services without having to download and use multiple separate apps.

Asia is a popular region for super apps because they increase user engagement and revenue for companies that offer them:

- Gojek (`https://www.gojek.com/en-id/`) – An Indonesian super app that allows users to use a wide range of services, such as messaging and payment processing

- Grab (`https://www.grab.com/sg/`) – An on-demand app that offers food delivery, payments, and other services

- Paytm (`https://paytm.com/`) – A popular Indian e-wallet and payment app that offers features such as shopping and investing, as well as booking tickets for travel, movies, and events

- LINE (`https://line.me/en/`) – A Japanese messaging app that also allows you to make payments and book hotel rooms

By providing convenience to users, super apps can enable them to access a variety of services without having to switch between multiple apps. Business owners can generate new revenue and reach new customers through super apps.

White-label apps

The white-label version of an app bears the logo and name of the company that is reselling it, rather than the name of the original developer who created it in the first place. Typically, these apps are customized to meet the specific needs of the company and are then resold to other businesses or clients in order to generate revenue for the company.

As a result, they are recommended as a way for companies to offer their customers a customizable app solution instead of having to invest the time and resources needed to develop an app from scratch, thereby increasing their customers' satisfaction.

E-commerce is a common example of white-label applications, in which businesses can purchase preexisting software and customize it with their own branding, products, and prices, such as Shopify (`https://www.shopify.com/`). This allows them to quickly and easily launch their own online store without having to build a platform from scratch.

Additionally, white-label apps are used in healthcare, education, and government. White-label apps, for instance, are used by healthcare providers to schedule and track patients' treatments, while schools use them to grade and track students' progress.

Using white-label apps has several benefits, including the following:

- An app that is developed from the ground up can be expensive and time-consuming. Apps with white labels are more affordable and efficient.
- Due to their pre-existing nature, white-label apps can be implemented and launched more quickly than custom-built ones.

Here are a few examples of white-label mobile apps:

- Branded and customized food delivery apps for local restaurant chains
- Hotel or resort-branded booking and reservation apps
- Customized and branded ticketing and event management software for concert and sports venues

Furthermore, developing an app that the target audience will find valuable and engaging, as well as optimizing the app's features, can be challenging.

Mobile teams can tackle these challenges by implementing best practices such as CI/CD and automated testing. Additionally, they can use tools such as mobile device clouds and test automation frameworks to streamline their processes and improve their mobile applications.

Let's summarize:

Since mobile app development is unique, DevOps should also be unique.

Summary

The concept of Mobile DevOps entails integrating development and operations (DevOps) practices to improve the efficiency and speed of mobile application development. To accomplish this, we use mobile-first features to test, build, and release mobile apps more quickly, as well as implement continuous integration, testing, deployment, delivery, and monitoring of mobile apps.

An effective Mobile DevOps process also involves collaboration and communication between the development, operations, and quality assurance teams, as well as the use of the right tools and technologies to achieve the desired results. To remain competitive and meet customer demands for high-quality mobile apps, businesses should adopt Mobile DevOps.

Make sure you don't copy someone else's process if you find it online. Develop a strategy and plan that suits the needs of your stakeholders and team members. Establish a standard process for your Mobile DevOps best practices upfront.

Our journey toward Mobile DevOps has just begun, and in the next chapters, we will explore more and learn how to effectively use Mobile DevOps.

2

Understanding the Mobile Ecosystem

The mobile ecosystem of an app encompasses all the elements it requires to function correctly on a mobile device, including the hardware, software, operating system, network, and services that make it work. To successfully implement Mobile DevOps and meet the needs of your customers, it is imperative to understand the mobile ecosystem in order to know the challenges and how to overcome them to deliver successful mobile applications.

In this chapter, we will cover the following topics:

- Mobile apps are like icebergs
- The greatest things about mobile apps
- The different mobile OSs, frameworks, and platforms in the market
- Mobile app functionalities such as monetization, push notifications, state management, deep linking, and more
- Mobile app architecture

Mobile apps are like icebergs

In my opinion, a mobile app is similar to an *iceberg*, in that there is an apparent part (**the user interface or UI**) and an unseen part (**the code and functionalities underneath the UI**). Even though the end user is the only one to see the finished product, this analogy often illustrates the amount of effort, complexity, and work involved in building and maintaining a mobile application, as shown in the following screenshot:

Figure 2.1 – A mobile app is an iceberg

When a user, for instance, downloads an app and begins using it for the first time, all they see is its interface, features, and functionalities. The user is unable to see much of what is going on behind the scenes, but it is much more important than they realize. A mobile application is connected to servers, databases, and APIs that allow it to communicate with other apps and devices, retrieve data, transmit data, and perform a variety of tasks.

A **mobile app** is, in its simplest sense, a piece of software that is designed to run on a certain platform (such as Android or iOS). Because of this, it requires a great deal of coding to be developed. As shown in *Figure 2.2*, it consists of a variety of programming languages, frameworks, libraries, and tools that are used to develop the app's functionality and features:

Figure 2.2 – Mobile app development

In addition to the technical aspects of a mobile app, a lot of work goes into its planning, design, testing, and releasing phases as well. Wireframes, prototypes, and user flows must be developed and user tests conducted to ensure the app is intuitive, user-friendly, and performs well.

Now that we've explored the foundations of mobile app development, let's shift our focus to the challenges that most mobile development teams face to build great apps.

What makes mobile apps great?

In order to make a great mobile app, it needs to have a straightforward and intuitive UI that is easy to use but it is different from a web app, for the following reasons (as also shown in *Figure 2.3*):

- It's more critical
- The platform is fragmented
- The tools change frequently

- It iterates rapidly:

Figure 2.3 – A mobile app is unique

Based on the nature and complexity of mobile apps, there are a few things to consider when looking at what makes mobile apps great, as follows:

- Mobile apps help users to solve problems or fulfill their needs, and they need to be well designed and reliable, with a range of useful features and functions

- They should be fast, responsive, and able to handle a variety of platforms and devices flawlessly without crashing or lagging

- It is important for mobile apps to be compatible with a wide range of devices and platforms so that as many users as possible are able to take advantage of them

- They are designed to protect sensitive data and prevent unauthorized access to it

- They need to be updated regularly with new features and improvements in order to keep users interested and ensure that they remain relevant in the future

Since we now understand the importance of mobile apps, let's now take a closer look at the platforms and frameworks that are available today on the market and what needs to be considered when we implement Mobile DevOps processes and practices.

Mobile platforms and frameworks available today

As of writing this book, there are a lot of different mobile platforms on the market these days, both **native** and **cross-platform**, so let's take a quick look at the differences between them to give you a better understanding of what we need to consider when thinking about Mobile DevOps.

> **Note**
>
> I do not want to make this a detailed explanation of mobile development because this is a book about Mobile DevOps and there are tons of books about mobile development. However, as we mentioned previously, we should be in a position to interpret the requirements of different platforms and then implement the DevOps process accordingly.

As a starting point, let's take a look at native apps such as iOS and Android.

iOS

As we know, **iOS** is the operating system that runs on iPhones and iPads. Now, we have the iPadOS for iPads. It is well known that iOS is compatible with other Apple products besides its user-friendly interface, integration with other Apple products, and the vast selection of apps that are available through the App Store. While I am writing this book, the latest version of iOS is version *16*.

When developing, testing, and releasing iOS apps, it is imperative that you always have the latest version of macOS with the latest SDKs and tools to meet the app requirements, which can be a big challenge when it comes to mobile CI/CD, because if you want to build and release iOS apps, then you need to always be on the latest.

To avoid wasting developer time setting up and maintaining infrastructure for our mobile CI/CD platform, we should always look for a platform that is ready to use. We will dive deep into how we can choose a suitable CI/CD provider for our team in *Chapter 4, Achieving Continuous Integration and Delivery with Mobile DevOps.*

New features available with iOS 16

In September 2022, Apple released its new operating system, *iOS 16*. This version of the iOS operating system was announced at Apple's *WWDC22* conference (`https://developer.apple.com/videos/wwdc2022/`). iOS consists of features and performance improvements that are available on a wide range of devices, such as the following:

- **New Lock Screen**: You can now create complications for Apple Watch and widgets for the iPhone Lock Screen using WidgetKit, extending the glanceable experience and embracing SwiftUI

- **Tap to Pay on iPhone**: With Apple Pay, Apple Watch, and other digital wallets on iPhone, payment apps can now accept contactless payments through contactless credit and debit cards

- **SwiftCharts** is a powerful and concise SwiftUI framework for transforming your data into informative visualizations

- **Maps in 3D**: Experience the highly detailed 3D city experience on the all-new map

- **App Intents** will provide your users with the ability to perform quick tasks by only speaking or tapping your app

- Improved in-app purchase experiences with new APIs and enhancements

- Use **live text** in videos and apps to perform simple tasks such as copying and pasting

All of these come with new features and enhancements in security, accessibility, and privacy to help developers build secure and rich iOS apps. All the details can be found here: `https://www.apple.com/ios/ios-16/features/`.

In addition to mentioning the new features here, I also want to stress the fact that we have different challenges in UI testing of these features, such as UI testing of widgets and charts as well as Lock Screens, and that's why we always need to think bigger when it comes to what the next challenge might be.

Just be prepared for a new version of iOS to be released during the time you are reading this book.

Besides the preceding features in iOS 16, Apple also released the latest version of **Xcode**, which is *15* (`https://apps.apple.com/us/app/xcode/id497799835?mt=12/`) while writing the book, the main developer IDE to develop iOS, tvOS, iPadOS, watchOS, or macOS apps. The Xcode binary is 30% smaller than before, so you can start faster than ever. With downloadable simulator runtimes for watchOS and tvOS, Xcode gives developers access to the latest platforms at their fingertips. And one of the important features is configuring a multiplatform app with a single app target. Let's learn more about what a multiplatform app is.

Configuring a multiplatform app

With a multiplatform app (`https://developer.apple.com/documentation/xcode/configuring-a-multiplatform-app-target`), you can share your app's project settings and code across platforms with the use of a multiplatform target, as shown in *Figure 2.4*, which will allow you to expand the experience of your app across multiple platforms supported by the app:

Figure 2.4 – Multiplatform target

> **Note**
>
> watchOS apps remain on a separate target, despite the fact that iOS, iPadOS, macOS, and tvOS apps can share one target. More information can be found here: `https://developer.apple.com/documentation/Xcode/configuring-a-multiplatform-app-target`.

We should take this into consideration when designing the CI/CD pipeline since we need to consider the **code signing** mechanism, **certificates**, and **provision profiles** for each target, as well as the steps that must be taken when archiving or building the application for testing.

Android

The **Android** (`https://www.android.com/`) operating system is an open source platform developed by Google for smartphones and tablets. This operating system, based on the Linux kernel, is primarily intended for mobile devices but it has also been implemented in watches, TVs, cars, and other equipments. There are many reasons why Android is so popular, including the ability to customize your device, and the wide selection of apps available through the Google Play Store.

As an alternative version of the Android operating system, there is **Android Go** (`https://www.android.com/versions/go-edition/`), which is designed to run smoothly on *low-spec* smartphones and tablets that have *limited resources*. With a *lighter* version of the Google Play Store, Google apps, and a wide range of apps optimized for low-end devices, it is designed to run smoothly on entry-level smartphones and tablets with limited resources.

The main objective of Android Go is to provide a smooth user experience that is reliable and easy to use for users with limited resources.

> **Note**
>
> You can learn more about how to develop an app for Android Go here:
>
> `https://developer.android.com/guide/topics/androidgo/develop`

New features available with Android 13

Likewise, iOS always has the latest version of Android, including new features and enhancements to existing ones. Let's explore a few of them together:

- As part of Android 13, Material You (`https://material.io/blog/announcing-material-you`) is incorporated into the operating system's look and style. By customizing non-Google apps, you can make your home screen more cohesive and unique by matching the theme and colors you have chosen.

- When you copy sensitive information such as your email address, phone number, or username and password, Android automatically clears your clipboard history after a period of time.

- It's even easier to multitask on your tablet now that Android 13 is available.

> **Note**
>
> And there's much more—you can find details of all the new features at the following link: `https://www.android.com/android-13/#a13-highlights`. You can check all releases and versions at the following link: `https://developer.android.com/about/versions`.

In terms of CI/CD, Android can be built on various operating systems such as macOS, Windows, or Linux, but in order to build Android apps, you'll need to have the SDKs and tools for Android, such as **Gradle**, which is the official and main tool for Android app development.

Next, let's examine the applications that can run on multiple platforms or cross-platform applications.

Flutter

Flutter (`https://flutter.dev/`) is a framework for developing mobile apps founded by Google. The Flutter platform enables developers to create mobile applications for Android and iOS that are highly responsive, visually appealing, and high performing, as well as desktop applications for macOS and Windows, web applications, and embedded applications, all from a single source of code (`https://flutter.dev/multi-platform/`).

As a result, Flutter is an ecosystem where you can build six apps from a single code base. As shown in *Figure 2.5*, with Flutter you can build web, mobile embedded apps, and desktop apps(Windows, macOS, and Linux):

Figure 2.5 – Flutter multiplatform

Flutter uses the **Dart** programming language (`https://dart.dev/`) and features a reactive programming model, allowing for smooth and seamless app interactions. It also includes a wide range of customizable widgets and tools for building UIs, as well as access to native device features such as camera and storage.

Flutter is an excellent tool to help you build web applications such as **progressive web apps** (**PWAs**) and extend your existing mobile apps to the web, but the web itself is a flexible platform.

It is challenging to think about the CI/CD pipeline when it comes to Flutter because each app requires specific tools and pre-requests when it comes to releasing it. Since Flutter has iOS apps, it also requires macOS machines with the latest tools and SDKs as well. For instance, with the Flutter SDK, Linux requires different tools in addition to the Flutter SDK, and for sure with Windows, you will need to have the Windows OS in order to build the app.

React Native

The **React Native** framework (`https://reactnative.dev/`) is one of Facebook's most popular frameworks since it allows developers to build native-like apps using JavaScript and the React library. React Native uses declarative programming and includes a large set of components and tools for creating high-performance applications. At this link, you can explore who is using React Native, such as Shopify, Microsoft, Facebook (Meta), and more: `https://reactnative.dev/showcase`. As shown in *Figure 2.6*, you can build iOS and Android apps from one single code base with React Native and JavaScript:

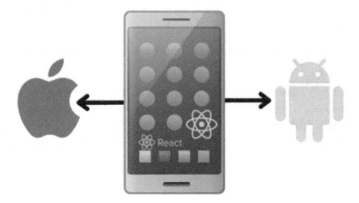

Figure 2.6 – React Native framework

A new version of React Native, 0.72.4 (`https://github.com/facebook/react-native/releases`), has been announced by the React Native team recently. Several improvements come with this version, including a new unified configuration for CodeGen, as well as CMake support for Android builds, and new documentation for the new architecture.

Additionally, they announced a new architecture because the old architecture had several challenges, including the following:

- Data being submitted *asynchronously* to the bridge and then asynchronously *waiting* for it to be processed by the other layer

- Since JS was single-threaded, all computations in that world happened in that thread

- It was decided that JSON would be the best format for simplicity and human readability, but it did impose some overhead as every time one layer had to use the other, it had to serialize some data

In spite of this, there will be several benefits associated with the new architecture, such as the following:

- The execution of *synchronous* functions is now possible. In the past, these functions were asynchronous.

- The new architecture does not have to serialize or deserialize data anymore, so there is no serialization tax to pay.

- By using C++, it is now possible to abstract all the *platform-agnostic* code and to share it easily between platforms.

- A layer of code automatically generated from one or more JavaScript specifications is included to ensure JavaScript can invoke C++ methods and vice versa.

> **Note**
>
> Read more about the new architecture at this link:
>
> `https://reactnative.dev/docs/next/the-new-architecture/why`

There's one more enhancement in the build time: from **React Native 0.71** onward, you will be able to consume prebuilt artifacts coming from **Maven Central**, which can be consumed from Android. As a result, the new architecture (`https://github.com/reactwg/react-native-new-architecture/discussions/105`) has seen massive improvements in build time.

Last but not least, **Shopify** (`https://www.shopify.com/`) announced recently that its whole mobile app had been migrated over to React Native.

> **Note**
> The following link explains in detail why Shopify did it, how it got there, and what the company gained from it: `https://shopify.engineering/migrating-our-largest-Mobile-app-to-React-Native`.

Ionic

Ionic offers integrations with major frameworks, including **Angular**, **React**, and **Vue**, to provide high-quality, performant mobile apps using web technologies. Ionic Framework (`https://ionicframework.com/docs/`) has a complete UI toolkit for building high-quality, performant mobile apps, as shown in the following screenshot:

Figure 2.7 – Ionic Framework

For developers who are building mobile apps, the advantage of using Ionic is that it offers a wide variety of pre-designed UI components and layouts so that they can easily develop apps that are user-friendly and visually appealing. In addition, Ionic has an active and large community that offers a variety of plugins and resources to extend its functionality in a wide range of ways.

A native app for Ionic Framework can be distributed via app stores and run on mobile devices as well since Ionic apps are usually deployed as native apps. As well as offering tools and services for developing PWAs, which are web applications that work offline like native applications and can be installed as native applications on a device.

Ionic has **Capacitor** (`https://capacitorjs.com/`), an open source cross-platform app runtime that allows web-based apps to run natively on iOS and Android. It's helpful to refer to these apps as native **PWAs**, as they represent the next evolution beyond the traditional hybrid app mentality, as shown in *Figure 2.8*:

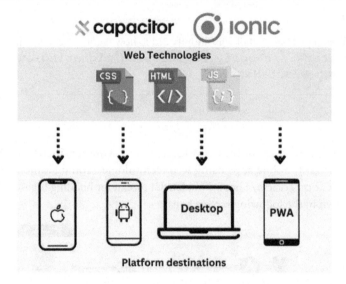

Figure 2.8 – Ionic and Capacitor

For Ionic CI/CD, **Appflow** (`https://ionic.io/appflow`) allows teams to build apps with hybrid mobile architectures, including Cordova, Capacitor, and React Native apps. Don't worry—in *Chapter 4, Achieving Continuous Integration and Delivery with Mobile DevOps*, we will learn more about Appflow and how to use it with Ionic apps.

Cordova

The **Cordova** framework (`https://cordova.apache.org/`) allows you to develop cross-platform applications using standard web technologies such as HTML5, CSS3, and JavaScript, as shown in *Figure 2.9*.

> **Note**
>
> More information can be found at this link:
>
> `http://cordova.apache.org/docs/en/11.x/guide/overview/index.html`

Each platform is targeted with its own wrapper, which provides access to sensors, data, network status, and so on, using standards-compliant API bindings:

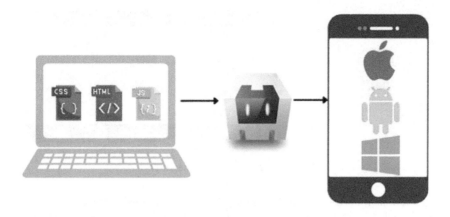

Figure 2.9 – Cordova framework

Apache Cordova can be used if you want to do the following:

- Extend your mobile application across multiple platforms; you don't have to re-implement it with each platform's language and tools

- Develop an app for distribution in app stores by packaging it for web deployment

As part of the Cordova community, a variety of plugins have also been developed to extend the features of Cordova apps, such as accessing native device features such as the camera, GPS, and accelerometer through Cordova plugins.

> **Note**
>
> At this link, you can find a comparison between Cordova and Capacitor from Ionic:
>
> `https://ionic.io/enterprise-guide/capacitor-vs-cordova`

Xamarin

In the **Xamarin** framework (`https://dotnet.microsoft.com/en-us/apps/xamarin`), developers are able to write code in C# and share it across multiple platforms by using platform-specific APIs to access native features and capabilities of the platform, as shown in *Figure 2.10*:

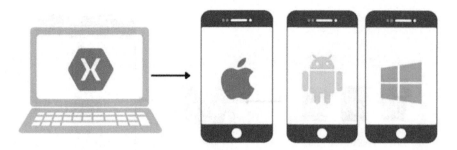

Figure 2.10 – Xamarin framework

As a part of its Xamarin.Forms toolkit, Xamarin provides developers with the ability to define UI layouts for their apps that can be reused across multiple platforms using a single UI toolkit.

Is Xamarin dead or alive?

Recently, we noticed that Microsoft announced that if you want to build native, cross-platform desktop and mobile apps from a single code base, you can use **.NET MAUI**.

So, we assumed that maybe it is the end of Xamarin, but actually, it is the beginning of .NET MAUI.

As shown in *Figure 2.11*, .NET MAUI (`https://dotnet.microsoft.com/en-us/apps/maui`) is designed to replace Xamarin.Forms and provide a more modern, feature-rich, and consistent UI toolkit for building mobile apps that run on iOS, Android, and Windows platforms.

.NET MAUI is built on top of .NET 6, but the current version of the framework at the time of writing is .NET 7 (`https://dotnet.microsoft.com/en-us/download`):

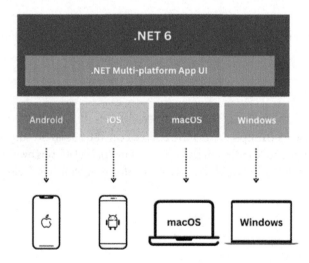

Figure 2.11 – Multiplatform target

> **Note**
>
> To migrate your app from Xamarin with .NET MAUI, visit the following link:
>
> `https://learn.microsoft.com/en-us/dotnet/maui/get-started/`
> `migrate?view=net-maui-7.0`

Finally, the differences between Xamarin, React Native, Ionic, Cordova, and Capacitor are shown in the following screenshot:

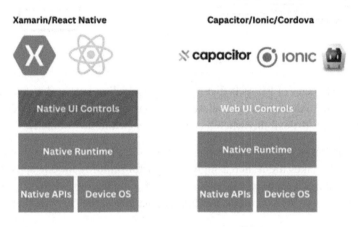

Figure 2.12 – Xamarin, React Native, Ionic, Cordova, and Capacitor

As we discussed previously, different frameworks use web technologies such as HTML, JavaScript, and CSS in building mobile apps to mimic the experience of native apps. Let's explain the concept behind PWAs.

PWAs

A PWA (`https://web.dev/progressive-web-apps/`) is a web application that is designed to mimic the experience of native apps. In addition to the fact that they can work on any device, regardless of whether it supports modern web standards, they are also referred to as *progressive* because they become more powerful as the device on which they are running becomes more powerful.

PWAs are accessed through a web browser by using web technologies such as HTML, CSS, and JavaScript. Users can also install them on their devices and use them as native apps with features such as offline support, push notifications, and access to hardware such as cameras and microphones, as shown in *Figure 2.13*:

Progressive Web App

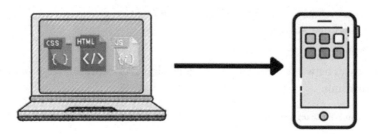

Figure 2.13 – PWAs

Among the main advantages of PWAs is that they are *easy to distribute and install* because they *do not require* an app store to download. This allows users to use the app more easily, and it also allows for faster updates and more flexibility when it comes to design and functionality.

In addition to offering many of the same benefits as native apps, PWAs can be easily accessed through a web browser, which makes them increasingly popular for building mobile apps. In cases where businesses or organizations want to provide their users with a mobile app experience but cannot afford to build and maintain separate native apps for different platforms, they can use them.

Here are a few examples of popular PWAs:

- **Twitter Lite**: This is an extremely lightweight version of the Twitter app that can be accessed directly from any device with a web browser

- **Starbucks**: This lets users order, pay, and track purchases from their mobile devices using the Starbucks PWA

- **Trivago**: This lets users search for hotels and book them, as well as access their past bookings

> **Note**
> Since there are a lot of books, articles, or videos talking about cross-platform frameworks, I will not waste your time by comparing them, but I would recommend choosing a framework based on the nature of the application, the business, the goal, and the target audience, as well as the skill level of the team.

Now we have briefly explored the different mobile app OSs, frameworks, and platforms, let's look at the most valuable features of mobile apps.

Mobile apps' most valuable features

There are numerous valuable features included in mobile apps that cater to the diverse needs and preferences of users. Some of the most useful features are described next.

Large screens and foldable devices

In order to make your app work well on a larger screen and foldable devices, you'll need to make sure it's optimized to work on different screen sizes. This might mean redesigning your layout to make the most of the extra screen space or setting your app to work on both portrait and landscape screens.

Foldables offer new ways for users to interact with their devices, such as being able to use them in **folded** or **unfolded** modes. As shown in *Figure 2.14*, when a foldable device is folded, it can affect the way your app is displayed and used. Make sure you consider this when designing your app, and test to ensure it works smoothly when the device is folded and unfolded:

Figure 2.14 – Foldable device

To ensure that your app looks good and works well on large screens and foldable devices, follow the design guidelines for the platform on which you are developing, such as Android (`https://developer.android.com/guide/topics/large-screens/get-started-with-large-screens`). Providing a consistent user experience will help your app feel cohesive with the rest of the operating system. You may also need to invest in some additional hardware for the best results.

In addition, developers must ensure their apps are *compatible with older devices without foldable screens*, even though foldable mobile devices are a relatively new technology. In order to ensure that an app works correctly on all devices, we need to develop and test different versions of the app. In this case, test automation can assist with achieving this goal.

Due to this, QA engineers will need to ensure that apps and automated tests will help them achieve this goal when testing apps on large screens and foldable devices. The challenge can be overcome by using screenshot testing or an **artificial intelligence** (**AI**) testing tool that detects UI screens and compares them. In *Chapter 5, Implementing a Robust Mobile App Testing Strategy*, we will cover testing practices for large screens and foldable devices.

Deep links

In mobile apps, **deep links** are links that allow users to access specific content or functions within an app by clicking on a link within the app, rather than having to navigate the app manually to reach the relevant content.

There are a number of ways in which deep links can be used to promote content within an app or allow users to access specific features or functions within an app. They can be included in email campaigns, social media posts, or other types of marketing material to encourage users to engage with the app.

In addition to improving the user experience, deep links can be used to direct users to content or functions that they wish to access quickly and easily. A deep link may, for example, be used to direct users to a specific product page within an e-commerce app or to a specific screen within a game, as shown in *Figure 2.15*:

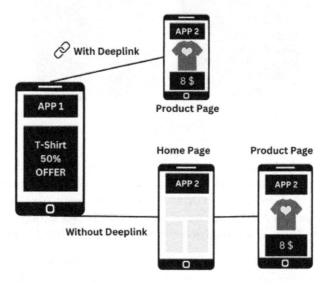

Figure 2.15 – How deep links work

It is important to note that in order to use deep links, the app must be installed on the user's device. If the app is not installed, the deep link will normally redirect the user to the app store to download the app.

Another challenge for developers and QA engineers is how to test deep links, which will be discussed in *Chapter 5, Implementing a Robust Mobile App Testing Strategy*.

Fragmentation

It is common for iOS and Android apps to fragment across devices and operating systems. It is essential to test mobile applications more frequently due to OS upgrades and the release of new devices. The fragmentation of devices and hardware-related bugs on Android and iOS are common problems.

The manufacturer of the device, the screen size, the connection type, the battery life, the resolution, and the version of the operating system may differ, as shown in *Figure 2.16*:

Figure 2.16 – Devices and OS fragmentation

For developers, it can be challenging to develop and maintain applications that work across all devices and operating systems as fragmentation can make it hard for them to create and maintain them. For instance, an app that works perfectly on one device might have performance issues or display problems on another device with a different configuration.

It is highly important that the teams test their mobile apps early and frequently on different devices and OS versions to increase the test coverage and ensure that our mobile apps behave correctly.

In addition to fragmentation, businesses may lose potential customers and revenue due to unsupported devices and operating systems.

In this case, you can use cloud device services to set up different devices and OS versions to ensure that you are supporting the desired devices. We will examine together the different types of device labs available on the market in *Chapter 5, Implementing a Robust Mobile App Testing Strategy*.

Localization

A mobile app's **localization** refers to the process of adapting it to a specific language or culture, as shown in *Figure 2.17*. Among the tasks involved are translating the text and interface of the app, adapting images and graphics to meet different cultural conventions, and adjusting the app's functionality to meet local requirements.

It is important to localize mobile apps for different reasons, as explained here:

- It helps to reach a wider audience, which can help you expand your user base and reach a wider audience

- It improves the user experience for users who are not fluent in the language of the app, as well as improving the experience of users who are fluent in the app's language. By providing content in the native language of the app, users can feel more connected to the app as they can receive content that pertains to their culture and language:

Figure 2.17 – Localization

To localize a mobile app, several factors need to be taken into consideration, including the languages and cultures that you intend to target, the resources and budget that you have available, and technical challenges that may arise during localization.

Additionally, you will need to think about the possibility of maintaining and updating the localized versions of your application over time, as languages and cultures can change and evolve. *Chapter 5, Implementing a Robust Mobile App Testing Strategy*, discusses how to test mobile apps for localization using screenshots and other methods.

Accessibility

In mobile apps, **accessibility** refers to the development and design of apps that are accessible to people with disabilities, such as vision or hearing impairments, as shown in *Figure 2.18*. You must ensure that your mobile app is accessible because it will allow a wider audience to use and benefit from it, as well as improve the user experience for everyone:

Figure 2.18 – Accessibility

Mobile apps can be made accessible in several ways, such as the following:

- For users with vision impairments, it is especially important to make sure that the *text is properly formatted and that there is enough contrast between the text and the background.*

- To ensure that users with vision impairments can understand the content, provide *alternative text for images, videos, and other media.*

- Users with hearing impairments may benefit from *captions and transcripts for audio and video content.*

- *Language should be clear and concise.* Avoid jargon or technical terms that may be confusing to some users.

- *Follow accessibility guidelines* and best practices.

- *Test it with assistive technologies,* such as screen readers or text-to-speech software. In *Chapter 5, Implementing a Robust Mobile App Testing Strategy,* we will discuss this point in greater detail.

By implementing these and other accessibility measures, you can ensure that your mobile app is accessible to a wider audience and improve the user experience for all users.

Push notifications

A **push notification** is a message sent from a server to a mobile device informing the user of new content, transactions, events, or updates.

Users can receive push notifications when new emails arrive, tasks are completed, or new features are available. Push notifications can be used to promote products and services or to encourage users to use an app, as shown in the following screenshot:

Figure 2.19 – Push notifications

Push notifications can only be received if users opt for and grant permission to the app to send them. In most cases, this can be done in the app's settings or the operating system's settings.

Users are notified with push notifications even when the app isn't running, which makes them a useful tool for engaging with it. It should not, however, be overused and should not be used excessively, as excessive notifications can be irritating and may result in users disabling them or uninstalling the app. Testing push notifications is challenging, but we will cover it in *Chapter 5, Implementing a Robust Mobile App Testing Strategy*.

Offline capability

The need for **offline functionality** in mobile apps is often the greatest. In addition to the fact that apps must function regardless of whether a user has a network connection, some applications, such as fieldwork apps, can be used in places where network connectivity is weak or nonexistent, as shown in the following screenshot:

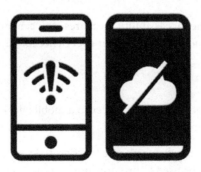

Figure 2.20 – Offline-enabled functionality

When internet connectivity is unreliable or unavailable, or users do not want to incur data charges, this app is designed to function even without an internet connection.

The following strategies can be used by developers to enable offline functionality in mobile apps:

- A mobile app can *cache data locally on the device*, such as images or text, and access these cached files when the device is offline, enabling users to access certain features of the app without connecting to the internet.

- Apps can *synchronize data between devices and servers* when an internet connection is available, enabling users to access up-to-date information whenever they are online.

- The devices can be used as local storage such as *SQLite* devices when apps are installed to store data and access it while offline.

- The content may be rendered on the server and cached on the device using server-side rendering. In some cases, it may be possible for the app to render certain content on the server and cache it on the device so that it can display this content even when the device is offline.

It is also challenging to test connectivity because you must use real devices in order to test a variety of connectivity types and conditions, which require a test lab and a good test design. Don't worry—this is discussed in detail in *Chapter 5, Implementing a Robust Mobile App Testing Strategy*.

Monetization

The goal of **monetization** is to generate revenue for the app developer while providing value to the user. Monetization strategies vary depending on the app and its audience and may involve a combination of different methods.

In-app purchases are a type of feature that allows users to purchase additional content or features within a mobile application. These purchases are made directly from within the app and are typically processed through the user's app store account, as shown in the following screenshot:

Figure 2.21 – Monetization

It is possible to make in-app purchases using a variety of payment methods, such as credit cards, PayPal, or mobile payment services such as Apple Pay. Developers can set the price for in-app purchases, and they can be one-time purchases or subscriptions.

Chapter 5, Implementing a Robust Mobile App Testing Strategy, will discuss how to test in-app purchases for both Android and iOS devices and what you need to do in order to do so.

Modularization

In mobile apps, **modularization** refers to the *division of an app into smaller, independent modules or components*. The code can be more easily reused in other parts of the app or future projects, saving time and effort.

The modularization process can also help to *increase an app's performance* by allowing you to load only the modules you need at a given time, as opposed to loading the entire app in one go. As a result, you can make changes to one module without affecting the rest of the application, making it easier to maintain and update the app over time.

The interaction between the different modules can then be managed by using techniques such as **dependency injection (DI)** or **inversion of control (IoC)**, as shown in the following screenshot:

Modularized App Architecture

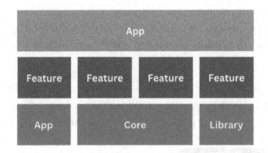

Figure 2.22 – Modularized app architecture

Mobile app development can benefit from modular architecture in several ways:

- *The ability to reuse modules* across different parts of the app or across different apps reduces the need to write new code and speeds up development

- Modular architecture *simplifies the maintenance and updating of applications* because changes can be made to individual modules without affecting the entire application.

- By adding new modules or modifying existing ones, the *modular architecture enables the app to scale as it grows and evolves*.

- It is easier to test an app with a modular architecture because *each module can be tested separately, reducing the risk of errors or bugs*

> **Note**
>
> For more information, you can visit the following link—for instance, to view how to modularize the Android app: `https://developer.android.com/topic/modularization`.

Performance optimization

As users expect mobile apps to be responsive and fast, **performance** is an important consideration.

It is important to test applications on a variety of devices and networks to ensure that it is performing well under real-world conditions. There are various mobile performance optimization tools and libraries, such as **Flipper** (`https://github.com/facebook/flipper`), which can be used for the same. Additionally, there are different practices we can use to optimize mobile apps' performance, such as the following:

- **Caching** reduces the number of network requests made by an app and improves its overall performance
- Write clean, efficient code to minimize resource usage and reduce the app's load time
- Using **profiling tools** can reveal any bottlenecks or problems with an app and provide detailed information about how it is performing
- Using smaller, more optimized versions of images and videos in the app will *minimize the use of resources*
- You can identify and diagnose performance issues in an application with the help of a **performance monitoring tool**
- If you *reduce the app's size*, its download and installation times will be faster

It will be discussed in the next chapters how caching can be used to improve the build process of an application, particularly in the CI/CD pipeline, and how tools can be used to reduce the size and performance of the app.

As we discussed that modularization refers to the division of an app into smaller, independent modules or components, it's important to know the mobile app architecture and what are the considerations and factors to design a good mobile app.

Mobile app architecture

It is the architecture of a mobile app that describes how the app is designed and structured, as shown in the following screenshot. It includes all the components and the relationships between them, as well as the design patterns and frameworks that have been selected for development:

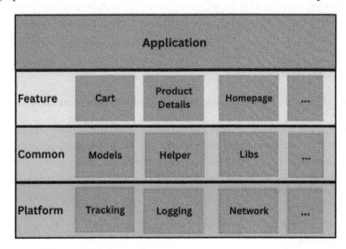

Figure 2.23 – Example of architecting a shopping app

Designing the architecture of a mobile app requires consideration of several factors, including the following:

- The architecture will be influenced by the platform the app is developed and runs on (for example, iOS; Android)

- Components and design patterns will be determined by the functionality of the app

- A well-designed architecture should consider the app's performance when designing the architecture

- A scalable architecture is important as the app grows in popularity and usage

A list of a few best practices for mobile app architecture is provided here:

- Design your app so that it can be easily updated or replaced by dividing it into smaller, independent modules.

- Make your code base easy to read and maintain by using clear naming conventions and following established coding standards.

- Consider using a **minimum viable product** approach. Start with the minimum set of features that your users will find valuable and iterate as needed.

- Make sure your app is scalable, and make sure it can handle large data volumes and multiple users without slowing down.

- Adapt your design to new technology and features: use an architecture that is flexible and adaptable. There are a variety of architectures available for mobile development based on the platform, such as the following:

  - **Model-View-Controller** (**MVC**) (`https://shorturl.at/bju00`)

  - **Model-View-Presenter** (**MVP**) (`https://shorturl.at/hkHWX`)

  - **Model-View-ViewModel** (**MVVM**) (`https://shorturl.at/fptP2`)

  - **View-Interactor-Presenter-Entity-Routing** (**VIPER**) (`https://www.objc.io/issues/13-architecture/viper/`)

  - **View - Interactor - Presenter** (**VIP**) (`https://github.com/thetay55/VIP-Architecture/blob/master/VIP_Architecture.md`)

  - **Composable** (`https://github.com/pointfreeco/swift-composable-architecture`)

  - **Redux** (`https://www.kodeco.com/books/advanced-ios-app-architecture/v3.0/chapters/6-architecture-redux`)

- Make sure your app is reliable by using automated testing and continuous integration.

- Create a maintainable architecture with design patterns and practices that make updating and maintaining the app easier.

- Make your app more flexible and testable by using DI.

- Ensure that the networking layer between your backend and your frontend is robust and efficient.

- Ensure that your app data is stored in an efficient and reliable database.

- Improve the user experience by implementing a robust error-handling mechanism.

- Troubleshooting and debugging can be made easier with the help of powerful logging mechanisms.

In order to provide their customers with a better user experience, mobile app developers should adhere to these practices to make their apps perform better and deliver a better user experience.

Summary

As we embark on this journey together, exploring the intricate world of mobile platforms, frameworks, and unique functions of mobile devices, it becomes increasingly apparent that these present a multitude of challenges for those in the field of mobile development, including developers, QA engineers, release engineers, and others. The complex and constantly evolving nature of these platforms and technologies demands that we stay vigilant and proactive in our approach, consistently seeking new and innovative solutions to overcome obstacles that stand in our way.

One way in which we can tackle these challenges is by utilizing automation to streamline and enhance the mobile app development process. Whether it be through building, testing, releasing, or monitoring, automation offers a multitude of benefits that can greatly assist us in producing high-quality, reliable, and efficient mobile applications.

With a thorough understanding of these various mobile platforms, frameworks, and functions, we can confidently approach challenges that lie ahead, utilizing automation as a powerful tool in our quest to create great mobile apps. So, let us continue our exploration and discovery, embracing obstacles and opportunities that come our way, and always striving to push the boundaries of what is possible in the ever-evolving world of mobile development.

Our next chapter will be about the fundamentals of Mobile DevOps and how the practical steps for implementing it will begin in the following chapters.

3
Mobile DevOps Fundamentals

There is no doubt that Mobile DevOps is quickly becoming a key part of the mobile development process, enabling teams and organizations to quickly develop and release mobile applications. We will discuss the fundamentals of Mobile DevOps and how it can help your team to reach your mobile development goals through the use of this process.

In this chapter, we will cover the following topics:

- Mobile continuous integration/continuous delivery (CI/CD) fundamentals
- Choosing between self-hosted and cloud-based continuous integration/continuous delivery (CI/CD
- Do we need a Mobile DevOps engineer?

Sounds interesting! Let's begin our journey toward Mobile DevOps.

The importance of Mobile DevOps

Businesses are increasingly relying on mobile applications today. DevOps is an essential part of the mobile development process because it manages the development and release of mobile applications. To streamline the development process and improve the quality of mobile apps, CI, **continuous testing** (**CT**), CD, and continuous deployment techniques are used.

It is an approach to developing mobile applications that *emphasizes collaboration* between development, quality, product, and operations teams to ensure mobile applications are delivered *quickly, frequently, and reliably*, as shown in the following screenshot:

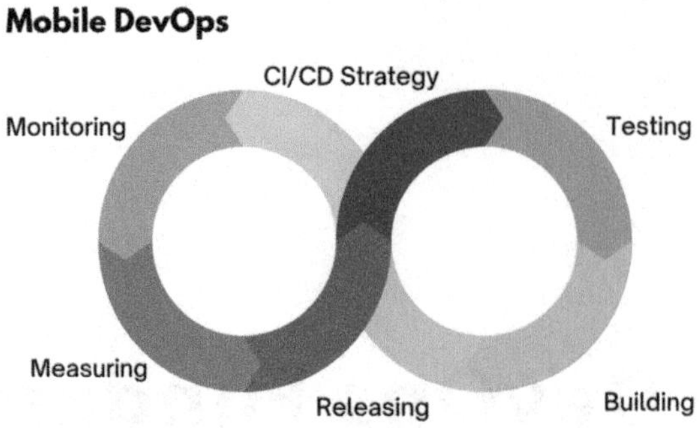

Mobile DevOps

Figure 3.1 – Mobile DevOps

With Mobile DevOps, teams can *collaborate more effectively and efficiently* as they *develop and release mobile applications faster* and with fewer errors (as much as possible) since they can work together more. This helps *reduce the time required to develop a mobile app*, while also ensuring that the app *complies with quality, security, and performance* standards at the same time.

In *Chapter 1, Resolving Challenges in Mobile DevOps*, we discussed how traditional mobile app development was often *slow, error-prone, and siloed*. It was common for developers to work in isolation, handing off their work to the quality team for testing, and then passing it on to operations teams for deployment and release. The process was often slow, resulting in *critical issues, delays, poor user experiences, and dissatisfaction*.

As a result, Mobile DevOps is shifting the way mobile apps are developed and maintained. It involves the use of DevOps principles and practices to improve the speed, security, and quality of mobile app development.

Many advantages of Mobile DevOps can be summarized as follows:

- Faster development cycles
- Improved collaboration between different teams
- Better QA practices
- Efficient deployment process
- Quick response to customer feedback
- Cost savings through automation
- Reduced deployment time
- Ensuring applications are secure and compliant

The Mobile DevOps process has proven invaluable to organizations seeking to maximize their mobile development efforts.

Let's deep-dive and learn more about Mobile DevOps fundamentals.

Mobile CI/CD fundamentals

If you are familiar with the fundamentals of DevOps for web apps, backend services, or other types of apps, you already know the concepts of **CI/CD**. In mobile, it's the same but with specific tasks that are required to build, test, and release the mobile apps.

But before jumping to the CI/CD part, I'd like to give you an idea about the preparation stage, which is the planning stage or phase.

Continuous planning

As a team, we should agree together about the process that we will use to implement Mobile DevOps and CI/CD. The **continuous planning stage** involves gathering requirements from stakeholders, creating a project plan, and determining the necessary resources. This is an important step in ensuring that the app meets the needs of the users and aligns with the overall business objectives.

Also, we need to clearly define what you want to achieve with your mobile CI/CD strategy. This may include improving the speed and quality of your releases, increasing collaboration between team members, or reducing the risk of errors.

One of the frameworks that can be used to improve DevOps practices is **CALMS** (`https://www.atlassian.com/devops/frameworks/calms-framework`), as shown in *Figure 3.2*. It can be applied to Mobile DevOps as well, to optimize the process of developing, testing, and releasing mobile apps:

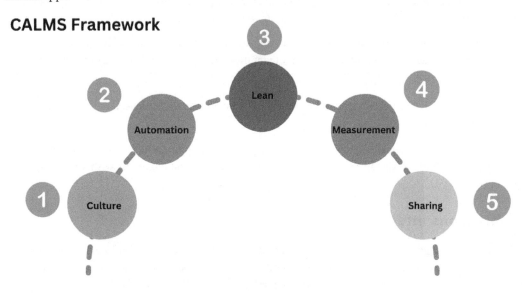

Figure 3.2 – CALMS framework

CALMS can be used to achieve the following:

- Teams can identify and resolve issues more quickly and deliver higher-quality apps by working together and sharing knowledge and resources

- Collaboration and communication can boost team morale and productivity, resulting in greater efficiency and productivity

- Team members can avoid misunderstandings and errors by keeping everyone informed about project goals and progress

- Communication and collaboration between team members can facilitate faster decision-making, resulting in more efficient project progress

There are five main components of CALMS, as follows:

- **Culture**: Essentially, this refers to the values and beliefs of the team, as well as the overall work environment and dynamics of the team. Every team needs a positive culture to succeed.

- **Automation**: Automating workflows reduces the need for manual intervention and minimizes the chance of error by using tools and processes.

- **Lean**: Throughout the development process, the lean approach seeks to maximize value and minimize waste. As part of this process, unnecessary steps are identified and eliminated, workflows are streamlined, and processes are continuously improved.

- **Measurement**: Identifying areas for improvement requires collecting and analyzing data. The metrics can include lead and cycle times, as well as defect rates.

- **Sharing**: Collaboration and efficiency are improved when knowledge and resources are shared within and across departments. Regular team meetings, pair programming, and code reviews can all contribute to this.

Now that we've determined what your mobile CI/CD strategy should achieve, let's learn more about the CI/CD process.

DevOps culture is a critical component of building a capable engineering team for organizations. It contributes greatly to signaling a company's quality to in-demand engineers with a wide range of job options.

Continuous integration

Continuous integration (CI) makes incremental code changes regularly and reliably. CI enables *automated build and test procedures* to make code updates reliable before they are *merged* into the repository or specially merged to the main or the master branch, and we must always do that to keep the main or master branch green at all times without conflicts or errors because it's the main source for our business. If we need to release a new version, this is the baseline, as shown in the following screenshot:

Continuous Integration

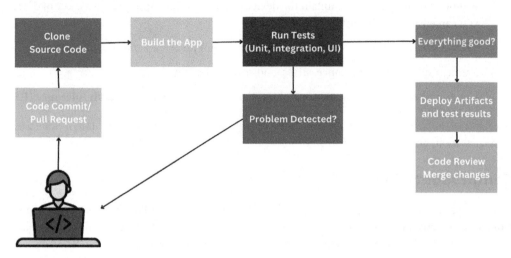

Figure 3.3 – The CI process

The process of CI for mobile apps mainly comprises the following steps:

- Cloning the source code from the repository
- Building the app binaries
- Running different test types such as unit tests, integration tests, UI tests, and so on
- Creating and deploying the artifacts (`.aab` or `.ipa`) based on the app type that can be later used in the distribution

Continuous testing

The practice of **continuous testing** (**CT**) involves testing software as part of the development process instead of waiting until the end of the cycle to test it. A high-quality app is especially important for mobile apps, which are often used by many users and use a large amount of data.

Mobile apps can be continuously tested in different ways, such as the following:

- Decide on a clear mobile testing strategy before you begin testing.
- Throughout the development process, ensure that tests are applied in the initial phase and progressively.
- Follow an automated testing process that involves the use of different testing tools to execute tests such as unit, integration, UI, and so on on the app without the need for human intervention. This is especially useful for running a large number of tests in a consistent and timely manner.

- Tests can be run on a wide variety of devices and operating systems using cloud-based testing without having to own or maintain the devices. By testing your app across a variety of devices, you can ensure that it works properly.

- Make sure you test the UI on a real mobile device, not just on an emulator or simulator.

- Perform sufficient performance, stress, and security testing.

- Conduct tests to assess app interoperability, battery consumption, and **fault tolerance** (**FT**).

In *Chapter 5, Implementing a Robust Mobile App Testing Strategy*, we will deep-dive into mobile testing strategies, tools, and frameworks.

Continuous Delivery

Once this process is finished without errors, the code can be quickly and easily deployed through the **Continuous Delivery** (**CD**) process; otherwise, if there is any error, the process will be stopped and the error reported back to the developer to fix it, as shown in the following screenshot:

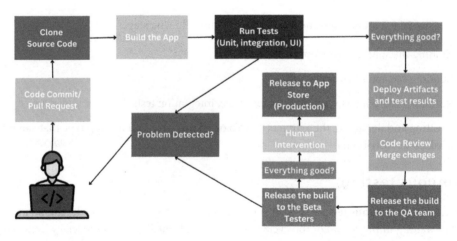

Figure 3.4 – The CI/CD process

Once the code commits or changes have been merged into the central branch (main, master, and so on), CD automatically delivers the builds that pass the CI checks to production environments (such as staging), where they will be tested and reviewed before being released into production.

The goal is to automate development and deployment processes to ensure the rapid, reliable, and budget-friendly delivery of mobile apps.

The process of CI/CD for mobile apps mainly comprises the following steps:

1. Release the build to the QA teams to do additional checks and tests.

2. Release the build to the Beta testers if the company or the team is already participating in the program.

3. If everything is good, after that, the release manager or anyone responsible for the release process can approve the build and release it to the app stores or the production environments.

Continuous deployment

Continuous deployment is often part of the CI/CD pipeline, which means that the code that is deployed to the repository will automatically be deployed to production or, in our cases for the mobile apps, to the App Store. CI/CD pipelines are often referred to as the combination of these practices, as shown in the following screenshot:

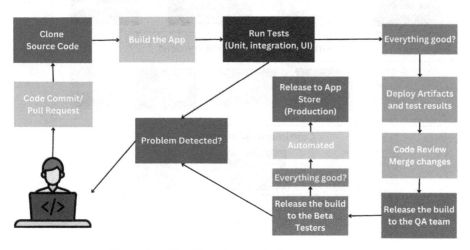

Figure 3.5 – The CI/continuous deployment process

The continuous deployment process automates the deployment of your app build, preventing human intervention. The only thing that will prevent a new change from being deployed into production is a failed build or test. This is used to speed up the app production and to get customer feedback faster.

Continuous monitoring

After we release the mobile apps to production, this is not the end of the CI/CD life cycle, but we have another stage. **Continuous monitoring (CM)** involves monitoring the app's performance and gathering data on user behavior, as shown in *Figure 3.6*.

This helps organizations improve the user experience, identify potential issues, and optimize the performance of their mobile applications. The data collected can include information on device performance, network conditions, app crashes, user behavior, and more. The analysis of this data is typically done using advanced analytics tools and techniques to provide insights into the mobile app performance and user experience. In *Chapter 7, Establishing Mobile App Monitoring, Observability, and Analytics*, we will deep-dive into monitoring and analytics tools for mobile apps and learn more about how to use them effectively with mobile CI/CD and DevOps:

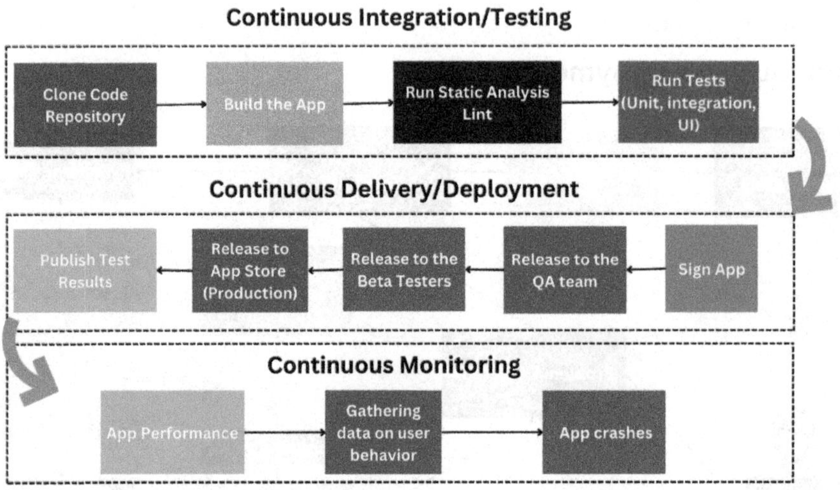

Continuous Integration/Testing

Clone Code Repository → Build the App → Run Static Analysis Lint → Run Tests (Unit, integration, UI)

Continuous Delivery/Deployment

Publish Test Results ← Release to App Store (Production) ← Release to the Beta Testers ← Release to the QA team ← Sign App

Continuous Monitoring

App Performance → Gathering data on user behavior → App crashes

Figure 3.6 – The full process of CI/CD

Effective and specific mobile CI/CD platforms consist of a progression of different Mobile DevOps tools used to address a particular business challenge. By connecting the mobile developers, quality engineers, and customers, they ensure a profitable cycle.

It is not easy to build Mobile DevOps processes, as we discovered. Automating processes requires continuous experimentation and refinement.

As a result, I highly recommend *starting small and building the Mobile DevOps toolchain and CI/CD pipelines incrementally* once you decide to embark on the Mobile DevOps journey.

Based on my previous experience, I believe if you try to implement all the processes and steps at once, you will fail and be frustrated. Instead, take it slowly and build it step by step; success is the sum of small efforts.

In my opinion, as shown in *Figure 3.7*, there are three phases to the Mobile DevOps journey:

- **The beginning phase/the CI phase**: Implement only the minimal CI pipeline by cloning the source code, running the static analysis code or lint, and running unit tests.

- **Keeping the promise phase—mobile CI/CD partial pipeline**: Continuously improve the pipeline from the first phase by adding a few other steps, such as running UI tests on cloud devices, generating UI test reports, and running security or performance tests depending on the requirements. This stage can also contain releasing the app to the QA teams or the stakeholders and sending notifications to different teams about the statuses.

- **The sustain phase—fully automated mobile CI/CD pipeline**: Add more steps toward the fully mobile CI/CD, such as steps to release the apps to the beta testers and the app stores as well as enhance the UI testing to reduce the build time by running them in parallel, or add other steps to improve the quality of the CI/CD pipeline:

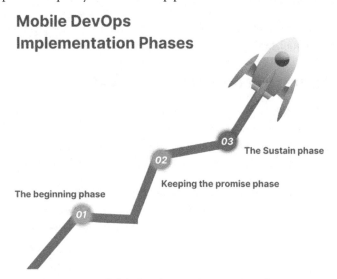

Figure 3.7 – Mobile DevOps implementation phases

Using this approach will always help the team to improve the Mobile DevOps process and enhance the performance of the release process. These duties can be the responsibilities of the platform engineering team, the internal developer productivity team, or the mobile engineering team, depending on the team topologies inside the organization. In *Chapter 4*, *Achieving Continuous Integration and Delivery with Mobile DevOps*, we will get started with the implementation phase of mobile CI/CD pipelines with different platforms.

Now we've discussed the fundamentals of Mobile DevOps and explained each stage of the process, let's explore together the benefits of Mobile DevOps and CI/CD for mobile app development.

The benefits of CI/CD for mobile app development

Having mobile CI/CD has more positive effects than only making an existing process a little more efficient for the following reasons:

- It allows developers to focus on writing code and monitoring mobile apps in production

- A faster deployment time and faster delivery to markets

- All versions of the mobile apps are accessible to QA and product stakeholders

- The test results, code change logs, and release logs are always available

- Enhanced communication and productivity

- Improved employee engagement

- Customers are more satisfied

Determine which tools and technologies will be used in your mobile CI/CD pipeline. A version control system, build automation tool, testing framework, or deployment platform may be included in this list.

The tools and infrastructure of Mobile DevOps

As we discussed before, Mobile DevOps is a set of practices, tools, and infrastructure aimed at streamlining the development and release of mobile applications. It enables continuous integration, testing, delivery, and monitoring, ensuring that developers can rapidly iterate, deploy, and maintain high-quality mobile apps. The key components of Mobile DevOps infrastructure are set out here:

- A version control management system, such as GitHub, allows teams to track changes to their code bases and collaborate on them. In *Chapter 9, Mobile DevOps Best Practices*, we will learn more about the different types of Git repositories such as monorepos, and how to use them.

- Tools that automate the build and test processes, such as Gradle, Gradle Enterprise for Android, or Fastlane for iOS, allow developers to focus on writing code instead of building and testing. In *Chapter 4, Achieving Continuous Integration and Delivery with Mobile DevOps*, we will learn more about the different build tools for mobile apps in practice and also how to use caching to speed up the build time with those tools.

- **Labs for testing apps on a wide range of physical devices**: These labs are often hosted in the cloud, allowing teams to test apps on a range of devices. In *Chapter 5, Implementing a Robust Mobile App Testing Strategy*, we will learn the best practices when using cloud devices to accelerate the testing processes.

- Infrastructure for deploying and managing backend services for mobile apps is provided by cloud platforms such as **Amazon Web Services (AWS), Google Cloud Platform (GCP),** or Azure. In *Chapter 9, Mobile DevOps Best Practices*, we will learn more about how to use cloud services with mobile apps.

- Testing tools such as Appium, Espresso, XCUITest, and Detox automate the testing of mobile apps across different platforms and devices. In *Chapter 5, Implementing a Robust Mobile App Testing Strategy*, we will learn the difference between the testing tools and what is a suitable tool or framework for our team.

- Managing the mobile app distribution process, such as automatically managing code signing, certificates, provisioning profiles, and key stores is made easier using tools such as fastlane and others. In *Chapter 6, Mobile App Release Management*, we will learn how to distribute our apps automatically to Beta users or the App Store using different tools such as Firebase App Distribution, fastlane, TestFlight, and more.

In my opinion, mobile CI/CD pipelines are like LEGO toys—you're always working with different tools, configurations, and dependencies. All you need to do is decide how you want your pipeline to look.

When you play with LEGO, you can feel like an architect. You can create different results by building different shapes and structures.

The idea behind building a mobile CI/CD pipeline for your specific needs and requirements is knowing how to use the pieces correctly. There is no set-in-stone template required for building a mobile CI/CD pipeline. Instead, you should always implement the steps that fit your needs.

Through Mobile DevOps, developers, testers, product managers, and release management teams can work together more effectively.

DevOps and CI/CD are based on the philosophy of rapid development, testing, and release, which allows technology to be iterated quickly.

It is a philosophy that closely aligns with the needs of companies, from start-ups to enterprises. They need to be able to deliver products to market quickly and constantly improve their quality in order to gain a competitive edge.

Developing a mobile CI/CD strategy is an essential part of ensuring the successful delivery of mobile applications. It involves creating a process that automates the development, testing, and deployment of applications, helping to ensure the applications are of high quality and are released quickly.

As a result, the team or the organization should choose which Mobile DevOps and CI/CD platforms are suitable for the business and **return on investment (ROI)**. Let's compare the options between self-hosted and cloud-based CI/CD to know which option or choice is a suitable fit for our organization.

Choosing between self-hosted and cloud-based CI/CD

With **self-hosted CI/CD**, organizations retain full control over their environment and data. As a bonus, this approach can be more cost-effective in the long run since organizations can avoid cloud service costs by using existing infrastructure.

For instance, if the team already uses CI/CD platforms for web apps and APIs and backend services, it needs to incorporate the mobile part.

This requires educating the DevOps team about the mobile apps requirements to be able to add the mobile part to the existing CI/CD platform, such as provisioning the required hardware and software as well as implementing the processes and the prerequisites that are necessary to support mobile release processes to app stores, such as signing apps, uploading certificates, provisioning profiles, and creating key stores.

Additionally, setting up a self-hosted CI/CD solution can be *time-consuming* and may require *specialized expertise*. Additionally, teams will need to take on the responsibility of *maintaining and updating their environment and infrastructure*, which can be a burden on resources.

On the other hand, **cloud-based CI/CD** solutions have several advantages over self-hosted solutions, such as the following:

- *The process of setting up and maintaining them is generally easier*, and they are more scalable. As cloud-based services can be *accessed remotely*, they are also more accessible. In addition, they can be more *flexible* since they can *easily be integrated with other tools and services*. Cloud-based CI/CD eliminates the need for on-site infrastructure by providing off-site hosting. By allowing CI/CD to be used immediately, cloud-based CI/CD can *both reduce costs and time* spent on setup.

- CI/CD in the cloud is also scalable, allowing for easy expansion or reduction of resources.

In addition to its benefits, cloud-based CI/CD also has some drawbacks. The lack of control over data can pose a security concern. Furthermore, cloud-based services can quickly add up in costs, especially if organizations need to use multiple services because it's required to have monitoring on the cost of machines and builds.

It's important to note that it also depends on the specific needs and requirements of the project, as well as the size and resources of the organization. As shown in the following screenshot, self-hosted CI/CD can be time-consuming but it's more customizable; on the other hand, cloud CI/CD can help developers to save time by managing required tasks such as updating the infrastructure or stacks:

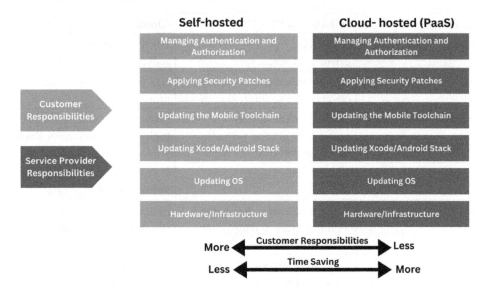

Figure 3.8 – Self-hosted versus cloud-hosted (PaaS) CI/CD

A cloud-based CI/CD solution might be the best option for a *small team or start-up*, while a larger organization might prefer to have *more control over its environment and choose a self-hosted solution*, but it always depends on the team's expectations and needs.

The cloud-based version of CI/CD is often referred to as **CI/CD as a service**. CI/CD tools are developed, maintained, and hosted by a dedicated organization that offers internet access to customers.

In contrast, self-hosted CI/CD means you either build your own CI/CD tool or use a third-party CI/CD tool (usually open source) hosted on your infrastructure. It can be on-premise servers or IaaS platforms such as AWS, **GCP**, or Microsoft Azure.

As a summary, this comparison table outlines the main differences between self-hosted and cloud-based CI/CD solutions, including factors such as control, cost, scalability, and security. The choice between the two depends on the specific needs and requirements of the project and organization:

Criteria	Self-Hosted CI/CD	Cloud-Based CI/CD
Control	Full control over environment and data	Less control over data and environment
Cost	More cost-effective in the long run; uses existing infrastructure	Costs can add up quickly; requires monitoring of machine and build costs
Setup and maintenance	Time-consuming setup; requires specialized expertise; team maintains infrastructure	Easier setup; less maintenance required; hosted off-site

Criteria	Self-Hosted CI/CD	Cloud-Based CI/CD
Scalability	Limited by existing infrastructure	Highly scalable; can expand or reduce resources easily
Accessibility	Access limited to an on-premises or internal network	Can be accessed remotely; more accessible
Flexibility and integration	Customizable; may require more manual integration with other tools and services	Easier integration with other tools and services; more flexible
Security	Higher control over data security	Potential security concerns due to less control over data
Suitability	Better for larger organizations with resources to manage the environment and data	Better for small teams or start-ups that need immediate access and lower upfront investment
Implementation	Build your own CI/CD tool or use a third-party tool hosted on your infrastructure	CI/CD as a service provided by a dedicated organization with internet access for customers

Table 3.1 – Differences between self-hosted and cloud-based CI/CD solutions

Mobile-specific CI/CD

Mobile CI/CD PaaS refers to the use of a cloud-based platform as a service to automate the build, test, and deployment of mobile apps. Mobile CI/CD PaaS providers offer a range of tools and services to help organizations streamline and optimize their mobile app development and release process. Different platforms on the market provide us with this type of service, such as **Bitrise** (`https://www.bitrise.io/`), **Codemagic** (`https://codemagic.io/`), or **Xcode Cloud** (`https://developer.apple.com/xcode-cloud/`) from Apple. All the platforms available in the market will be discussed and examples will be shown in *Chapter 4, Achieving Continuous Integration and Delivery with Mobile DevOps*.

Mobile CI/CD as a service has the following benefits:

- These platforms often come with tools for managing code changes and collaborating on projects that integrate with version control systems such as GitHub, Bitbucket, and GitLab

- Developers can focus on writing code by automating the build and test processes with mobile CI/CD as a service

- Integration of cloud devices: These platforms offer tools for testing and deploying mobile apps across a variety of devices and platforms

- Identify and resolve issues with mobile apps using monitoring and analytics tools: Mobile-CI/CD-as-a-service platforms often provide tools for tracking the performance and usage of mobile apps

- In comparison to setting up and maintaining an in-house mobile CI/CD infrastructure, mobile CI/CD PaaS involves a monthly subscription fee rather than an upfront investment

- Organizations can adjust their mobile CI/CD capabilities as needed with mobile CI/CD-as-a-service scalability

- For organizations that are new to mobile CI/CD or do not have in-house expertise in this field, a mobile CI/CD PaaS can be very valuable

- It typically frees up IT staff to focus on other tasks by allowing mobile CI/CD-as-a-service providers to maintain and update the infrastructure

- The integrity of the mobile CI/CD process and sensitive data is protected by robust security measures offered by many providers of mobile CI/CD as a service

The release processes may also need to be accelerated since mobile requires fast machines with high performance to build, test, and release apps. In *Chapter 4*, *Achieving Continuous Integration and Delivery with Mobile DevOps*, we will deep-dive more and learn about the different mobile CI/CD platforms and the pros and cons of each one.

After discussing the pros and cons of self-hosted and cloud-hosted CI/CD for our team, each team should decide for itself which is the best option. It's time to discuss whether we need a Mobile DevOps engineer for our team or whether we can manage it by ourselves.

As we discussed Mobile DevOps and CI/CD fundamentals and learned about self-hosted and cloud CI/CD platforms, you may have been thinking, *Do we need a mobile SRE or DevOps engineer?* This is an important question, so let's answer it.

Do we need a Mobile DevOps engineer?

The best answer always is that it depends on the team's objectives, goals, scale, skill sets, and experience. You can have different team members responsible for the Mobile DevOps stages, but don't forget that we mentioned previously that it's a team effort and collaboration. However, if the team already has a DevOps engineer responsible for the DevOps implementation in general in the company, it can also help the mobile team, or involve it in the mobile part by doing the following:

- Understand DevOps practices for mobile, such as code signing and releasing mobile apps.

- Learn the basics of mobile app development. Learn a new programming language, such as Kotlin or Swift, and gain experience building mobile apps.

- Create, deploy, and manage mobile apps in the cloud as you develop your knowledge of cloud computing.

- Contribute to open source projects or work on personal projects to get hands-on experience working on Mobile DevOps projects.
- Keep up to date with the latest trends and best practices in Mobile DevOps.

On the other hand, experienced mobile developers may be able to take the responsibility of implementing Mobile DevOps because they are familiar with the mobile development process, most of the challenges, and the need to increase their knowledge of CI/CD for mobile applications.

There is an opinion that it's a way of doing things and a process you use at work. By understanding these four essential DevOps practices, even solo or indie developers can improve their productivity.

But for me, I believe that it can be a combination of both approaches because we can have both DevOps engineers and experienced mobile engineers working together to assist the mobile teams in achieving their goals and delivering apps more quickly and reliably. It is imperative that someone takes care of the infrastructure of the servers and someone takes care of the tools and frameworks.

Summary

Mobile DevOps is a crucial practice for the development of high-quality mobile apps. It is a powerful process that can help teams develop and deploy mobile applications quickly and efficiently. By leveraging automation, testing, and continuous deployment, teams can ensure that their applications are stable, secure, and up to date. With Mobile DevOps, teams can achieve their mobile development goals more quickly and efficiently.

Mobile DevOps also helps to simplify the development process by automating repetitive tasks. This allows developers to focus on the creative aspects of development, such as creating innovative features without having to worry about mundane tasks. Additionally, it ensures that the mobile app follows best practices and is optimized for specific platforms and devices. This allows organizations to create high-quality mobile applications that are well suited to their users' needs.

By using automation, version control, cloud services, monitoring and analytics, and security, developers can streamline the development process and improve the overall quality of the app. With the help of these practices, mobile app developers can deliver better apps faster and with more reliability.

CI/CD pipeline implementation will be discussed in the next chapter, starting with the CI part, exploring different CI providers and the steps that need to be followed, and then integrating the CD part to create the automated CI/CD pipeline that we will be using for our mobile app development.

Part 2: Implementing the Mobile DevOps Environment

Mobile DevOps relies on automated processes for the continuous integration and delivery of mobile apps. This means that code changes are automatically built, tested, and deployed to staging and production environments, without the need for manual intervention.

This part has the following chapters:

- *Chapter 4, Achieving Continuous Integration and Delivery with Mobile DevOps*
- *Chapter 5, Implementing a Robust Mobile App Testing Strategy*
- *Chapter 6, Mobile App Release Management*

4

Achieving Continuous Integration and Delivery with Mobile DevOps

In continuous delivery, code changes in mobile apps are automatically built, tested, and released. With Mobile DevOps, software developers, testers, release managers, and DevOps engineers work together to improve mobile app development speed and quality. Mobile app delivery can be continuously delivered when these practices are combined.

In this chapter, we will discuss the following topics:

- Factors to consider when selecting a CI/CD provider
- Choosing a CI/CD provider
- Implementing a CI/CD pipeline for mobile apps
- Setting up the build and unit tests for mobile apps

Introduction

CI/CD for mobile apps is a process that enables the organization to quickly and efficiently release and update their mobile applications. It also allows teams to quickly test and release their mobile applications, ensuring the code is stable, secure, and up to date. Furthermore, it allows teams to quickly address any bugs or issues found in their mobile applications.

In the rapidly evolving world of mobile app development, **Continuous Integration** (**CI**) and **Continuous Deployment** (**CD**) have emerged as vital practices to streamline the development process, improve code quality, and enable rapid, iterative releases. This chapter will explore the significance of CI/CD in mobile app development, illustrating its benefits and providing real-world examples to demonstrate its impact on the mobile development life cycle.

As mentioned in *Chapter 3, Mobile DevOps Fundamentals*, we will discuss the steps to implement CI and CD in Mobile DevOps, but first, let's discuss how to choose a CI/CD provider for your mobile app that is also suited to your team's scale and business:

Continuous Integration

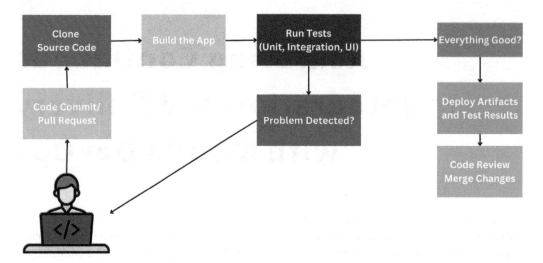

Figure 4.1 – The continuous integration workflow

We will begin with the CI part for automating the build and test processes, which includes doing the following:

- Choosing a CI/CD provider for mobile apps
- Setting up a CI server for mobile apps
- Setting up the build and unit tests for mobile apps

Before that, let's discuss how to choose CI/CD for Mobile apps, how to set up the CI server with the most popular CI/CD providers in the market, and the pros and cons of each.

Choosing the right CI/CD provider for your mobile app is extremely important to ensure a seamless development, testing, and release process. The following are some factors to consider when choosing a CI/CD provider for a mobile app development project:

- **Platform support**: Make sure the CI/CD provider supports the platforms your app targets (for example, iOS, Android, React Native, Flutter, and so on). Certain providers specialize in one platform, such as Xcode Cloud, while others support multiple platforms, such as Bitrise. Consider this factor if your team is building multiple mobile apps.

- **Performance and reliability**: A provider should be able to deliver high performance, minimal downtime, and quick build times. For example, CI/CD platforms provide us with insights and mentoring features to track our CI/CD performance and health status. This will ensure a smooth and efficient development process.

- **Build configuration and environment**: To select the right CI/CD provider for your mobile apps, consider the available build configuration and build environment options. Look for a provider with flexible build pipelines and customizable environments that support your project's needs. These features can save you time and effort while ensuring a streamlined build process and successful project deployment. For instance, most companies are building white label apps that require them to build the apps with different configurations so that they can reuse the same build pipeline with different values.

- **Scalability**: Scaling and growing your team requires this factor to make sure the CI/CD provider can handle the growing complexity, build frequency, and the number of developers of your app. Your provider should offer scalable infrastructure and resources to meet your growing needs, sometimes providing dedicated machines for your teams or changing the machines types and the technical specifications.

- **Integration**: Providers should integrate seamlessly with your existing tools, such as version control systems, project management tools, bug tracking tools, cloud tools, monitoring tools, or feature flagging tools, to be able to measure the success of the whole Mobile DevOps process.

- **Security and compliance**: The provider should adhere to strict security standards and offer features such as encryption, access control, and audit logs. Ensure the provider supports your app's compliance with specific regulations, especially if it's a cloud provider and your data and customers' data will be stored in the cloud, such as in e-banking apps.

- **Ease of use**: Choose a provider with a user-friendly interface, comprehensive documentation, and good support. CI/CD pipelines can be set up, maintained, and troubleshooted more easily if you follow these steps; Bitrise and Codemagic, for example, provide GUIs for building them.

- **Community and support**: You can easily resolve issues and get answers to your questions from a provider with an active community and strong customer support. You can find out whether professional services or consulting are available through professional forums, support channels, or community forums.

- **Pricing**: In my opinion, this factor is important, and even if the CI/CD provider has different features when it comes to purchasing a tool, various factors affect this decision, so you need to compare the pricing plans of different CI/CD providers while taking factors such as the number of builds per month, parallel builds, build minutes, and storage into consideration. The best provider will offer the most value for your budget without compromising on features.

As a result, deciding on a CI/CD provider is ultimately a decision that needs to be made by a team based on the business and team needs.

An overview of the six most popular CI/CD providers for mobile apps

Having discussed the factors that need to be considered, let's explore the CI/CD providers available in the mobile CI/CD market. The following are six of the most popular mobile CI/CD providers:

- Bitrise
- Codemagic
- GitHub Actions
- Xcode Cloud
- Visual Studio App Center
- Ionic AppFlow

To find the best fit for your mobile app project, you need to evaluate each provider based on the aforementioned factors.

Bitrise

Bitrise (`https://bitrise.io/`) is a cloud-based CI/CD platform specifically designed for mobile application development. It streamlines the process of building, testing, and deploying iOS, Android, and cross-platform apps, helping developers ensure their applications are reliable and high-quality:

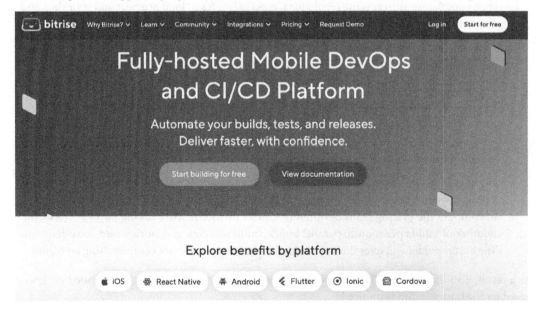

Figure 4.2 – Bitrise home page

Bitrise's mobile-first approach makes it a CI/CD solution for mobile app developers and offers specialized features and tools tailored to mobile development workflows.

Bitrise provides seamless integrations with popular version control systems such as GitHub, GitLab, self-hosted GitLab, and Bitbucket, as shown in *Figure 4.3*, as well as with mobile app development tools such as fastlane, Xcode, and Android SDKs:

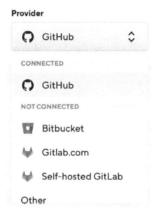

Figure 4.3 – Bitrise's version control system

Bitrise's visual workflow editor allows developers to easily design and configure their CI/CD pipelines without manually editing configuration files, as shown in *Figure 4.4*:

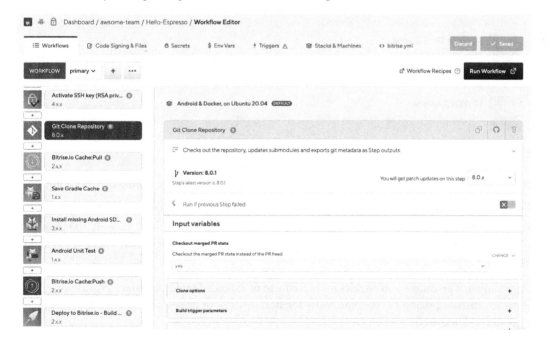

Figure 4.4 – Bitrise's workflow editor

Bitrise offers a wide range of pre-built and community steps that can be easily added to workflows, simplifying the process of setting up common mobile app development tasks, as shown in *Figure 4.5*:

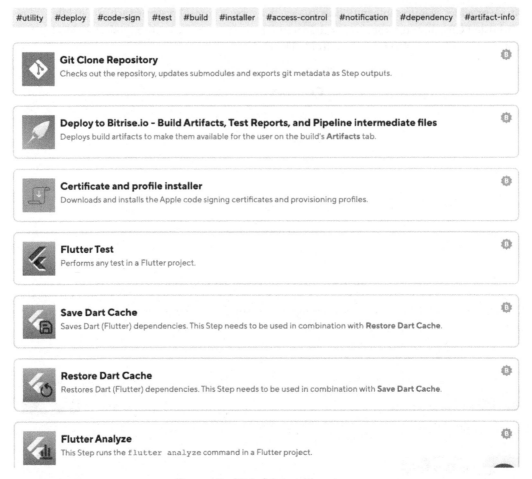

Figure 4.5 – Bitrise's integration steps

Bitrise supports iOS simulators and Android emulators, simplifying the testing of mobile apps on various devices and setups.

The platform offers a complimentary (hobby) plan with 90-minute build durations, 300 monthly credits, and up to 5 simultaneous builds with macOS M1 VMs, making it cost-effective for small projects and individual users.

Upgrading to a premium plan enables more frequent or extended builds for larger projects or teams. However, Bitrise's pricing can become costly for sizable teams or projects that need additional build capabilities or features.

By seamlessly integrating with well-known app stores and beta testing services such as Google Play, Apple App Store, and TestFlight, Bitrise streamlines the release process.

Developers can leverage Bitrise Insights to pinpoint and address bottlenecks, enhance build processes, and use credits more effectively.

Data and configuration settings can be stored securely, ensuring unauthorized individuals cannot access them. Using Bitrise's team management functionality, developers can collaborate on projects and control access to specific workflows and environments.

Example

Let's look at an example of creating a Bitrise application for Android and configuring it.

The prerequisites

You will require the following:

- A Bitrise account (`https://app.bitrise.io/users/sign_up`)
- A GitHub account (`https://github.com/join`)
- An Android app
- A Google Play Console account or Apple Developer ID to be able to release your mobile apps to the relevant app stores afterward

Let's get started!

Getting started

Follow these steps:

1. To get started with Bitrise for Android, you need to select **Add new app**, as shown in *Figure 4.6*:

Figure 4.6 – Add new app

2. Then, select the workspace type to specify whether the app will have private or public access, as shown in the following figure:

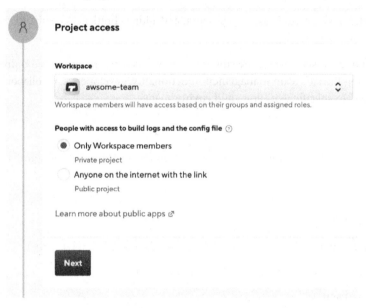

Figure 4.7 – Selecting the app's privacy

3. The next step is selecting the repository from the provider, such as GitHub, as shown in the following figure:

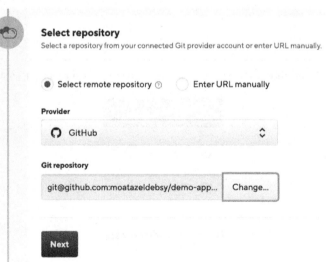

Figure 4.8 – Selecting a repository

4.   Then, choose to add an SSH key to be able to access the source code, as shown in the following figure:

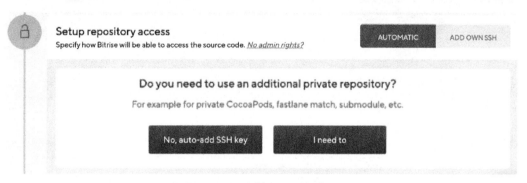

Figure 4.9 – Adding an SSH key

5.   Select the branch name from the list and choose the **Yes, auto-detect configuration** option to let Bitrise automatically detect the application type, as shown in the following figure:

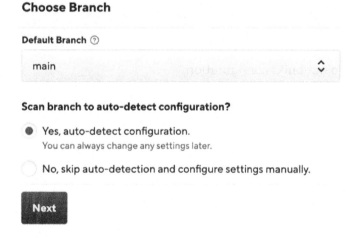

Figure 4.10 – Choosing a branch

6.   Bitrise will detect that the app is an Android one and will give you the appropriate machine type and stack. Now, you can add the app module and variant, as shown in the following figure:

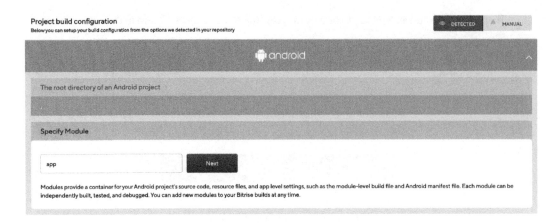

Figure 4.11 – Selecting the app's module

This is the project configuration, including the Android stack and all the other information:

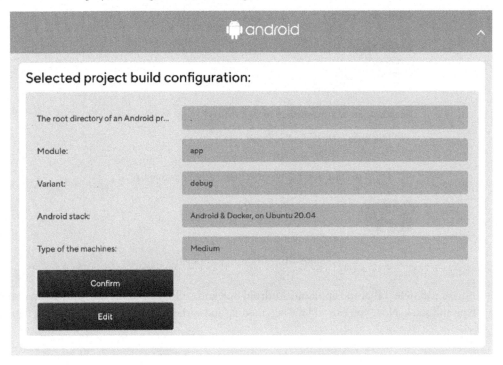

Figure 4.12 – Confirming the configuration

7. The next screen will be **App icon**. Here, you can upload a custom image or use the icon from the app's directory, as shown in the following figure:

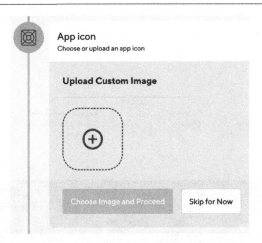

Figure 4.13 – App icon

8.   Next, you must register a webhook and trigger the first build, as shown in *Figure 4.14* and *Figure 4.15*:

Figure 4.14 – Registering a webhook

Figure 4.15 – Running the first build

9.   The first build will be started. At this point, you can check the build log and the build's details, as shown in the following figure:

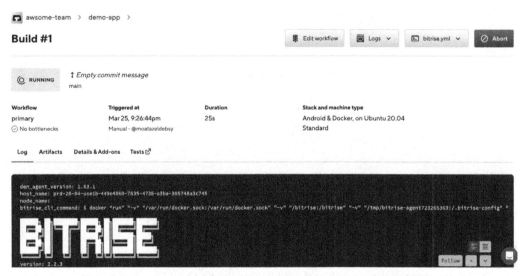

Figure 4.16 – Build log details

10. Once the build has finished, you can check the build's status to see whether it was a success or a failure, as shown in the following figure:

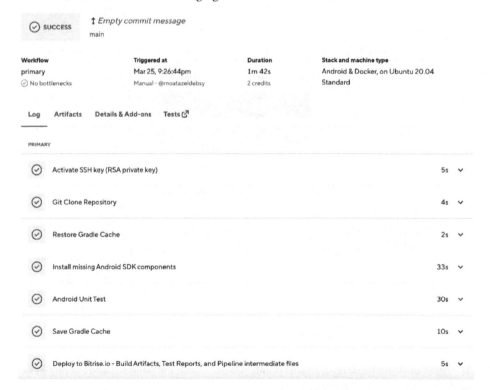

Figure 4.17 – Success build on Bitrise

11. After that, you can click on the **Workflow Editor** button to view or modify the CI workflow by adding or removing steps, as shown in the following figure:

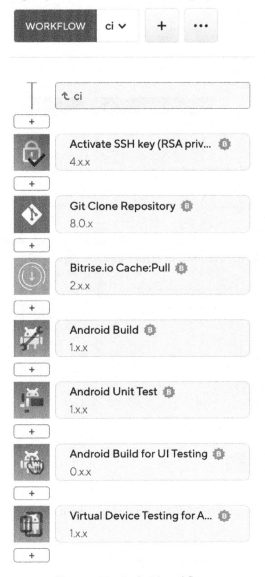

Figure 4.18 – Android workflow

12. From the **Workflow Editor** area, you can configure the trigger map or when you run the workflow based on Gitflow, such as running on every pull request, a new tag, or when pushing new code, as shown in the following figure:

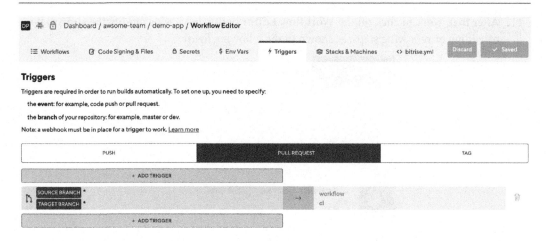

Figure 4.19 – How to trigger the build on Bitrise

13. Additionally, you can add secret environment variables for any third-party tools or services such as a Slack webhook, as shown in *Figure 4.20* and *Figure 4.21*:

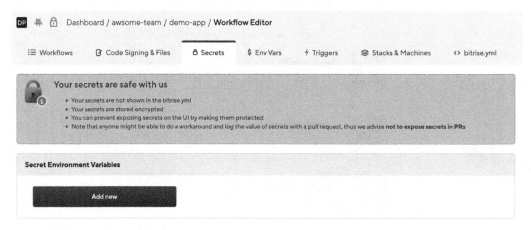

Figure 4.20 – Adding secret environment variables

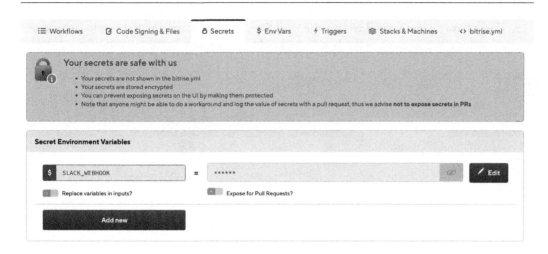

Figure 4.21 – Adding a Slack webhook

14. You can also change the stack and machine types, as shown in the following figure:

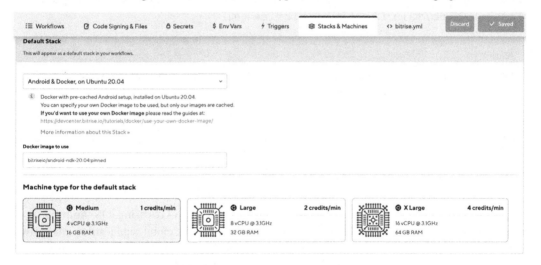

Figure 4.22 – Changing the stack and machine types

15. If you have any unit or UI tests in the workflow, you can access the test results, which are automatically generated, in the **Test Reports** add-on, as shown in the following figure:

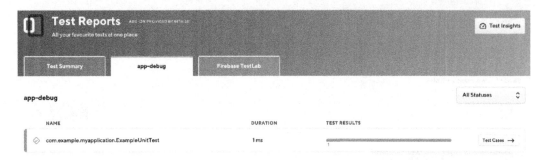

Figure 4.23 – The Test Reports add-on

Bitrise also has a `bitrise.yml` file that saves all of the configurations you did in a `yml` file; you can save it with the source code or on the Bitrise website. Here's a link to an example of a `bitrise.yml` file: `https://github.com/PacktPublishing/Mobile-DevOps-Playbook/blob/main/Chapter-4/bitrise.yml`.

> **Note**
> Other apps, such as iOS, macOS, Flutter, React Native, Ionic, and Cordova, use the same process, but the steps vary depending on the type.

Codemagic

Codemagic (`https://codemagic.io/start/`) is a fully cloud-hosted and managed CI/CD solution specifically designed for mobile app development, emphasizing cross-platform projects.

The platform streamlines the process of constructing, examining, and releasing iOS, Android, and cross-platform apps, empowering developers to produce high-quality mobile applications efficiently. This analysis will cover the advantages, disadvantages, and features of Codemagic, as well as how Codemagic measures up against other CI/CD alternatives in the market:

Figure 4.24 – Codemagic home page

Developers can easily configure Flutter builds via the user interface or the highly customizable codemagic.yaml file, allowing for app creation on Android, iOS, web, and desktop platforms.

Codemagic seamlessly integrates with well-known version control systems such as GitHub, GitLab, and Bitbucket and is compatible with various app stores, beta testing services, and notification tools.

The platform's uncomplicated setup procedure allows developers to swiftly establish their CI/CD pipelines without requiring in-depth technical knowledge.

With Codemagic, developers can design custom workflows using either YAML configuration files or the web-based configuration editor, granting flexibility and authority over the CI/CD process.

The platform offers a generous free tier, including 500 build minutes per month, a 120-minute build timeout, and macOS M1 virtual machines, making it suitable for smaller projects and individual developers, but you need to enable billing to have the full features.

Codemagic provides dedicated support for Flutter projects, automatically detecting project settings and applying optimizations for building and testing Flutter apps.

The platform supports iOS simulators and Android emulators, enabling developers to assess their mobile applications on various devices and configurations.

Codemagic integrates with popular app stores such as Google Play and Apple App Store, as well as beta testing services such as TestFlight, simplifying the deployment process.

Sensitive data and configuration settings can be securely stored, ensuring they are not disclosed in logs or accessed by unauthorized users.

Codemagic also includes unlimited team seats and an access management feature that facilitates project collaboration and allows developers to regulate access to specific workflows and environments.

Example

In this example, we'll build and test a Flutter application using Codemagic and configure it according to our needs.

The prerequisites

You will need the following:

- A Codemagic account (`https://codemagic.io/signup`)
- A GitHub account (`https://github.com/join`)
- The Flutter app
- A Google Play Console account or Apple Developer ID to be able to release your mobile apps to the relevant app stores afterward

Let's get started!

Getting started

Follow these steps:

1. After creating your account, you can start setting up your first app on Codemagic by selecting the repository and the project type, as shown in the following figure:

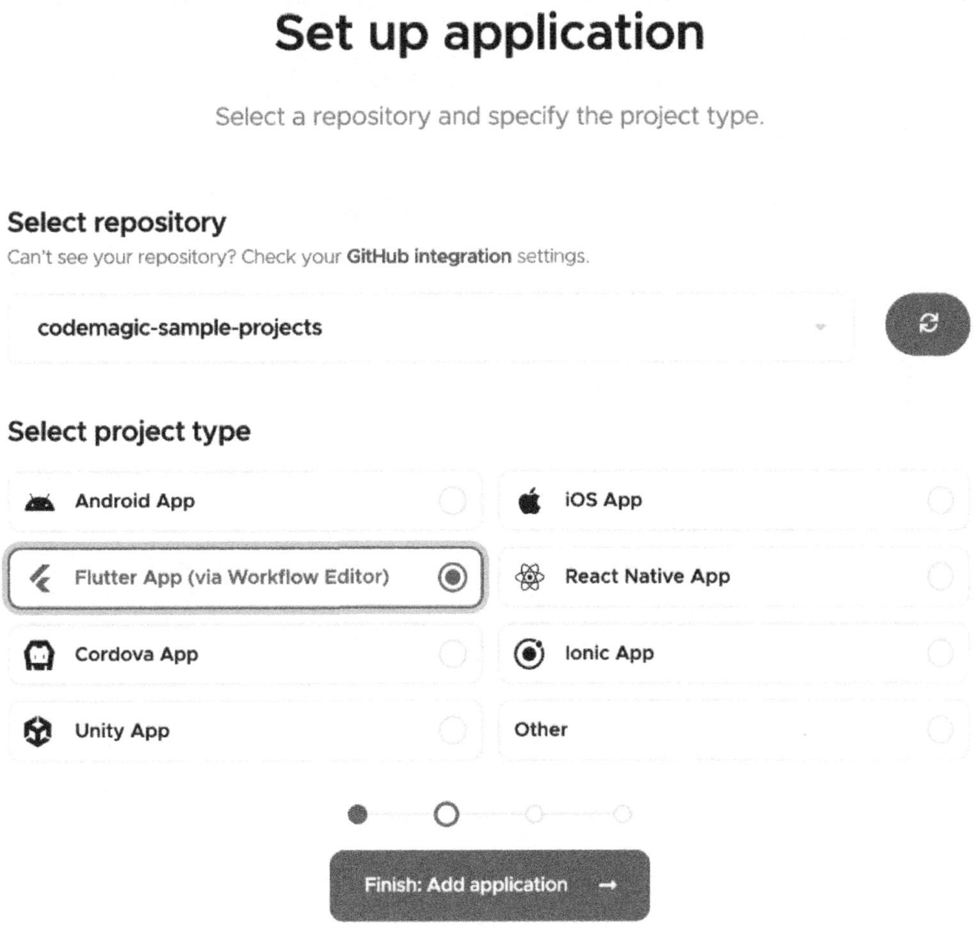

Set up application

Select a repository and specify the project type.

Select repository

Can't see your repository? Check your **GitHub integration** settings.

codemagic-sample-projects

Select project type

Android App	iOS App
Flutter App (via Workflow Editor)	React Native App
Cordova App	Ionic App
Unity App	Other

Finish: Add application →

Figure 4.25 – Choosing the repository and project type

2. Next, from the **Workflow Editor** area, select your preferred configuration such as iOS, Android, or both from your Flutter app, as well as your machine type, as shown in *Figure 4.26* and *Figure 4.27*:

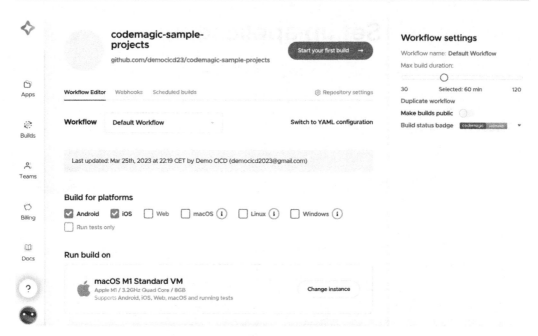

Figure 4.26 – Codemagic's Workflow Editor area

Figure 4.27 – Machine types on Codemagic

3. Then, you can configure the build triggers or make the build fail if the tests fail, as shown in *Figure 4.28* and *Figure 4.29*:

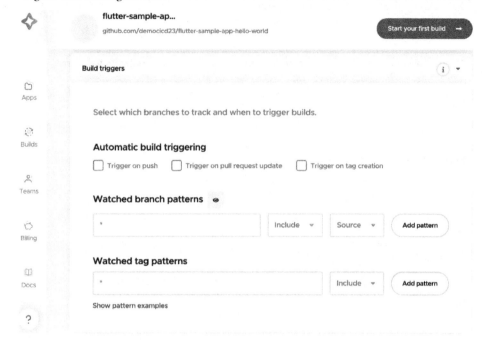

Figure 4.28 – Build trigger

Figure 4.29 – Configuring the tests

4. Next, you can configure the Android Flutter configuration, including **Flutter version**, **Project path**, and **Android build format**, as shown in the following figure:

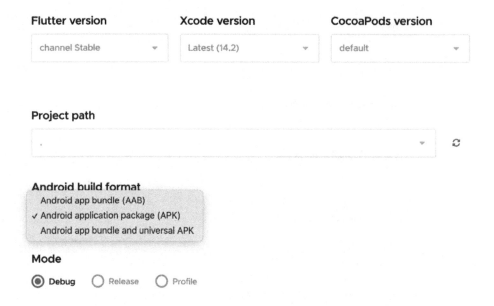

Figure 4.30 – Specifying the Flutter configuration

5. After that, you can set up notifications and select whether you need to send emails or Slack notifications, as shown in the following figure:

Figure 4.31 – Configuring notifications

6. Now, you can trigger your first build by selecting the workflow's name and the branch's name, as shown in the following figure:

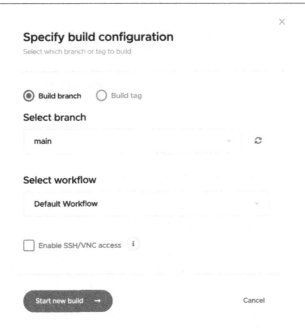

Figure 4.32 – Starting a new build

7. Now, you can check the build log and its status, as shown in *Figure 4.33* and *Figure 4.34*:

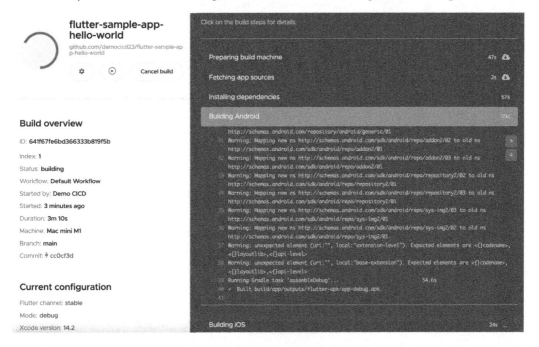

Figure 4.33 – Build view

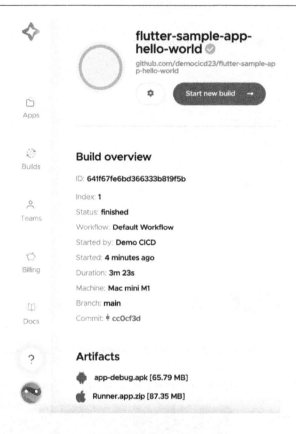

Figure 4.34 – Successful build

With Codemagic, similar to Bitrise, you can save the `.yaml` file on the Codemagic website via the **Workflow Editor** area or as a `codemagic.yml` file, as shown in *Figure 4.35* and *Figure 4.36*:

Figure 4.35 – Changing the settings to codemagic.yaml from the Workflow Editor area

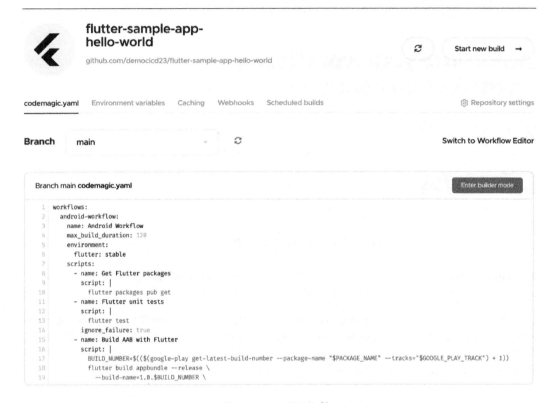

Figure 4.36 – YAML file

Here is an example of the YAML file for building Flutter via iOS and Android: `https://github.com/PacktPublishing/Mobile-DevOps-Playbook/blob/main/Chapter-4/codemagic.yml`.

GitHub Actions

GitHub Actions (`https://github.com/features/actions`) is an automation platform designed to streamline mobile development by enabling CI/CD workflows:

Figure 4.37 – GitHub Actions home page

As a part of the GitHub ecosystem, GitHub Actions is tightly integrated with the platform, making it easy for mobile developers to set up and use their existing repositories.

GitHub Actions allows developers to create custom workflows using simple YAML syntax, enabling highly specific and complex automation tasks. While there is a GUI available during the CI build to display the steps and connections, it's not currently feasible to construct the workflow using GUI platforms such as Codemagic or Bitrise:

Figure 4.38 – The workflows folder inside the app repository

The GitHub Actions Marketplace offers a wide range of pre-built actions that the community contributes, which can be easily incorporated into workflows, saving time and effort.

GitHub Actions supports various platforms, including Windows, macOS, and Linux, similar to Codemagic, allowing mobile developers to test and release projects on multiple environments such as Flutter apps. You can build and release mobile, web, and desktop apps from a single code base:

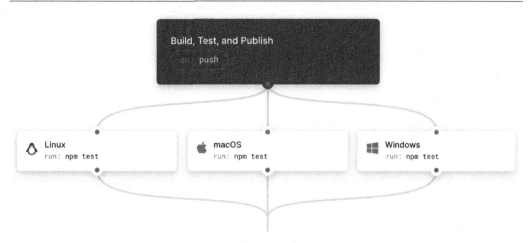

Figure 4.39 – Machine types in GitHub Actions

Self-hosted runners are available on GitHub, and you can customize the environment to run jobs in your GitHub Actions workflow.

It offers a generous free tier, with 2,000 minutes per month for private repositories for individuals and organizations. However, larger projects and teams may quickly exceed the allotted minutes and be required to upgrade to a paid plan.

In addition, GitHub offers features such as Codespace, a cloud developer environment with flexible compute and preconfigured containers, package storage, GitHub issues such as bugs or security issues, and project management, and the new GitHub Copilot add-on, which gets suggestions for whole lines or entire functions inside your editor.

Setting up GitHub Actions may require a steep learning curve for users unfamiliar with YAML or CI/CD concepts. As GitHub Actions is part of the GitHub ecosystem, migrating to a different version control platform may prove challenging.

While the Marketplace offers many pre-built actions, GitHub Actions may not have native support for some third-party services, requiring users to create custom actions or find alternative solutions.

GitHub Actions supports many triggers, including push and pull requests, issue creation, and scheduled events. This feature lets developers simultaneously test their code on multiple versions of programming languages, platforms, and configurations.

Caching is another feature offered by GitHub Actions. It allows you to cache dependencies, speed up build times, and reduce resource usage. GitHub Actions stores build artifacts and logs, making it easy to access and share results with team members.

In addition to providing security, GitHub includes features such as code scanning, secret scanning, dependency review with dependabot alerts, and preventing sensitive data or configuration settings from being exposed in logs or shared with unauthorized individuals.

Example

Let's look at an example of setting up GitHub Actions for an Android app to build and run unit and lint tests.

The prerequisites:

- A GitHub account (`https://github.com/join`)
- An Android app
- A Google Play Console account or Apple Developer ID to be able to release your mobile apps to the relevant app stores afterward

Let's get started!

Getting started

Let's get started:

1. If you already have an Android application, you can click on the **Actions** button to start using GitHub Actions, as shown in the following figure:

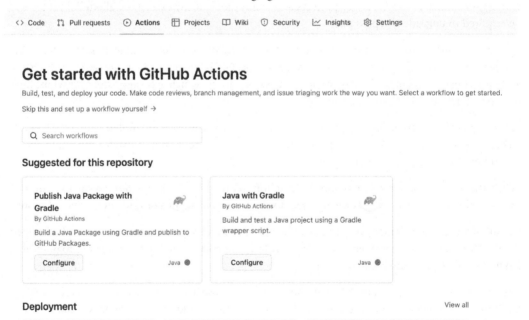

Figure 4.40 – Getting started with GitHub Actions

2. Click on **Java with Gradle** or search for `Android` to find a template for this, as shown in the following figure:

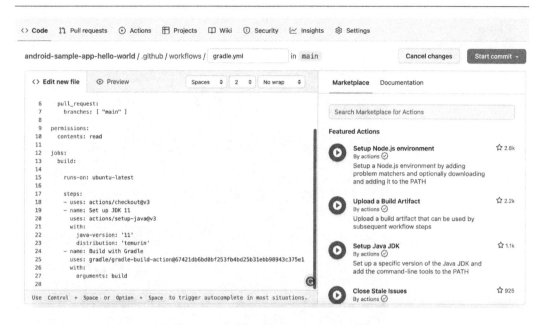

Figure 4.41 – The default gradle.yaml file

3.   Trigger the build after committing the change. GitHub Actions will start a new build. At this point, you can check the log, as shown in *Figure 4.42* and *Figure 4.43*:

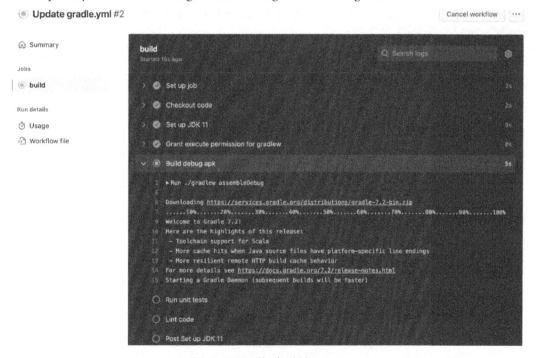

Figure 4.42 – The build log view

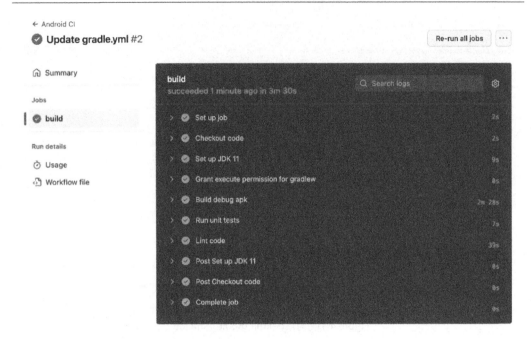

Figure 4.43 – Successful build

Here is an example of a GitHub Actions Android CI YAML file: `https://github.com/PacktPublishing/Mobile-DevOps-Playbook/blob/main/Chapter-4/.github/workflows/android.yml`.

Example

For our next example, we will set up GitHub Actions for an iOS app so that we can build the app and run the necessary unit tests:

Choose a workflow

Build, test, and deploy your code. Make code reviews, branch management, and issue triaging work the way you want. Select a workflow to get started.

Skip this and set up a workflow yourself →

Q Search workflows

Suggested for this repository

Swift	
By GitHub Actions	
Build and test a Swift Package.	
Configure	Swift ●

iOS	
By GitHub Actions	
Build and test an iOS application using xcodebuild and any available iPhone simulator.	
Configure	

Xcode - Build and Analyze	
By GitHub Actions	
Build Xcode project using xcodebuild	
Configure	Objective-C ●

Figure 4.44 – Getting started with the iOS app

Here is an example of the YAML file for the iOS app: `https://github.com/PacktPublishing/Mobile-DevOps-Playbook/blob/main/Chapter-4/.github/workflows/iOS.yml`.

> **Note**
>
> You can remove the Install CocoaPods step if your app doesn't include a podfile.

Xcode Cloud

Xcode Cloud (`https://developer.apple.com/xcode-cloud/`) is a CI/CD service built by Apple and integrated directly into the Xcode development environment. It is designed to streamline the process of building, testing, and deploying iOS, macOS, watchOS, and tvOS applications:

Figure 4.45 – Xcode Cloud home page

Xcode Cloud is fully integrated with the Xcode development environment, providing a seamless experience for Apple developers.

The integration with Xcode means that setting up a CI/CD pipeline is straightforward, with minimal configuration required.

To use Xcode Cloud, you must have Apple Developer Program membership.

There is a free version of Xcode Cloud, but it only comes with 25 compute hours per month. Xcode Cloud is optimized for building and testing Apple platform applications, ensuring optimal performance and compatibility. It supports parallel testing across multiple devices and configurations, speeding up the testing process and improving overall efficiency.

As an Apple service, Xcode Cloud is designed to protect source code and build artifacts throughout the CI/CD process. Xcode Cloud is specifically designed for Apple platforms and so is unsuitable for Android or other non-Apple application development.

Xcode Cloud's tight integration with Xcode may limit the level of customization available compared to more general-purpose CI/CD solutions.

As Xcode Cloud is integrated with Xcode, developers who prefer other development environments may find it less appealing.

Features

Xcode Cloud provides automated code diagnostics, allowing you to identify issues and get recommendations for improvement.

Xcode Cloud integrates with App Store Connect, streamlining the process of distributing applications to testers and submitting them to the App Store. It supports collaboration, allowing team members to collaborate on projects, share results, and coordinate their efforts.

Example

Let's look at an example of using Xcode Cloud to build, test, and archive an iOS application.

The prerequisites:

You must have the following:

- An Apple Developer ID to be able to release your mobile apps to the App Store
- A GitHub account (`https://github.com/join`)
- An iOS app

Let's get started!

Getting started

Follow these steps:

1. To get started with Xcode Cloud, open the iOS app in Xcode and click **Report Navigator** in the left-hand side menu, then click **Get Started with Xcode Cloud**. After that, you must select a product, which is the app that you want to build:

Figure 4.46 – Xcode Cloud inside the Xcode IDE

2. At this point, the **Workflow Editor** area will open. Here, you can modify the steps as you wish, as shown in *Figure 4.47* and *Figure 4.48*:

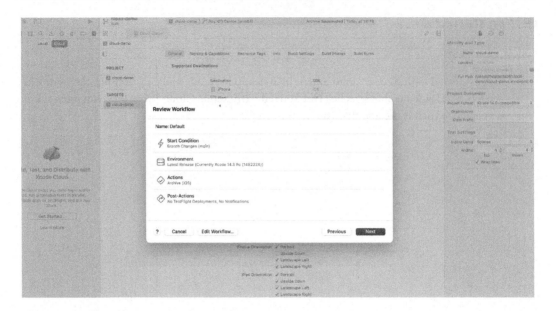

Figure 4.47 – The Workflow Editor area

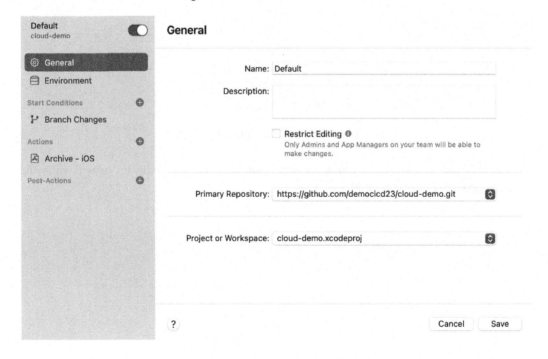

Figure 4.48 – Editing the workflow

3. You can add different steps such as **Build**, **Test**, **Analyze**, and **Archive** for your iOS app, as shown in the following figure:

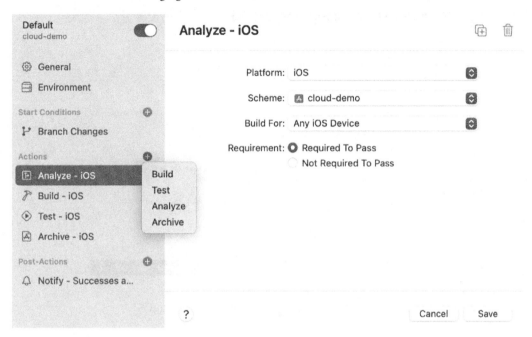

Figure 4.49 – Adding different steps, such as Test and Analyze

4. Next, you need to connect Xcode Cloud to your GitHub repositories so that you can access your source code and install the Xcode Cloud app, as shown in *Figure 4.50*, *Figure 4.51*, and *Figure 4.52*:

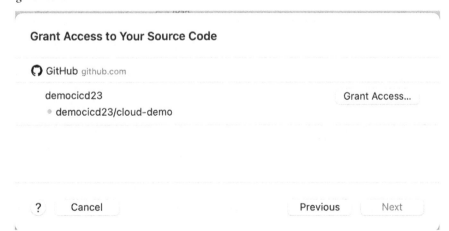

Figure 4.50 – Granting access to your source code

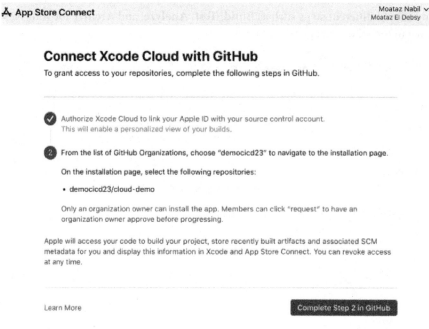

Figure 4.51 – Connecting Xcode Cloud with GitHub

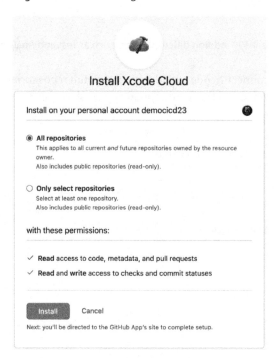

Figure 4.52 – Installing the Xcode Cloud app

5. Select your repository for the Xcode Cloud app, as shown in the following figure:

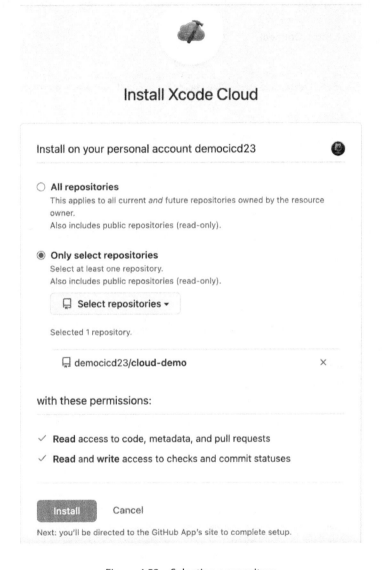

Figure 4.53 – Selecting a repository

6.   Next, from Xcode Cloud, you can create an app record via App Store Connect to be able to release the app to the App Store if you don't have an existing one, as shown in the following figure:

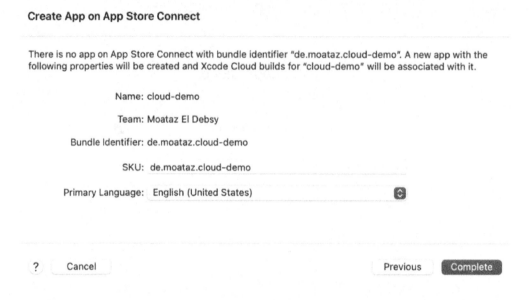

Figure 4.54 – Create App on App Store Connect

7.   Now, you can start the build by selecting the branch name and clicking the **Start Build** button, as shown in the following figure:

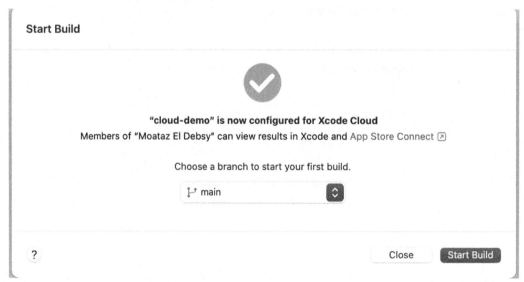

Figure 4.55 – Starting the build

8.   You can now view the build log via the Xcode IDE, as shown in the following figure:

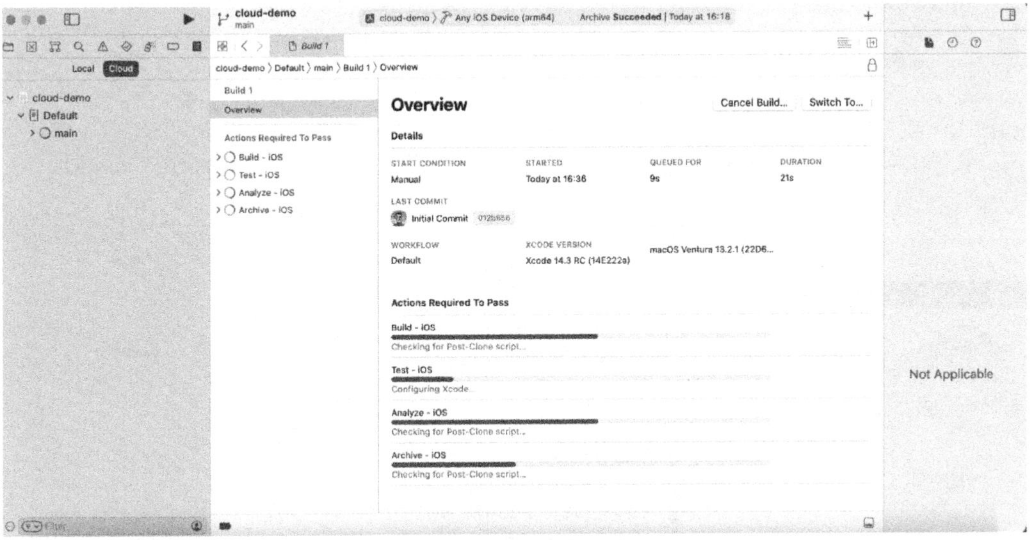

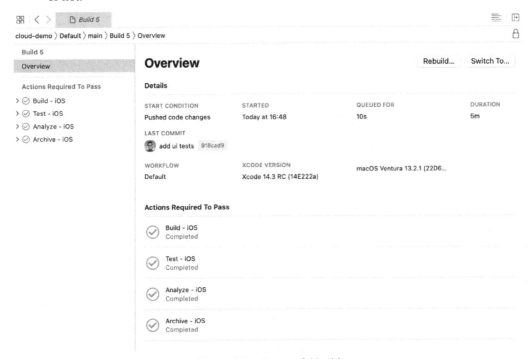

Figure 4.56 – Build view

9.   Once the build has finished, you can check its status to see whether it's completed successfully or not:

Figure 4.57 – Successful build

10. Additionally, you can check the test results in the logs and test artifacts, as shown in *Figure 4.58* and *Figure 4.59*:

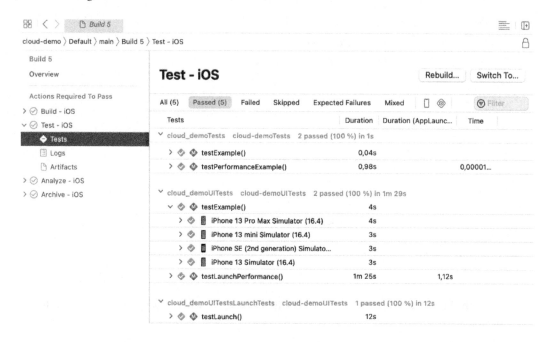

Figure 4.58 – The Test - iOS view

Figure 4.59 – The Archive - iOS view

> **Note**
>
> There is no YAML file for the workflow with Xcode Cloud. However, you can modify or access the workflows from the Xcode IDE or App Store Connect, as shown in the following figure: 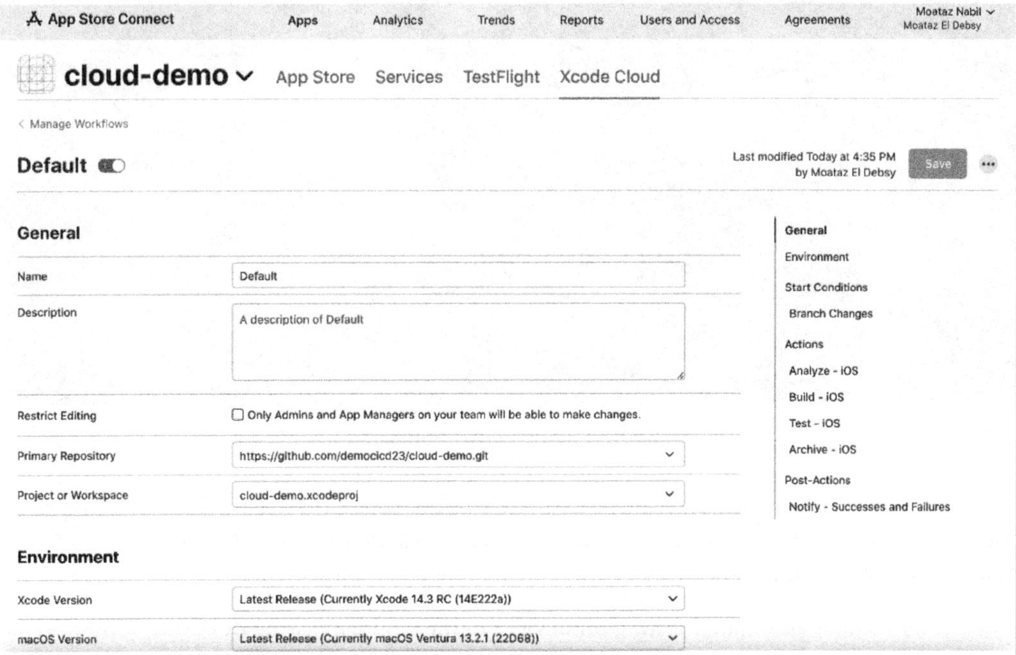
>
>
> Figure 4.60 – Xcode Cloud on App Store Connect

Visual Studio App Center

Visual Studio App Center (`https://appcenter.ms/`) is a cloud-based CI/CD platform developed by Microsoft, specifically designed for mobile app development.

It supports iOS, Android, React Native, and Xamarin projects, streamlining the process of building, testing, distributing, and monitoring mobile applications. This section will discuss the pros, cons, and features of Visual Studio App Center, as well as how it compares to other CI/CD solutions on the market:

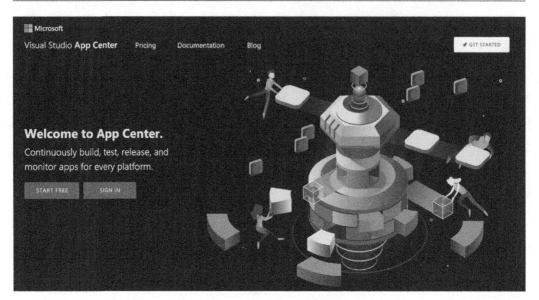

Figure 4.61 – App Center home page

The platform boasts a user-friendly setup process, allowing developers to establish their CI/CD pipelines quickly. You can integrate with widely used version control systems such as GitHub, Bitbucket, and Azure Repos, along with connections to app stores and beta testing services.

App Center enables automated testing on devices in the cloud, assisting developers in verifying compatibility and performance across multiple target platforms. Although its pricing may be costly for larger teams or projects that need increased build capacity or features, its streamlined setup process compensates for this drawback. However, it might lack the customization options other CI/CD platforms offer.

As App Center focuses on mobile app development, it may not be the ideal choice for non-mobile or web development projects. The platform simplifies the process of building and signing iOS and Android apps, ensuring consistency throughout releases. It facilitates testing on various real devices in the cloud, guaranteeing compatibility and performance across target platforms.

App Center streamlines the distribution of applications to beta testers, app stores, or enterprise environments, with support for **over-the-air** (**OTA**) updates. In addition, it offers crash reporting and analytics features, enabling developers to monitor app performance and detect issues in real time. Lastly, the platform manages and sends push notifications to users, supporting segmentation and targeting.

Example

Let's learn how to set up Visual Studio App Center for an Android app.

The prerequisites

You will need the following:

- An App Center account (`https://appcenter.ms/create-account`)
- A GitHub account (`https://github.com/join`)
- An Android app
- A Google Play Console account or Apple Developer ID to be able to release your mobile apps to the relevant app stores afterward

Let's get started!

Getting started

Follow these steps:

1. After creating an App Center account, the next step is to add a new app by selecting the app type and then connecting the source code provider, as displayed in *Figure 4.62* and *Figure 4.63*:

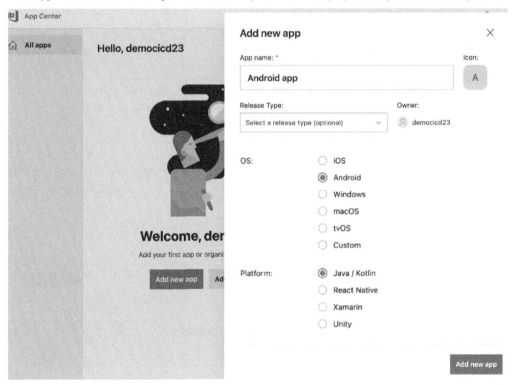

Figure 4.62 – Add new app

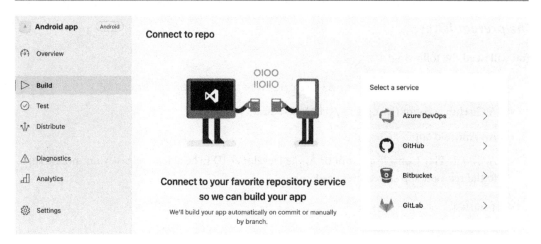

Figure 4.63 – Connecting the source code service

2. Next, select the app module, variant, and the other configuration options, then click the **Save & Build** button to start a new build, as shown in *Figure 4.64* and *Figure 4.65*:

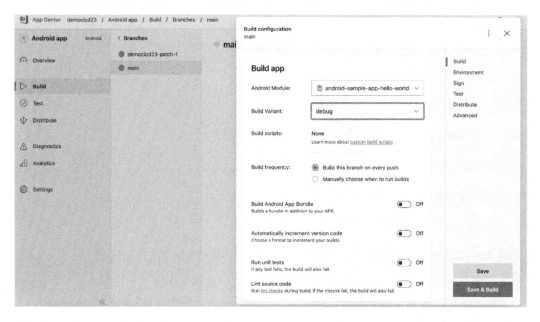

Figure 4.64 – Configuring the build

Figure 4.65 – Running the build

> **Note**
>
> There is no YAML file for the workflow with App Center; you can only modify or access the workflows from the website.

Ionic AppFlow

Ionic AppFlow (https://ionic.io/appflow) is a cloud-based CI/CD platform specifically designed for mobile app development using the Ionic framework. It streamlines the process of building, testing, and deploying iOS, Android, and **progressive web app** (**PWA**) applications built with Ionic, helping developers deliver high-quality applications efficiently:

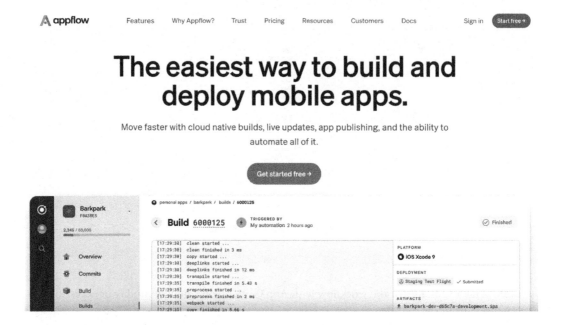

Figure 4.66 – AppFlow home page

Designed for Ionic framework projects, Ionic AppFlow delivers specialized features and enhancements for building and deploying Ionic apps. The platform streamlines the setup process, enabling developers to efficiently configure their CI/CD pipelines without in-depth technical expertise. Live updates are supported, allowing for direct deployment of changes and bug fixes to users' devices without app store reviews.

Ionic AppFlow seamlessly integrates with popular version control systems such as GitHub, GitLab, and Bitbucket, as well as app stores, beta testing services, and notification tools. It also automates the build process for iOS and Android, simplifying mobile app deployment.

However, Ionic AppFlow's focus on the Ionic framework might not be suitable for non-Ionic or non-mobile app development projects. Its pricing can be costly for larger teams or projects that require extra build capacity or features compared to alternative CI/CD solutions. While it streamlines the setup, Ionic AppFlow may lack customization options of other CI/CD platforms.

Developers who favor other mobile app development frameworks might find Ionic AppFlow less appealing due to its specific focus on Ionic projects. Nevertheless, it offers dedicated support and is optimized for building and deploying Ionic apps.

Ionic AppFlow automatically generates iOS and Android builds for distribution through app stores or internal testing and deploys updates and bug fixes directly to users' devices without necessitating app store downloads.

Example

Let's learn how to set up Ionic AppFlow for an Ionic app.

The prerequisites

You must have the following:

- An AppFlow account (`https://ionic.io/signup?source=appflow&product=appflow`)

- A GitHub account (`https://github.com/join`)

- An Ionic app

- A Google Play Console account or Apple Developer ID to be able to release your mobile apps to the relevant app stores afterward

Let's get started!

Getting started

Follow these steps:

1. After creating your account, you can start creating a new app or import an existing one into AppFlow, as shown in the following figure:

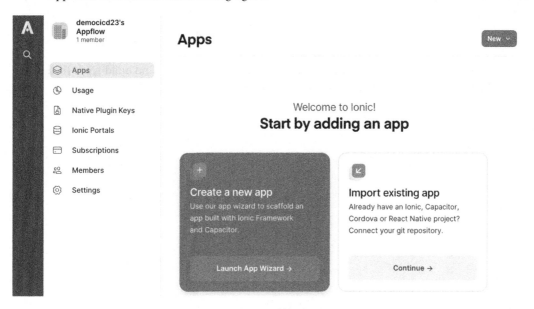

Figure 4.67 – Adding a new app or importing an existing Ionic app

2. Next, click on **Create your first build**, as shown in the following figure:

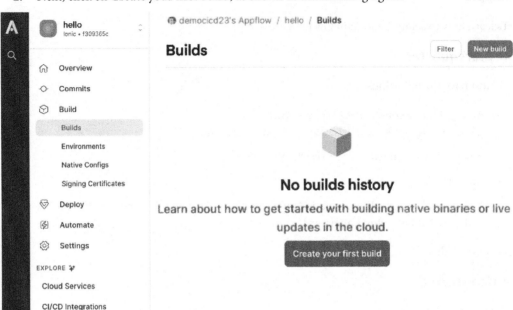

Figure 4.68 – Create your first build

3. Next, choose the app type, such as Android, then select the stack and build type. Then, click the **Build** button, as shown in the following figure:

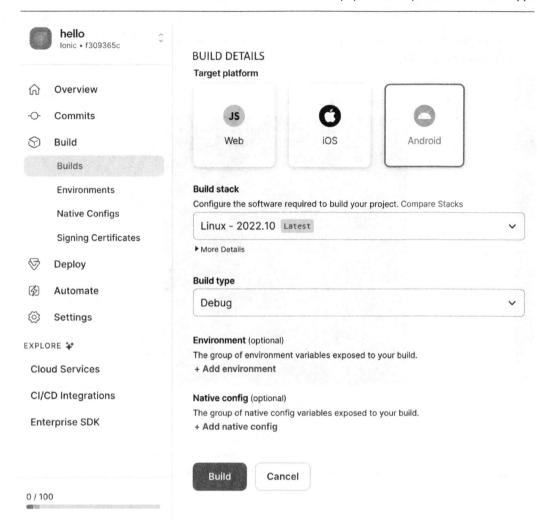

Figure 4.69 – Choosing the app to build

4.   Once the build has started, you can view the build's log view and build's status, as shown in the following figure:

Figure 4.70 – Build log view

Now that we have discussed the different CI/CD providers for mobile apps and how they work, we can create a workflow to build, test, and release mobile apps. You now better understand Mobile DevOps and which CI/CD provider is suitable for your apps, business, team, and, as we mentioned earlier, your budget.

> **Note**
>
> In addition, there are different CI/CD providers on the market, but they are not mobile-focused, such as CircleCI, GitLab, Azure Pipelines (DevOps), and Jenkins. A company may choose one of them if the rest of the teams use it for the backend and web applications.

In the previous examples, we covered the test steps that are integrated into the workflow or pipeline quickly because, in *Chapter 5, Implementing a Robust Mobile App Testing Strategy*, we will dive deep into testing, from designing the testing strategy to running a different type of testing in the CI/CD pipeline. As we move on to *Chapter 6, Mobile App Release Management*, we will complete the CI/CD cycle and learn more about app releases.

Summary

CI/CD for mobile apps is a process that enables organizations to quickly and efficiently release and update their mobile applications, ensuring that the code is stable, secure, and up to date.

Choosing the right CI/CD provider for a mobile app development project is crucial for ensuring a seamless development, testing, and release process. We explored the most popular CI/CD providers on the mobile CI/CD market, including Bitrise, Codemagic, GitHub Actions, Xcode Cloud, Visual Studio App Center, and Ionic AppFlow.

Each provider offers unique features, pricing plans, and levels of support, and it is essential to choose a provider that meets the team's specific needs.

One of the critical factors to consider is platform support, ensuring that the selected provider supports the platforms that the app targets. For example, some providers specialize in one platform, such as Xcode Cloud, while others support multiple platforms, such as Bitrise. Organizations should also consider performance and reliability, build configuration and environment, scalability, integration, security, ease of use, community and support, and pricing.

We also discussed implementing CI and provided detailed steps for setting up different CI servers for mobile apps, including setting up the necessary build and unit tests.

In the next few chapters, we will continue our journey toward implementing full CI/CD with test automation, release management, and DevSecOps.

5

Implementing a Robust Mobile App Testing Strategy

As discussed in the previous chapters, mobile applications have become integral to our daily lives. With the proliferation of smartphones and tablets, developing and delivering mobile apps that provide a seamless user experience across different devices and platforms has become essential. Mobile app testing involves testing different aspects of the application, including its functionality, performance, security, usability, and compatibility. In addition, testing should be done on various devices, operating systems, and network configurations to ensure the app works seamlessly across all possible scenarios.

It cannot be argued that mobile app testing plays a critical role in ensuring the application performs well, booms, and has a positive user experience. By investing time and resources into testing, developers are more likely to develop responsive applications and deliver exceptional user experiences.

Test automation for mobile apps in Mobile DevOps is like the wheels on a car – it provides the necessary traction for driving the project forward efficiently and with minimal risk. With it, you will find yourself able to reach your destination.

However, developing and testing mobile apps can be challenging due to the diverse range of devices, operating systems, and network configurations. In this chapter, we will discuss how to implement a robust mobile app testing strategy that can help you deliver high-quality mobile apps, including the following topics:

- Understanding mobile app testing
- The importance of test automation for mobile apps
- Mobile app testing challenges and pitfalls
- What is a mobile app testing strategy?
- Testing tools, frameworks, and services for mobile apps
- Mobile app UI and functionality testing

- Testing on cloud devices
- How AI and ML are changing mobile testing
- Test case management
- Achieving successful mobile test coverage

Let's begin by understanding more about mobile app testing.

Understanding mobile app testing

Mobile app testing involves testing different aspects of the application, including functionality, performance, security, usability, and compatibility. In addition, testing should be done on various devices, operating systems, and network configurations to ensure the app works seamlessly across all possible scenarios. Mobile apps should be tested before and after they have been launched to identify and fix any bugs and new features that might improve the user experience.

First, let's discuss the different testing levels in software development and mobile development specifically.

Testing levels

The field of software development is constantly evolving, particularly in the realm of mobile development. This is because we are always striving to introduce new and improved features and technologies that can better assist our customers in their daily tasks. Therefore, all mobile developers need to adopt testing as a necessary practice to ensure that all functionalities are performing as intended.

There are various types of testing, each with its own scope. Typically, we categorize these types using the test pyramid as a reference.

Unit testing

These are tests that focus on individual components that have a single responsibility. Essentially, this is the lowest level of testing. In this level of testing, the developer asserts a set of conditions that must be true, along with some that need to be false.

Imagine we are developing a calculator app – the developer will assert what will happen when we click on the plus (+) button, and the expected results will be narrowly defined.

As a unit of code, unit testing cannot detect integration errors or system-level errors, which are covered in integration and **end to end** (**E2E**) testing.

When it comes to verifying different aspects of a program, unit testing can be used in various ways to find the following:

- The expected cases or "happy paths"
- The edge cases

- The boundary conditions
- The program's logic

In iOS, we can use the **XCTest** framework to write unit tests for our Xcode projects that integrate seamlessly with Xcode's testing workflow.

In Android, unit tests are compiled to execute on the **Java Virtual Machine** (**JVM**) to reduce the amount of time it takes. If your tests rely on objects within the Android framework, you can use the **Robolectric** (`https://robolectric.org/`) tool. In cases where your tests depend on your dependencies, mock objects can be utilized to emulate the expected behavior of those dependencies.

In Flutter, a unit test can be written using the `test` package, and a widget can be tested using the `flutter_test` package.

In React Native, developers use testing frameworks such as **Jest** (`https://jestjs.io/`) and testing utilities such as **React Testing Library** (`https://testing-library.com/docs/react-testing-library/intro/`) to facilitate unit testing.

When it comes to writing efficient unit tests, there are certain criteria to keep in mind:

- Tests should be fast and efficient.
- Tests must be fully automated and should only indicate "pass" or "fail" outcomes.
- Tests should be independent and isolated from one another, meaning they should not share states.
- It is advisable to write tests before writing the production code. This is known as **test-driven development** (**TDD**).

Unit testing and code coverage

The purpose of code coverage testing is to determine how much code is being tested. The following formula can be used to calculate it:

```
Code Coverage Percentage = (Number of lines of code executed)/(Total
number of lines of code in an application) * 100
```

Here are the different techniques for code coverage that are utilized in unit testing:

- Statement coverage
- Decision coverage
- Branch coverage
- Condition coverage

There are also different code coverage tools, such as the following:

- **JaCoCo** (`https://docs.gradle.org/current/userguide/jacoco_plugin.html`) can generate an HTML report for your Android unit tests and integrate it with your continuous integration server.

- **Flutter Console Coverage Test** (`https://pub.dev/packages/test_cov_console`) is a Dart tool that's used to generate a Flutter Coverage Test report.

- **dlcov** (`https://pub.dev/packages/dlcov`) is a CLI that's used to verify the code coverage threshold.

- **SonarQube** (`https://www.sonarsource.com/products/sonarqube/`) integrates with various build systems and supports Android projects. It provides a comprehensive quality analysis platform that includes code coverage metrics.

- **Codecov** (`https://about.codecov.io/`) is a service that provides code coverage solutions for various programming languages, including mobile app development platforms. It can integrate with your CI/CD pipeline to gather and display coverage reports.

Another technique can be used alongside unit testing to improve the quality of a code base: **TDD**. Let's explore the concept and its benefits.

Test-driven development

TDD is an approach to testing that differs from traditional methods. Instead of waiting until the code or feature is fully developed to test it, TDD involves creating tests based on the feature requirements and then writing code to ensure the tests pass, as shown in the following figure:

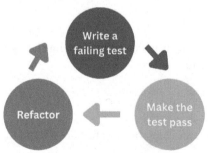

Figure 5.1 – How TDD works

Using TDD is an incredibly valuable technique for improving the internal quality of your code base. It also serves as a great tool for training yourself and your team to design better software in a disciplined manner.

Here is an overview of the TDD process and how it works:

1. Write a test. In this stage, the developers create tests for each functionality they want to add. These tests serve as requirements that the new code must meet and writing them first ensures that developers consider potential issues before writing any code.

2. Run the test and intentionally cause it to fail. This step confirms that the test is valid and that new code is necessary.

3. Write code that passes the failed test. While the code may not be perfect, it must meet the test requirements. If it fails, the code must be revised until it passes and ensures that the new code does not break any existing features.

4. Refactor the code for better readability and maintainability. Running tests at this stage ensures that the functionality is preserved.

5. Repeat the process from *Step 1* for each piece of functionality.

What are the benefits of TDD?

By writing tests before writing code, TDD challenges us to think more clearly and critically about the problem we are trying to solve.

Breaking down the problem into smaller parts leads to the creation of more modular code, which ultimately results in higher-quality code and lower maintenance costs.

To summarize, the benefits of TDD are as follows:

- Improves code quality

- Gives developers the confidence to make changes

What are the cons of TDD?

While TDD can improve software quality, it also has drawbacks. Some developers have expressed concerns about the approach and argue that it may not always be the best option.

The main criticisms are that TDD can slow down development and create additional code maintenance work.

When should you avoid using TDD?

While TDD helps teams prioritize their code base's internal quality early on, it's not the only way to do so. Whether you adopt TDD should depend on the reality of your project and the surrounding situation.

Here are some scenarios or situations where it may not make sense to use TDD:

- When experimenting or creating a proof of concept

- When dealing with language/framework methods

- When dealing with GUI development

To TDD or not to TDD

Implementing TDD involves a fundamental shift in culture and testing practices, requiring the support of both the engineering team and management.

If you work in an organization that utilizes extensive legacy code, you may be curious about how TDD can benefit you. While it may not affect the existing code base, you can gradually integrate TDD for new features and bug fixes, resulting in an improved code base over time.

Integration testing

These tests are meant to check the integration of individual components. This process ensures that all the different layers of the app, such as the UI, business logic, data storage, and external services, work together seamlessly. Integration testing helps uncover any issues that may arise due to the interactions between these different parts of the app.

Acceptance/E2E testing

Acceptance testing focuses on verifying whether a mobile app meets the specified requirements and is ready for release. It aims to ensure that the app aligns with the intended functionality, user expectations, and business requirements.

E2E testing focuses on testing the complete flow of an application, often spanning multiple components and systems. In the context of mobile apps, E2E testing ensures that all the different parts of the app work seamlessly together, from the UIs to the backend systems.

The difference between TDD and unit testing

Unit testing involves writing many small tests that each test one very simple function's or object's behavior. TDD is a thinking process that results in unit tests, and "thinking in tests" tends to result in more fine-grained and comprehensive testing and an easier-to-extend software design.

Let's move on and learn more about the different types of mobile app testing.

Types of mobile app testing

When it comes to mobile app testing, there are several types of testing that you can perform to ensure that your app is robust and reliable and provides an excellent user experience. Here are some of the most common types of mobile app testing:

- **Functional testing**: This aims to determine whether the app's functionality meets the requirements and works as expected. It involves testing a variety of aspects of the app, such as the UI, navigation, data processing, and business logic.

- **Regression testing**: This ensures that new features or changes do not affect the app's functionality. A regression test checks whether the app's existing features work correctly after introducing new features or changes.

- **Usability testing**: This focuses on the user experience and checks whether the app is easy to use, navigate, and understand. It involves testing the app's design, layout, colors, font sizes, and other elements that affect the user experience. Some of the popular testing activities here are **snapshot** and **visual testing**; we will discuss both in this chapter.

- **Compatibility testing**: This checks the app's compatibility with different devices, operating systems, and screen sizes. Testing the app's compatibility with hardware, network, and software configurations is necessary. Using cloud device testing such as Sauce Labs or Firebase Test Lab helps you run your test suites on different devices and configurations to ensure that the app works as expected.

- **Localization testing**: This checks whether the app is compatible with different languages, regions, and cultures by testing the language support, the date and time formats, the currency format, and other cultural elements, especially if the app supports languages such as Arabic since it changes the UI to **Right to Left** (**RTL**).

- **Performance testing**: This checks the app's performance and responsiveness under different scenarios, such as low battery, weak network connectivity, or high usage. It tests the app's load, response, memory usage, and battery consumption. In *Chapter 7, Establishing Mobile App Monitoring, Observability, and Analytics*, we will discuss how to monitor the performance of mobile apps using different tools and services.

- **Accessibility testing**: This tests the application's UI for accessibility to people with disabilities, such as those with visual impairments. Testing for accessibility can identify issues with an application's layout, design, and UI that may prevent users with disabilities from using it.

- **Security testing**: This checks the app's security features and identifies vulnerabilities that can compromise user data. It includes testing the app's authentication, authorization, encryption, and data storage mechanisms. In *Chapter 8, Keeping Mobile Apps and DevOps Secure*, we will discuss security testing and how to inject security into Mobile DevOps processes.

By performing these types of mobile app testing, you can ensure that your app is high quality, meets user expectations, and provides an excellent user experience.

Test automation is essential for mobile apps as it enhances efficiency, reduces costs, improves app quality, and ensures a positive user experience across a variety of devices and operating systems. By investing in test automation, mobile app developers can create and maintain high-quality apps that meet users' expectations and stand out in a competitive market.

Now, let's discuss the importance of test automation for mobile apps.

The importance of test automation for mobile apps

In mobile DevOps, test automation is essential as it makes the mobile development life cycle faster and more reliable.

Mobile DevOps cannot exist without test automation for the following reasons:

- **Faster release cycles**: Mobile DevOps aims to deliver mobile apps rapidly and consistently. Test automation helps achieve this by allowing teams to execute tests quickly and repeatedly, reducing the time it takes to identify and fix issues before deployment.

  Test scripts can be reused, making it easy to retest the app after updates or modifications.

- **Continuous integration and deployment/delivery (CI/CD)**: Mobile DevOps relies on **CI/CD** to streamline the mobile release process. Test automation is crucial to these processes. As part of the development cycle, automated tests are run every time code is committed or changes are made, ensuring the mobile app remains stable and functional. For example, the CI workflows and pipelines we implemented in the previous chapter can use different test automation tools such as **Espresso**, **XCUITest**, and **Appium** to ensure app quality.

- **Increased test coverage**: In this way, more tests can be run quickly, resulting in better test coverage. Continuous testing identifies issues earlier in the development process and reduces the possibility of final production defects. We will discuss how to achieve successful mobile test coverage, continuous testing, and shift-left testing later in this chapter.

- **Improved collaboration**: Automated mobile tests enable developers and testers to collaborate more efficiently by providing immediate feedback on how code changes impact the application. They prevent errors from entering the production environment and enhance communication among team members.

- **Cost-efficiency**: Manual testing can result in reduced test automation, saving time and money. By automating repetitive tasks, teams can focus on more complex tasks and increase productivity and the **Return On Investment(ROI)**.

Now, let's discuss the challenges we come across in mobile development before we discuss the need for a robust mobile testing strategy.

Mobile app testing challenges and pitfalls

Mobile technology is rapidly evolving, presenting unique challenges to mobile testing teams. Let's examine the most common challenges teams face when testing mobile apps so that we can overcome them:

- Finding suitable automation tools and frameworks can be challenging as mobile application testing becomes increasingly essential.

- With the growing number of devices and operating systems, testing mobile device compatibility and cross-platform compatibility can be challenging.

- To determine how an app will perform on different networks, such as 2G, 3G, 4G, and 5G, it is necessary to test the app on each network.

- To guarantee the app's compatibility with an **Internet Protocol version 6 (IPv6)** setup, various checks need to be conducted. This includes assessing address compatibility, network configuration, and the firewall and NAT, and determining how to mitigate any issues that arise.

- Mobile applications should be tested for performance under various conditions to ensure an optimal user experience. Teams should ensure that the applications are tested for speed, responsiveness, and stability.

- Security and privacy are increasingly important in mobile testing. Teams must ensure that all applications are tested for vulnerabilities and that user data is protected.

These challenges require teams to have a comprehensive testing strategy that covers all mobile application testing aspects. Teams should focus on developing a strategy to manage complexity, automate testing, optimize performance, improve security and privacy, and ensure cross-platform compatibility.

Additionally, teams should seek out tools and services that can help them simplify the mobile testing process. By planning and preparing strategically, teams can effectively face mobile testing challenges.

For their testing strategies to remain relevant and up to date, teams should regularly review their processes, evaluate new tools, and adapt their approaches as necessary.

Mobile testing strategies should be developed and maintained continuously.

This should include defining your testing efforts' scope, objectives, and priorities. Identify the types of testing required for your app and allocate resources accordingly. Review your testing processes, evaluate new tools and technologies, and adjust your approaches as needed.

Teams can ensure their mobile applications succeed by taking the right direction and leveraging suitable tools. Teams need to review their testing processes regularly and evaluate emerging technologies that can help simplify their mobile testing process.

The need for a robust testing strategy

As discussed in *Chapter 1, Resolving Challenges in Mobile DevOps*, it is essential for Fintech companies or any other companies to implement mobile DevOps and follow a testing strategy. Failure to do so can lead to numerous issues with manual testing, such as consuming significant time and effort, which can ultimately affect the release process and delay the rollout of new features. To ensure optimal functionality and user experience in a mobile app, a mobile testing strategy encompasses various testing types, tools, and techniques, all of which are addressed meticulously to cover every possible scenario. This includes **unit**, **integration**, **system**, **performance**, **compatibility**, and **usability** testing.

In my opinion, *Don't follow the test pyramid. It is a model.* There is no silver bullet or magic wand; each team or company should create its own testing strategy. Some businesses focus more on functional tests, others on performance tests, and others on security tests.

> **Note**
>
> The **Mobile Native Foundation** has an interesting discussion (`https://github.com/MobileNativeFoundation/discussions/discussions/6`) about how companies such as Lyft, Spotify, Uber, and more conduct testing and implement testing strategies.

What is a mobile app testing strategy?

A mobile app testing strategy is a comprehensive plan that outlines the testing process for a mobile app. It includes various testing techniques and tools that help ensure the quality and reliability of the app.

Here are some essential elements to consider when creating a mobile app testing strategy:

- **Clearly define your testing goals and objectives** by considering what you want to achieve through testing, such as ensuring the app works correctly on all devices and platforms, identifying and fixing bugs before releasing the app, or improving the app's overall user experience.

- **Identify the target devices and platforms** on which you want to test your app. To ensure compatibility, consider testing your app on various devices with different operating systems, screen sizes, and hardware configurations.

- **Choose testing techniques** that best suit your app's needs and objectives. Consider techniques such as functional testing, usability testing, performance testing, security testing, compatibility testing, and localization testing.

- **Use tools that can help you automate your testing** and provide comprehensive coverage. Consider tools such as Appium, XCUITest, Espresso, and Detox.

- **Define test cases and scenarios** that cover all app features, functionalities, and user scenarios. Test cases and scenarios should be designed to cover both positive and negative test scenarios.

- **Establish a test execution plan** that outlines the testing process, test schedules, and resources required to execute the tests. This plan should also outline the roles and responsibilities of the testing team.

- **Implement test automation** to save time and ensure consistent testing results. Automate repetitive tests that can be executed quickly, such as regression testing.

- **Involve end users in user acceptance testing** (**UAT**) to get feedback (beta testing) on the app's usability and functionality. This feedback can help you identify any issues and improve the overall user experience. In *Chapter 6, Mobile App Release Management*, we will discuss the concept of beta testing for mobile apps.

However, sometimes, people confuse a testing strategy with a test plan. Let's take a look at the differences between them:

Test Plan	Test Strategy
A document that outlines the scope, approach, resources, and schedule of the intended testing activities	A high-level document that defines the overall approach for testing a system or product, including the testing methodologies, tools, and processes to be used
Defines the specific test objectives and acceptance criteria	Determines the overall testing goals and objectives
Provides detailed information on how testing will be conducted	Provides a general overview of the testing approach
Outlines the roles and responsibilities of the testing team	Outlines the testing process and the roles and responsibilities of the testing team
Provides a detailed schedule of testing activities	Provides a high-level plan of testing activities
Includes a test schedule, test cases, scripts, and data	Includes testing methodology, testing tools, and testing process
Focuses on the testing process and the execution of test cases	Focuses on the overall testing approach and the testing goals and objectives

Table 5.1 – Test plan versus test strategy

As we mentioned earlier in this chapter, test automation helps us increase our test coverage, and more tests can be run quickly and continuously in the development process, resulting in better test coverage. From this, we got the concept of continuous testing and shift-left testing. Let's explore these concepts in more detail.

Continuous testing

Continuous testing encourages testing throughout the software development process rather than simply at the end. Through early and ongoing input on the software's quality, continuous testing seeks to help teams find and address problems as quickly as feasible.

Modern software development methodologies, such as Agile and mobile DevOps, where frequent releases and updates are the norms, depend heavily on continuous testing. Teams can ensure that every release is high quality and satisfies the end user's needs by incorporating testing into the development process.

The practice of continuous testing entails testing software while it is still being developed, as opposed to waiting until the end of the development cycle or releasing the mobile app, as we covered in *Chapter 3*, *Mobile DevOps Fundamentals*. A high-quality app is crucial for mobile applications, which are frequently used by many users and consume a lot of data:

Continuous Integration

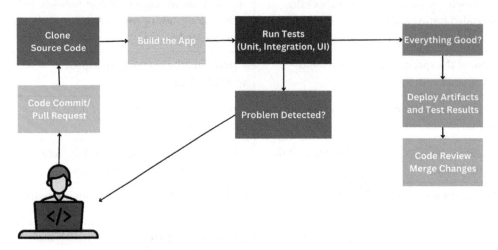

Figure 5.2 – Continuous testing with CI

As a result of the continuous testing process, shift-left testing is becoming more and more popular.

You can measure your team's maturity level and receive expert advice from domain experts with Katalon's Continuous Testing Maturity Assessment (`https://katalon.com/continuous-testing-self-assessment`).

Traditionally, testing is performed toward the end of the development process, once the code has been written. However, with the shift-left testing approach, testing is integrated into the development process from the very beginning.

Let's explain the concept and advantages of shift-left testing.

What is shift-left testing?

Shift-left testing is a methodology for software testing that focuses on the early phases of the software development life cycle. In conventional software development, testing is usually carried out after the majority of the code has been produced, toward the conclusion of the development phase.

In contrast, shift-left testing entails incorporating testing tasks into the early stages of development, such as requirement collection, design, and implementation, as shown in the following figure:

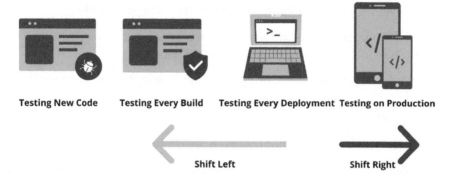

Figure 5.3 – Shift left in testing

There are several advantages to continuous testing as well as shift-left testing, such as the following:

- **Early detection of defects (test early and often)**: By testing early in the development process, defects can be identified and fixed before they propagate and become more expensive and difficult to resolve.

- **Improved collaboration and communication**: Shift-left testing encourages cooperation and communication between developers and testers, which can help identify and address potential issues early on and improve the overall quality of the software.

- **Faster delivery and deployment**: By shifting testing to the left, teams can deliver and deploy software faster. They can start testing earlier and avoid delays and bottlenecks at the end of the development process.

Organizations need to adopt a continuous testing approach to implement shift-left testing, where testing is integrated into the development process and performed throughout the life cycle. This may require a shift in culture and mindset and adopting the appropriate tools and technologies to support continuous testing.

Now, let's take a closer look at some of the testing tools, frameworks, and cloud services available in the market today for mobile apps to help you decide which is most suitable for your company.

Testing tools, frameworks, and services for mobile apps

There are numerous testing tools, frameworks, and services available for developers and testers to assist them in testing their mobile apps rapidly.

But first, let's begin by discussing the factors to consider when choosing a test automation framework or tool for mobile applications.

When selecting a mobile test automation tool, there are several factors to consider:

- The tool should integrate with other tools in your test automation ecosystem, such as CI and test management tools, so that you can use it in CI/CD pipelines

- The tool should be compatible with the different mobile devices and operating systems you plan to test

- The tool should be easy to set up, configure, and use

- The tool should provide clear, detailed reports on test results

- The tool should have a robust support system and a large community of users who can provide help and guidance

- The tool should be able to handle large-scale testing as your mobile app and user base grow

It's always a good idea to evaluate a few different tools and conduct a pilot test or a **proof of concept** project with a small set of tests before you decide that a tool or framework is suitable for your business, app, and team.

Mobile app UI and functionality testing

An excellent user experience requires testing the UI of a mobile application. Testers can identify and address issues with the application's functionalities and UI by performing automated testing in the testing process, resulting in a positive customer experience.

Here are some native and cross-platform mobile testing frameworks to consider when testing an app's functionality:

- iOS:

  - XCUITest

  - EarlGrey

- Android:

  - Espresso

  - Jetpack Compose

- Cross-platform:

  - Appium

  - Detox

- Flutter Driver and Flutter integration tests
- Maestro

Let's start with the native frameworks for iOS apps.

XCUITest

XCUITest (`https://developer.apple.com/documentation/xctest`) is a mobile testing framework created by Apple specifically for iOS, macOS, tvOS, and watchOS app testing. Designed to help developers and QA teams automate their testing processes, it supports Swift and Objective-C languages, offering flexibility in choosing the preferred language.

Built on Apple's XCTest framework, XCUITest enables unit and UI testing within a single framework, streamlining the process.

XCUITest advocates for accessibility by mandating proper **accessibility identifiers** in apps, ensuring universal usability.

Additionally, test engineers unfamiliar with Swift or Objective-C may also experience a steeper learning curve.

To use XCUITest, developers must import the XCTest framework and create a subclass of XCTestCase. They can then define test methods and interact with the app's UI using XCUITest's API:

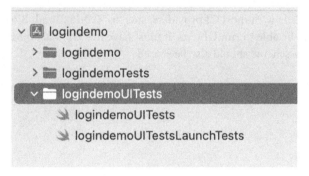

Figure 5.4 – The XCUITest directory in the iOS app

The framework also offers additional capabilities, such as taking screenshots, performing gestures such as swipes and pinches, and various other element interactions. Further information can be found in Apple's official documentation and API reference.

Example

Here is some simple XCUITest code to test the login functionality: `https://github.com/PacktPublishing/Mobile-DevOps-Playbook/blob/main/Chapter-5/iOS/XCUITest/simpleTest.swift`.

You can also use the Page Object pattern with XCUITest, which involves creating separate classes for each screen in your app. These classes will contain the UI elements and actions specific to that screen. This promotes better code organization and maintainability.

For the given SwiftUI app, we can create two page objects: `LoginPage` and `WelcomePage`. Here are some examples of how to use the Page Object pattern with XCUITest:

- Create the `LoginPage.swift` file (`https://github.com/PacktPublishing/Mobile-DevOps-Playbook/blob/main/Chapter-5/iOS/XCUITest/PageObjects/LoginPage.swift`)

- Create the `WelcomePage.swift` file (`https://github.com/PacktPublishing/Mobile-DevOps-Playbook/blob/main/Chapter-5/iOS/XCUITest/PageObjects/WelcomePage.swift`)

- Update your test class to use these page objects (`https://github.com/PacktPublishing/Mobile-DevOps-Playbook/blob/main/Chapter-5/iOS/XCUITest/TestClassWithPO.swift`)

XCUITest integrates easily with most CI providers, such as Xcode Cloud, Bitrise, GitHub Actions, and Codemagic, but to be able to run UI tests, it must have macOS machines with target iOS SDK and iOS simulators. The scheme should also be shared:

Figure 5.5 – Shared scheme in an iOS app

Then, you can run the tests on your preferred CI provider if you have the prerequisites.

For example, on Codemagic, you can use the code at the following link in your `codemagic.yml` file: `https://github.com/PacktPublishing/Mobile-DevOps-Playbook/blob/main/Chapter-5/iOS/XCUITest/codemagic.yml`.

On Bitrise, you can add an Xcode test for the iOS integration step to build the app for testing and running the UI tests:

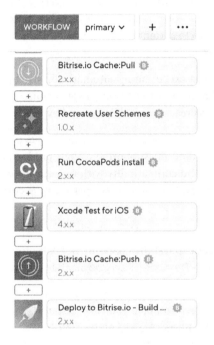

Figure 5.6 – Bitrise iOS workflow

EarlGrey

EarlGrey (`https://github.com/google/EarlGrey`), developed by Google, is a specialized iOS testing framework tailored to support native iOS app testing. It allows developers and QA teams to automate UI testing for their iOS apps using either Objective-C or Swift, according to their preference.

EarlGrey ensures smooth and reliable test execution by automatically synchronizing with the application's UI. It also offers a wide range of assertions and matchers, enabling developers to create thorough and expressive tests.

To create a UI test for the given SwiftUI app using EarlGrey, you'll need to set up EarlGrey in your project. After that, you can write your test cases. Here's a UI test for the given SwiftUI app using EarlGrey: `https://github.com/PacktPublishing/Mobile-DevOps-Playbook/blob/main/Chapter-5/iOS/EarlGrey/EarlGreyTest.swift`.

The same page objects concept can be applied to EarlGrey as well as when you're running the necessary tests in CI/CD workflows.

Now, let's discuss the native testing frameworks for Android apps.

Espresso

Espresso (`https://developer.android.com/training/testing/espresso`), created by Google, is a dedicated Android testing framework designed to support native Android app testing. It allows developers and QA teams to automate UI testing for their Android apps using either Java or Kotlin, according to their preferences.

It ensures smooth and reliable test execution by automatically synchronizing with the application's UI, which results in faster and more accurate testing. Espresso also provides various assertions and matchers, allowing developers to create comprehensive and expressive tests.

Easily integrated with AndroidJUnit4, Espresso allows developers to perform both unit and UI testing within a single framework. As an officially supported Google product, developers can rely on up-to-date documentation, resources, and compatibility with new Android versions. Additionally, those unfamiliar with Java and Kotlin may experience a steeper learning curve when starting.

Example

Here is some simple Espresso code to test the login functionality: `https://github.com/PacktPublishing/Mobile-DevOps-Playbook/blob/main/Chapter-5/Android/LoginTest.kt`.

You can use the Page Object pattern to make your Espresso tests more maintainable and easier to read (`https://github.com/PacktPublishing/Mobile-DevOps-Playbook/blob/main/Chapter-5/Android/PageObjects/LoginPage.kt`).

Here's an example of how you can implement the Page Object pattern in your Espresso test for a login screen using Kotlin: `https://github.com/PacktPublishing/Mobile-DevOps-Playbook/blob/main/Chapter-5/Android/LoginScreenTest.kt`.

Additionally, you can use **UI Automator** (`https://developer.android.com/training/testing/other-components/ui-automator`) with Espresso for cross-app functional UI testing across the system and installed apps.

Espresso integrates easily with most CI providers, such as Bitrise, GitHub Actions, and Codemagic, but to be able to run the UI tests, you must have Ubuntu or Windows machines with Gradle installed and the target Android SDK with Android Emulator. Then, you need to run the Gradle command `./gradlew connectedDebugAndroidTest`. This command combines the building and installation of the main app and the test app in a single step using the connectedDebugAndroidTest Gradle task. This task builds both the main app and its associated Android test app, installs them on the connected device, and then runs the tests defined in the test app.

Once you've done this, you can run the tests on your preferred CI provider if you have the prerequisites.

For example, on Codemagic, you can use the code at the following link in your `codemagic.yml` file: `https://github.com/PacktPublishing/Mobile-DevOps-Playbook/blob/main/Chapter-5/Android/codemagic.yml`.

On Bitrise, you can add the **Android Build for UI Testing** and **Virtual Device Testing for Android** integration steps to build the app for testing and run the UI tests on Firebase Test Lab, which is integrated internally with this Bitrise step:

Figure 5.7 – Bitrise Android workflow

Finally, with GitHub Actions, you can use the following YAML file: `https://github.com/PacktPublishing/Mobile-DevOps-Playbook/blob/main/Chapter-5/.github/android.yml`.

Open source project based on Espresso

There are many open source UI testing libraries built on top of Espresso for Android applications to simplify and streamline the process of writing UI tests, enabling developers to create robust and maintainable tests with ease. These include Kaspresso (`https://github.com/KasperskyLab/Kaspresso`), Barista (`https://github.com/AdevintaSpain/Barista`), and Kakao (`https://github.com/KakaoCup/Kakao`). Their fluent interfaces, advanced test interceptors, automatic screenshots, and enhanced logging capabilities make them a strong choice for Android developers looking to improve their UI testing experience.

Jetpack Compose

Jetpack Compose (`https://developer.android.com/jetpack/compose`) is Google's modern UI toolkit for Android applications. The Jetpack Compose Testing library (`https://developer.android.com/jetpack/compose/testing`) aims to simplify the process of writing and maintaining UI tests for applications built using Jetpack Compose.

Jetpack Compose Testing provides a Compose Test Rule, which sets up the necessary environment for testing Compose UIs and makes it easy to create and manipulate composable UIs within tests.

Jetpack Compose Testing supports screenshot testing, allowing developers to compare the visual appearance of UI elements against a reference image during test execution.

It is possible to use Espresso as a test framework since Jetpack Compose is an instrumentation test, but Compose already includes testing APIs to find, verify, and perform user actions on elements. Time manipulation and other advanced features are included.

In general, if you have a particular type of UI element or component, you should have specific APIs or methods to test them in their various scenarios.

To learn more about Compose testing, there is a cheat sheet (`https://developer.android.com/jetpack/compose/testing-cheatsheet`) that acts as a quick reference to some of the most useful Compose test APIs.

The same Page Object concept can be applied to Jetpack Compose and running the tests in the necessary CI/CD workflows (`https://github.com/PacktPublishing/Mobile-DevOps-Playbook/blob/main/Chapter-5/Android/JetpackCompose/CounterTest.kt`).

Here is an example from Reddit about their E2E UI automation framework for Android apps and how they use page objects and Fluent design patterns: `https://shorturl.at/ajH78`.

Appium

Appium (`https://appium.io`) is an open source, cross-platform mobile testing framework that enables developers and QA teams to automate testing for their mobile applications on Android, iOS, and Windows platforms.

Appium supports multiple programming languages, including Java, Ruby, Python, C#, and JavaScript, allowing developers to choose their preferred language.

Appium integrates with popular testing frameworks such as JUnit and TestNG, allowing developers to utilize their preferred testing tools.

Appium can easily be integrated with CI tools, such as Bitrise, GitHub Actions, and CircleCI, streamlining the testing process within the development workflow.

Appium's large, active community offers extensive documentation, resources, and regular updates. But usually, the initial setup and configuration of Appium can be time-consuming and requires significant effort to ensure proper functioning (`https://github.com/PacktPublishing/Mobile-DevOps-Playbook/blob/main/Chapter-5/Appium/AppiumDemo.java`).

You can use also the Page Object pattern to make your Appium tests more maintainable and easier to read.

To run Appium tests in your CI workflow, you need to install and run the Appium Server, along with Android Emulator or the iOS simulator. You can use the following shell script to do this: `https://github.com/PacktPublishing/Mobile-DevOps-Playbook/blob/main/Chapter-5/Appium/emulator.sh`.

Then, you can run the tests using the command line with Gradle or Maven.

Detox

Detox (`https://github.com/wix/Detox`) is an E2E mobile testing framework designed specifically for React Native applications. It enables developers and QA teams to automate testing for their React Native apps on both Android and iOS platforms.

Detox operates as a gray box testing framework, balancing the speed and reliability of white box testing and the realism of black box testing. Detox integrates seamlessly with Jest, a popular JavaScript testing framework, allowing developers to utilize their preferred testing tools and methodologies.

Detox automatically synchronizes test execution with the application's UI, ensuring that tests run smoothly and reliably.

Detox can easily be integrated with CI tools, such as Jenkins, Travis CI, and CircleCI, streamlining the testing process within the development workflow.

Detox has an active community of developers and users who provide resources, support, and regular updates.

Example

Here's an example of a Detox test for a simple React Native login app: `https://github.com/PacktPublishing/Mobile-DevOps-Playbook/blob/main/Chapter-5/Detox/LoginTest.js`.

Detox also requires you to have a configuration JSON file, such as the following: `https://github.com/PacktPublishing/Mobile-DevOps-Playbook/blob/main/Chapter-5/Detox/config.json`.

To run Detox tests in a CI/CD workflow or a pipeline such as GitHub Actions, you need Android Emulator or the iOS simulator. Also, install Node.js and NPM and build the app using the preceding configuration file. You can use the following YAML file for this: `https://github.com/PacktPublishing/Mobile-DevOps-Playbook/blob/main/Chapter-5/Detox/.github/detox.yml`.

Similar to the approaches for Bitrise, Codemagic, and the rest of the CI providers we have mentioned, you need to use a script step to install the prerequisites and then run your Detox tests.

Flutter Driver

Flutter Driver (`https://api.flutter.dev/flutter/flutter_driver_extension/flutter_driver_extension-library.html`) is a testing framework for Flutter applications, enabling developers and QA teams to automate integration and UI testing for their Flutter apps.

It supports testing on Android and iOS platforms, allowing developers to test their Flutter apps on various devices and operating systems.

Flutter Driver is designed for integration testing, enabling developers to test how different components of their application work together.

It uses Dart, the same programming language for developing Flutter applications, making it easier for developers to write tests in a familiar language.

Flutter Driver automatically synchronizes test execution with the application's UI, ensuring that tests run smoothly and reliably – Flutter Driver's automatic synchronization with the application's UI results in stable and reliable test execution.

In addition, testers unfamiliar with Dart or the Flutter framework may face a steeper learning curve when they start using Flutter Driver.

Example

Here's an example of a Flutter Driver test for a simple Flutter login app: `https://github.com/PacktPublishing/Mobile-DevOps-Playbook/blob/main/Chapter-5/Flutter/Flutter%20Driver/LoginTest.dart`.

There is also an integration test (`https://docs.flutter.dev/testing#integration-tests`) that can be used to test the Flutter app. Here's an example for a simple Flutter login app: `https://github.com/PacktPublishing/Mobile-DevOps-Playbook/blob/main/Chapter-5/Flutter/Integration%20Test/LoginTest.dart`.

To run Flutter tests in a CI/CD workflow or pipeline such as GitHub Actions, you need Android Emulator or iOS simulator and the Dart SDK. You can use the following YAML file to aid with this: `https://github.com/PacktPublishing/Mobile-DevOps-Playbook/blob/main/Chapter-5/Flutter/.github/FlutterIntegration.yml`.

Here's an example of a YAML file that runs a Flutter Driver test on both Android Emulator and the iOS simulator via GitHub Actions: `1https://github.com/PacktPublishing/Mobile-DevOps-Playbook/blob/main/Chapter-5/Flutter/.github/FlutterDriver.yml`.

On Bitrise, there are integration steps for building and testing Flutter apps:

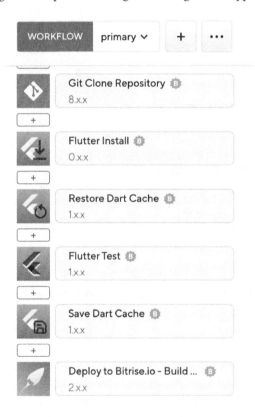

Figure 5.8 – Bitrise Flutter workflow

Similarly, on Codemagic, there are steps that support Flutter Driver and Flutter tests:

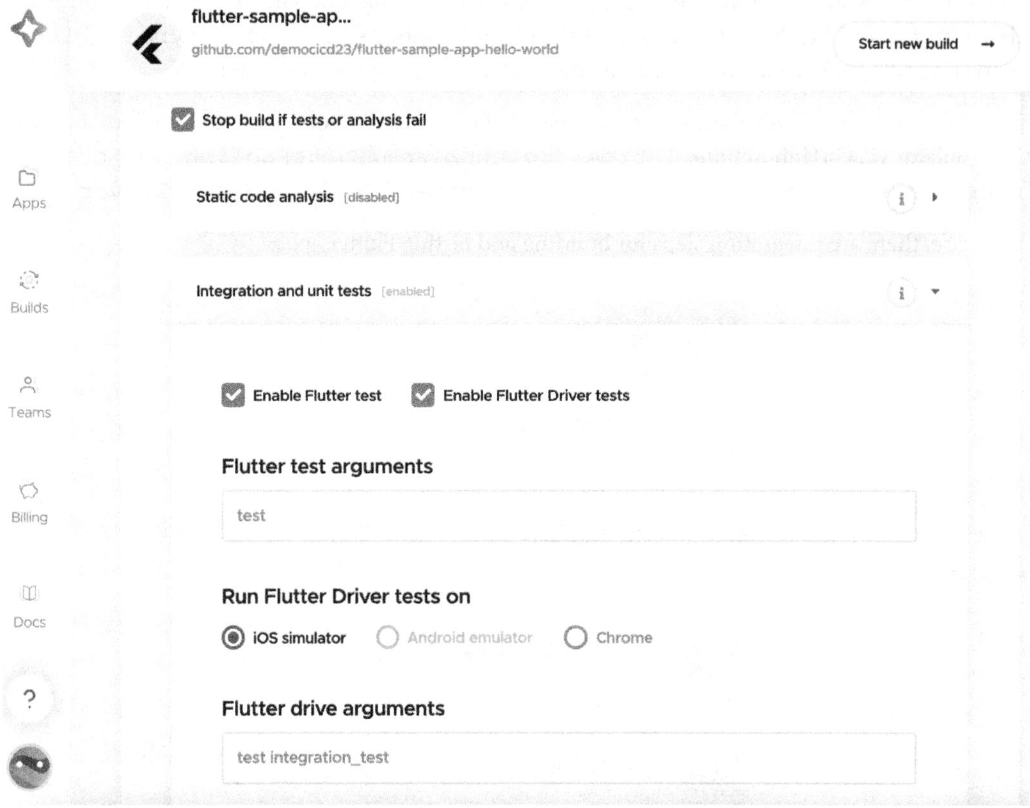

Figure 5.9 – Codemagic Flutter workflow

Maestro

Maestro (`https://maestro.mobile.dev/`) is the simplest and most effective open source mobile UI testing framework and is developed by mobile.dev. It allows you to easily define and test your flows (the user journey in the app – in other words, the E2E scenarios).

Maestro is YAML-based, meaning you define the test flows inside a `flow.yml` file (`https://github.com/PacktPublishing/Mobile-DevOps-Playbook/blob/main/Chapter-5/Maestro/flow.yml`) and run them on your devices.

Maestro has different features, such as the following:

- With Maestro, flakiness is tolerated. Apps and devices are built to be unstable, and UI elements are designed to counteract this.

- It is not necessary to call `sleep()` repeatedly in your tests. Maestro waits for the content to load automatically (but not too long) when this process takes a long time (for example, over a network).

- Maestro automatically reruns your tests when your test files change, so there's no need to compile anything.

- Maestro supports all of the major mobile development platforms, including Android, iOS, Flutter, React Native, and Web Views.

- Additionally, there is Maestro Studio, Maestro's personal assistant that will assist you in writing your Maestro flows.

You can easily test your flows on Maestro Cloud since they run in the cloud, so you don't have to configure any simulators or emulators.

Flows can also be run via the Maestro CLI on Android devices/emulators that support ADB connections and iOS devices/simulators that support Facebook's IDB. You can manually orchestrate your flow execution against any provider that supports these protocols. You can run your flows as you would locally with the Maestro CLI.

Bitrise has an integration step to help you run your Maestro tests on the cloud. If you are using another CI provider, you can use the Maestro CLI:

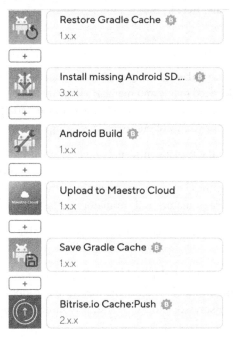

Figure 5.10 – Bitrise and Maestro workflow

By exploring the testing frameworks that we have on the market today and how to run them in a CI workflow, we have noticed that we have a new challenge: running tests on different devices with different operating system versions simultaneously. Let's talk about how to run our tests on cloud devices using different services to maximize coverage.

Testing on cloud devices

Developers and QA teams can test their applications on a wide range of devices and platforms without using physical devices via cloud device testing, a modern approach to mobile application testing.

A cloud-based infrastructure hosts several emulators or real devices remotely. Here is a list of the most popular cloud device testing for mobile apps:

- Sauce Labs
- BrowserStack
- AWS Device Farm
- Firebase Test Lab
- LambdaTest

Let's take a look at these in greater detail.

Sauce Labs

Sauce Labs (`https://saucelabs.com/products/mobile-testing`) streamlines the testing process by removing the need to buy and manage a large inventory of devices, enabling users to test their apps on actual devices in the cloud. Thanks to the platform's comprehensive device coverage, users can identify problems before they are published by testing apps on the most recent devices.

Sauce Labs supports Android and iOS platforms, enabling developers to test their apps across multiple devices and operating systems. It offers access to a vast range of real devices to test mobile apps, ensuring accurate results and minimizing the chances of encountering issues on real-world devices. In addition to real devices, Sauce Labs offers emulators and simulators for faster and more cost-effective testing.

This feature allows multiple tests to be executed simultaneously, significantly reducing the overall testing time.

Sauce Labs integrates seamlessly with popular CI tools such as Bitrise, GitHub Actions, and Codemagic, allowing for automated testing in the development workflow. It supports popular test automation frameworks such as Appium, Espresso, and XCUITest, providing flexibility in choosing the proper framework for a project.

Additionally, Sauce Labs provides detailed test reports, logs, and video recordings of test sessions, facilitating efficient debugging and issue resolution.

You can use the `saucectl` CLI with any CI provider to configure your account and run the tests from the relevant `config.yml` file (`https://github.com/PacktPublishing/Mobile-DevOps-Playbook/blob/main/Chapter-5/SauceLabs/config.yml`).

You can change the configuration to increase concurrency as you need to run the tests in parallel on different devices.

BrowserStack

BrowserStack (`https://www.browserstack.com/app-automate`) is a cloud-based testing platform that enables developers to test their mobile applications across various devices and operating systems. With a wide range of features and a user-friendly interface, BrowserStack aims to provide a comprehensive testing solution for developers and QA teams.

BrowserStack provides access to an extensive collection of real devices for the accurate testing of mobile apps, ensuring that they perform well on actual devices consumers use. In addition to real devices, BrowserStack offers emulators and simulators for quick and cost-effective testing.

This feature enables multiple tests to be executed simultaneously, reducing overall testing time and increasing productivity.

BrowserStack integrates with widespread CI tools such as Jenkins, TeamCity, Bamboo, CircleCI, Travis CI, Azure, Bitrise, and GitLab CI/CD, streamlining the testing process within the development workflow.

For example, Bitrise has integration steps for BrowserStack to upload and run Espresso and XCUITest tests:

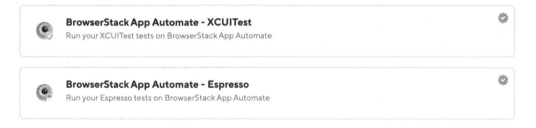

Figure 5.11 – Bitrise and BrowserStack integration steps

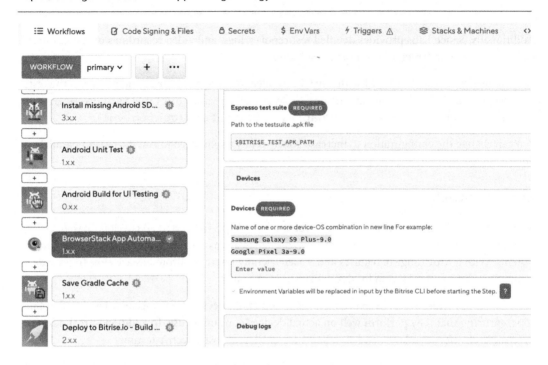

Figure 5.12 – Bitrise and BrowserStack workflow

If you have another CI provider or server, you can use the `curl` command to upload your tests to BrowserStack from the command line:

```
curl -u "YOUR_USERNAME:YOUR_ACCESS_KEY" -X GET "https://api-cloud.
browserstack.com/app-automate/recent_apps"
```

BrowserStack supports various test automation frameworks, including Appium, Espresso, and XCUITest, providing flexibility in selecting the most suitable framework for a project.

You can test native and hybrid mobile apps with BrowserStack App Automate using the Appium automation framework on a wide range of real Android and iOS devices.

LambdaTest

LambdaTest (`https://www.lambdatest.com/mobile-app-testing`) is a cloud-based testing platform that provides developers and QA teams with access to a wide range of devices and operating systems for web and mobile app testing.

LambdaTest supports Android and iOS mobile app testing, allowing developers to test their applications on various devices and operating systems.

LambdaTest also offers real mobile device testing, ensuring accurate results and a more realistic testing environment.

LambdaTest integrates with many popular testing frameworks, such as Appium, XCUITest, and Espresso, making it easy to incorporate into existing test suites. It also enables parallel testing, allowing multiple tests to run simultaneously and speeding up the overall testing process.

LambdaTest's cloud-based infrastructure provides scalability and collaboration features, making it suitable for small and large teams.

Finally, LambdaTest integrates with widespread CI tools such as AWS CodePipeline, Jenkins, CircleCI, Travis CI, GitLab CI, Azure Pipelines, and Bitrise.

Using the `curl` command from the command line, you can upload and run your tests on LambdaTest Cloud, just like you can with Sauce Labs and BrowserStack.

Here is an example of uploading the iOS app and then running the XCUITest test:

```
curl -u "YOUR_LAMBDATEST_USERNAME:YOUR_LAMBDATEST_ACCESS_KEY" \
--location --request POST 'https://manual-api.lambdatest.com/app/
uploadFramework' \
--form 'appFile=@"/Users/macuser/Downloads/proverbial.ipa"' \
--form 'type="xcuit-ios"'
```

```
curl -u "YOUR_LAMBDATEST_USERNAME:YOUR_LAMBDATEST_ACCESS_KEY" \
--location --request POST 'https://manual-api.lambdatest.com/
app/uploadFramework' --form 'appFile=@"/Users/macuser/Downloads/
proverbial_ios_xcuitest.ipa"' --form 'type="xcuit-ios"'
```

Here is an example of uploading the Android and test app:

```
curl -u "YOUR_LAMBDATEST_USERNAME:YOUR_LAMBDATEST_ACCESS_KEY" \
--location --request POST 'https://manual-api.lambdatest.com/
app/uploadFramework' --form 'appFile=@"/Users/macuser/Downloads/
proverbial_android.apk"' --form 'type="espresso-android"'
```

```
curl -u "YOUR_LAMBDATEST_USERNAME:YOUR_LAMBDATEST_ACCESS_KEY" \
--location --request POST 'https://manual-api.lambdatest.com/
app/uploadFramework' --form 'appFile=@"/Users/macuser/Downloads/
proverbial_android_expressotest.apk"' --form 'type="espresso-android"'
```

If your CI provider supports integration steps, such as Bitrise, you can use it directly instead of the command line:

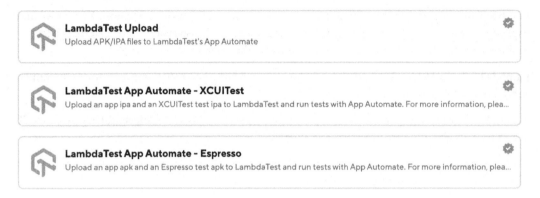

Figure 5.13 – Bitrise and LambdaTest integration steps

Figure 5.14 – Bitrise and LambdaTest workflow

AWS Device Farm

AWS Device Farm (`https://aws.amazon.com/device-farm/`) is a mobile application testing service provided by **AWS**. It supports testing on Android and iOS platforms, allowing developers to test their apps on various real mobile devices.

AWS Device Farm provides access to a selection of real devices for the more accurate testing of mobile apps, ensuring better compatibility with real-world devices consumers use.

Developers can remotely access devices for manual testing, allowing interactive debugging and troubleshooting.

AWS Device Farm supports popular test automation frameworks such as Appium, Espresso, and XCUITest, enabling developers to automate their testing processes.

AWS Device Farm integrates with popular CI tools, such as AWS CodePipeline, GitHub Actions, Codemagic, and Bitrise, streamlining the testing process within the development workflow.

With AWS Device Farm, you can upload the mobile app and test file manually to run your tests, as shown in the following screenshot. You can also upload the app with the CI build:

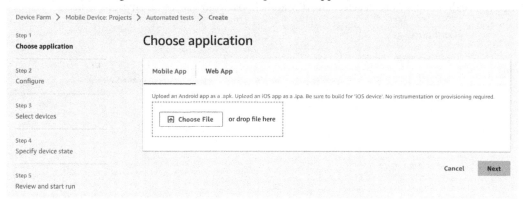

Figure 5.15 – AWS Device Farm – Choose application

Next, you can configure the test type and set up the test framework, such as **Instrumentation**, as shown here:

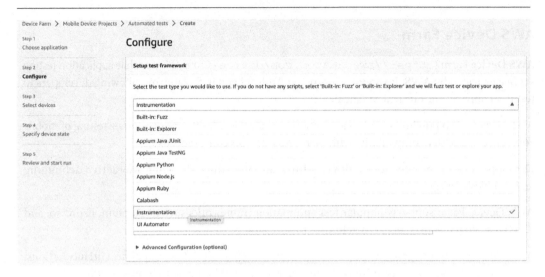

Figure 5.16 – AWS Device Farm – setting up the test framework

Once you've done this, you can select an APK and choose your execution environment:

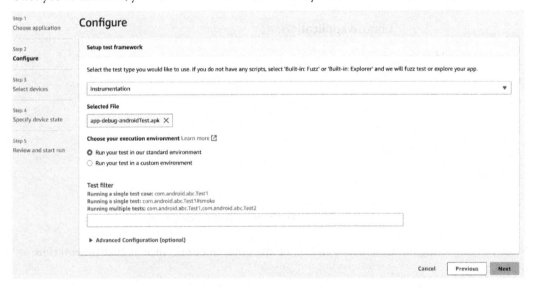

Figure 5.17 – AWS Device Farm – uploading the test app

Next, you can select the devices you wish to use. You can combine different device manufacturers, such as Google and Samsung, as shown in the following screenshot:

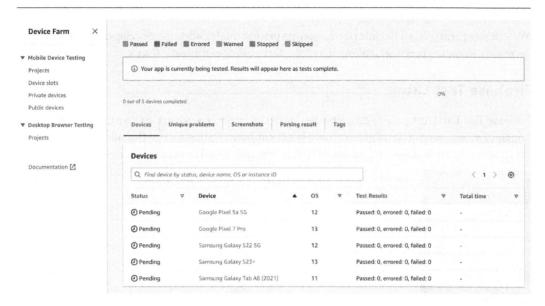

Figure 5.18 – AWS Device Farm – selecting devices

Once you've run the tests, you will see the test results, including videos, logs, and screenshots, as shown here:

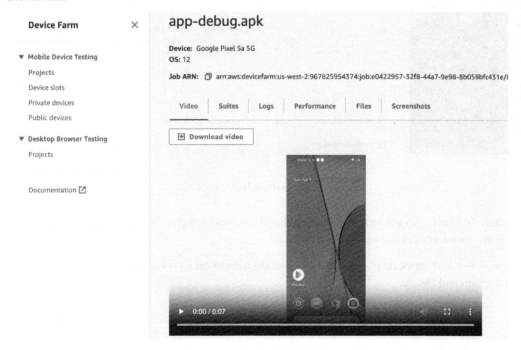

Figure 5.19 – AWS Device Farm – the test results

AWS Device Farm offers a flexible pay-as-you-go pricing model, allowing developers to pay only for the testing resources they use, making it a cost-effective option for some teams.

Firebase Test Lab

Firebase Test Lab (`https://firebase.google.com/products/test-lab`), a part of Google's Firebase suite of development tools, is a cloud-based testing service that allows developers to test their mobile applications on a variety of real devices and virtual devices (emulators and simulators):

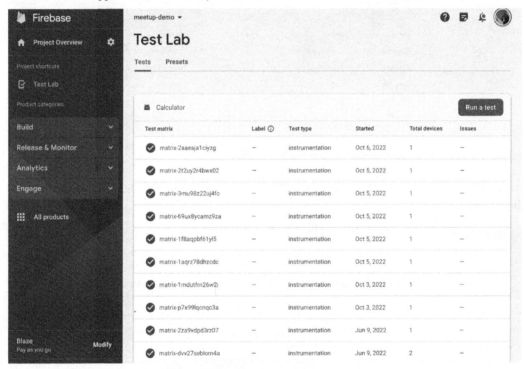

Figure 5.20 – Firebase Test Lab matrix

Firebase Test Lab supports testing on Android and iOS platforms, enabling developers to test their apps on various devices and operating systems.

Firebase Test Lab supports popular test automation frameworks such as Espresso and XCTest but not Appium and Detox:

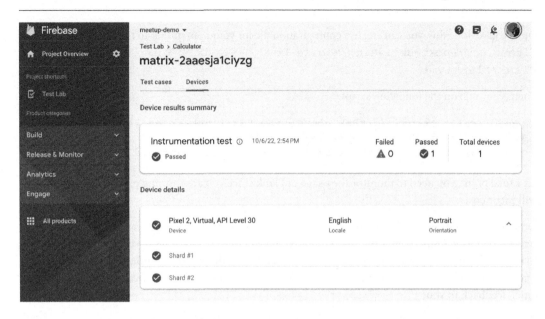

Figure 5.21 – Firebase Test Lab results

Firebase Test Lab integrates with popular CI tools, such as Jenkins, GitLab CI, and Bitrise, streamlining the testing process within the development workflow.

Firebase Test Lab automatically generates a pre-launch report with detailed test results, performance metrics, and screenshots, helping developers identify and resolve issues before they launch their app.

As part of the Firebase suite of tools, Firebase Test Lab seamlessly integrates with other Firebase services, such as Cloud Functions, simplifying the overall testing and development process.

You can run tests in parallel with **Flank** (`https://github.com/Flank/flank/`), a massively parallel Android and iOS test runner for Firebase Test Lab.

Flank is YAML-compatible with the `gcloud` CLI. It provides extra features to accelerate velocity and increase quality.

You can use Flank by performing the following steps:

1. Create a Google Cloud project and account.
2. Create a Firebase account.
3. Add your project to Firebase.
4. Create a service account to get access to the API.
5. Download the service account JSON file. This will contain a private key that can be added directly to your CI server and used for authentication.

Once you've done this, you can create a configuration file for your app, similar to the one at `https://github.com/PacktPublishing/Mobile-DevOps-Playbook/blob/main/Chapter-5/Flank/flank.yml`.

Then, you can run the following script:

```
wget --quiet https://github.com/TestArmada/flank/releases/download/
v22.05.0/flank.jar -O /usr/local/bin/flank.jar
java -jar /usr/local/bin/flank.jar firebase test android run
```

As a final point, you need to monitor the usage of Flank since you are running parallel devices, which will incur costs.

Other services provide us with cloud devices, such as **Genymotion** (`https://www.genymotion.com/`), a popular Android emulator and mobile testing platform that enables developers and QA teams to test their mobile applications on various virtual devices. Additionally, **emulator.wtf** (`https://emulator.wtf/`) is an Android cloud emulator that's laser-focused on performance to deliver quick feedback to your PRs.

Kobiton (`https://kobiton.com/`) is a cloud-based mobile testing platform that enables developers and QA teams to test their mobile applications on various real devices and simulators. It provides extensive features to ensure comprehensive app testing across different platforms and devices.

Also, **Perfecto** (`https://www.perfecto.io/`), the mobile testing platform by Perforce, enables developers and QA teams to test their mobile applications on various real devices and simulators in a secure cloud environment. It provides extensive features to ensure comprehensive app testing across different platforms and devices.

How AI and ML are changing mobile testing

Mobile testing has been revolutionized by AI and ML. Developers can test applications more swiftly and precisely because they automate testing. With the help of predictive analytics, bugs can be fixed more quickly. Intelligent test case generation develops test cases based on user behavior and utilization trends, exposing potential problems.

Additionally, the expense of mobile testing can be decreased with the assistance of AI and ML in addition to the advantages already stated. Companies can reduce the expenses associated with manual labor and simplify their testing processes by automating them.

Codeless and AI-based testing tools

AI can be a game-changer in automation testing. AI-powered testing tools can help improve test coverage, reduce the time and effort required for testing, and provide more accurate test results.

Here are some tools that can help software testers unleash the power of AI in automation testing:

- Applitools
- Katalon
- Waldo

Let's take a closer look.

Applitools

Applitools (`https://applitools.com/solutions/mobile-testing`) is a visual testing platform designed to help developers and QA teams automatically validate the appearance of their mobile applications across different devices and screen resolutions. It aims to streamline testing and reduce manual effort by leveraging AI-powered visual comparison and validation.

It uses AI to visually compare application UIs, detecting differences with high accuracy and reducing false positives, which can be beneficial in usability testing and snapshot testing.

Applitools integrates with many popular testing frameworks, such as XCUITest, Appium, and Espresso, making incorporating visual validation into existing test suites easy.

It offers extensive coverage of different browsers, devices, and screen resolutions, ensuring that applications are visually tested on diverse configurations.

Katalon AI Visual Testing

In addition to the Katalon ecosystem, Katalon Visual Testing helps you optimize your testing performance and save time by integrating seamlessly without any setup effort. On top of functional testing, it identifies unexpected visual changes to the UI.

Using AI, Katalon identifies and matches various zones between the baseline image and the checkpoint image, then highlights changes in the layout. In addition, ML models are used to extract and compare texts from the two images, which can help users identify texts that have been modified from the original version regardless of font family, font size, or color.

You can also run it in parallel with functional tests to cover E2E scenarios and visual regressions.

Waldo

Other services provide us with AI testing tools and platforms, such as **Waldo** (`https://www.waldo.com/`) from Tricentis. This is a codeless mobile app testing platform that's designed to help developers and QA teams automate and simplify the testing process for iOS and Android applications. Its codeless approach minimizes the learning curve and reduces the time spent on test script creation and maintenance.

Waldo enables users to create test scripts without writing code, using a visual interface to define and record test scenarios. Waldo automatically runs tests on every build, streamlining the process and ensuring that applications are constantly tested.

Waldo offers real mobile device testing in the cloud, providing accurate results and a realistic testing environment. Waldo's codeless approach simplifies the test script creation process, making it accessible to testers with varying programming skills.

Two other tools worth mentioning are Testsigma and Sofy.ai.

Testsigma (`https://testsigma.com/ai-driven-test-automation`) integrates seamlessly with mobile CI/CD tools, making it easy to incorporate into existing development workflows.

Sofy.ai (`https://sofy.ai/`) is an AI-powered mobile app testing platform designed to help developers and QA teams automate and simplify the testing process for Android and iOS applications. Its AI-driven approach aims to reduce the time spent on test script creation and maintenance while enhancing overall testing efficiency. In this review, we will focus on Sofy.ai's mobile testing capabilities, discuss its key features, pros, and cons, and compare it with other technologies on the market. Sofy.ai integrates seamlessly with mobile CI/CD tools, making it easy to incorporate into existing development workflows.

By effectively managing test cases, testing teams can ensure comprehensive coverage of software functionality, identify and fix defects, and ultimately deliver high-quality software to end users.

Test case management tools play a vital role in streamlining this process and enhancing the efficiency of the testing effort. Let's discuss the concept of test case management and cover some popular test case management tools.

Test case management

To ensure high-quality mobile applications are delivered to customers, test case management must be integrated with test automation and mobile DevOps. Integration involves using a test case management system that integrates seamlessly with automation tools and offers real-time reporting.

This integration allows developers to automate tests for different scenarios and execute them across multiple devices in a controlled environment.

In addition, integrating testing into the DevOps pipeline facilitates automated testing, early defect identification, and rapid feedback.

Test case management integrated with test automation and mobile DevOps can improve the quality of mobile apps, reduce development time, and increase efficiency.

A popular test case management tool that integrates well with test automation and mobile DevOps is **TestRail**. It is a web-based test case management tool that allows teams to create, manage, and organize test cases. TestRail can be embedded into CI/CD pipelines such as Jenkins, GitLab, GitHub Actions, and more, as well as mobile testing frameworks such as Appium, Espresso, and XCUITest.

With TestRail's extensive API, webhooks, or CLI, you can easily customize your QA processes so that they fit your specific testing workflows and integrate with your tech stack.

Some other test case management tools are **Zephyr** (`https://smartbear.com/test-management/zephyr/`) and **Testmo** (`https://www.testmo.com/`).

Test reports, insights, and analytics are critical components of a successful testing process and strategy. When you're measuring the success of your test automation progress, test reports, insights, and analytics help stakeholders understand the root causes of defects and make data-driven decisions.

Let's look at the difference between test reports, test insights, and test analytics:

- **Test reports**: With reports, you can summarize the testing results, including the number of tests executed, the number of tests that are passed and failed, and the overall test coverage. Test reports should be easy to understand and provide insights into the quality of the software.

- **Test insights**: Test insights provide deeper insights into the testing process by analyzing the root causes of defects and identifying areas for improvement. Test insights can help stakeholders understand the reasons behind test failures and take corrective actions to improve the quality of the software.

- **Test analytics**: Test analytics involves analyzing test data over time to identify trends and patterns. Test analytics can help stakeholders identify application areas that are prone to defects and make data-driven decisions on improving the software's quality.

Here are some examples of testing insights and analytics:

- Test coverage metrics show how much of the application has been tested and remains untested

- Failure rates and defect density provide information on the number of defects found and the rate at which they are discovered

- Test execution time and efficiency can help identify bottlenecks and areas for improvement in the testing process

- Test results and pass/fail rates summarize the overall quality of the application and the effectiveness of the tests

Many tools and techniques can be used to gather testing insights and analytics, such as **Buildkite Test Analytics** (`https://buildkite.com/test-analytics`), **Bitrise Insights** (`https://bitrise.io/bitrise-insights`), and **Sauce Labs Insights** (`https://saucelabs.com/products/sauce-insights`).

When it comes to software testing, test automation tools and test case management are crucial for creating, organizing, and managing test cases. This helps ensure that software applications are thoroughly tested. However, achieving mobile test coverage is also important. Let's learn how to do this.

Achieving successful mobile test coverage

When ensuring mobile app quality and functionality, it can be challenging to test mobile apps and even more difficult to get successful mobile test coverage. The following guidelines can be helpful:

- **Understand the app's goals and requirements**: It is essential to thoroughly understand the needs and goals of the mobile app before you start the testing process. The purpose and functionality of the app should be understood, as well as their specific features and capabilities.

- **Determine the most essential features and functions**: Prioritize test cases based on impact and risk. A mobile app's most critical features and functions should be prioritized since not all features and functions are equally important. It may be necessary to identify which features and functions are most commonly used by users or which are most likely to affect the app's performance or stability.

- **A comprehensive test plan should be developed**: After identifying the key features and functions of the mobile app, you can develop a comprehensive test plan that covers all of these features and functions. This test plan includes various test cases and scenarios to identify and address potential app defects and issues.

- **Combine manual and automated testing**: Manual and automated testing are essential. The use of manual testing can be effective for identifying defects and issues that are hard to automate, while automated testing can quickly and efficiently run large numbers of tests. Incorporate continuous testing into the development process and use appropriate testing tools and frameworks.

- **Collaborate with developers and other stakeholders**: To achieve successful mobile test coverage, it's crucial to collaborate with developers and other stakeholders throughout the testing process. Working together to identify and fix potential app issues and defects can involve sharing test results and feedback.

These guidelines will help you ensure your mobile app is thoroughly tested, ready for release, and effective.

Tips for successful CI/CD pipelines and test automation

Any successful software development project needs to have a CI/CD pipeline and test automation.

Here are some tips for ensuring success in these areas:

- Building a solid foundation for your CI pipeline and test automation strategy involves identifying your requirements, selecting the right tools and technologies, and developing a clear implementation plan.

- It is important to choose the right testing tools and frameworks for the testing you'll be doing. There are many tools available for manual, automated, and performance testing.

- Provide the necessary devices, emulators, simulators, and network conditions to set up the required environment.

- Select the target devices and platforms for your testing based on your market analysis. Use both real devices and emulators/simulators. To ensure wide coverage, ensure a mix of popular devices, operating system versions, screen resolutions, and form factors are included.

- Analyzing the results of your CI pipeline and test automation can help you identify trends, areas for improvement, and potential issues. Using these insights, you can continuously refine and improve your processes.

- Investing in training for your team can help them develop the necessary skills and knowledge to implement and maintain your CI pipeline and test automation strategy successfully.

- Ensure the highest level of quality for your mobile application by continuously improving your testing strategy based on results and feedback. Update your test cases, scripts, and tools as needed.

Skills for mobile testers

Mobile testers play a critical role in ensuring the quality and reliability of mobile applications. Here are some essential skills that mobile testers should have:

- A mobile tester should be able to communicate and collaborate effectively with other stakeholders, including developers, product owners, and business analysts.

- A mobile tester must be able to identify, analyze, and troubleshoot issues and defects in mobile applications.

- Mobile testers need to understand the operating system, device types, and screen sizes of the mobile platforms they are testing on.

- To identify potential issues and defects, mobile testers should be familiar with the mobile app architecture, including how the frontend and backend interact.

- To automate repetitive tests and increase test coverage, mobile testers should be familiar with test automation tools and techniques, including frameworks such as Appium, Espresso, and XCUITest.

- Mobile testers need to be able to test the performance of mobile applications, including checking for issues such as app crashes and slow loading times.

- To be a successful mobile tester, testers should have a strong understanding of app security and be able to test for potential security issues such as malware and unauthorized access.

- Mobile testers must be proficient in using bug tracking and reporting tools so that they can log, track, and report bugs to the development teams effectively.

How to improve your mobile testing skills

Now that we've discussed the skills that mobile testers require, let's discuss how to improve our mobile testing skills.

Keeping up with the ever-evolving world of mobile applications requires improving your mobile testing skills. You can do this in various ways:

- Understanding the various mobile platforms and operating systems available, such as Android and iOS, is a great place to start.

- Participate in real-world projects to experience mobile testing in the real world.

- Keeping up with the latest trends in mobile technology, such as 5G or IoT, will enable you to anticipate challenges and opportunities in the future.

- Become familiar with different mobile devices, operating systems, and browsers.

- Learn about Appium, XCUITest, Espresso, Detox, and Maestro, some of the most popular mobile testing tools and frameworks available today.

- To exchange knowledge and best practices, join a community of mobile testers, such as an online forum or a local meetup.

- Continue your education by taking online courses, reading blogs, joining webinars, and attending industry events. Keeping up with these resources will help you stay informed and adaptable in the rapidly changing mobile testing world.

- Testers should be able to combine technical skills, such as knowledge of mobile platforms and test automation, with soft skills, such as communication and problem-solving. Mobile testers must have a diverse skill set to assist with ensuring the quality and reliability of mobile applications, ultimately ensuring the best possible customer experience.

Summary

In this chapter, we examined the numerous aspects of mobile app testing. We learned how vital it is to test mobile applications to provide users with high-quality experiences. We also explored the advantages of test automation, such as quicker testing cycles and consistent results across platforms and devices. This helped us understand the significance of a well-planned testing strategy to overcome the challenges and obstacles in mobile app testing.

In addition, we gained valuable insights into the various testing tools, frameworks, and services available for mobile apps. We understood the importance of testing the mobile app UI and functionality to ensure seamless user experiences. Our exploration of testing on cloud devices and the impact of AI and ML on mobile testing deepened our understanding, leading us to recognize the necessity of comprehensive test case management.

This streamlines the testing process, resulting in successful mobile test coverage across various devices, operating system versions, and network conditions. By incorporating these concepts, developers can implement effective mobile app testing strategies to create robust and reliable applications that meet user expectations.

The next chapter will cover mobile app release management. It's important to release mobile apps efficiently due to fast-paced technology and user experience needs. We'll also discuss the top practices and challenges.

6

Mobile App Release Management

We are now in the sustain phase of our Mobile DevOps and CI/CD progress. Once the application has been successfully developed and tested, it is ready to be released to app stores. This typically involves releasing the mobile application to beta testing or production and making it available to users. Mobile app release management is essential for businesses to optimize the user experience and maintain high quality. It involves planning and implementing new features/updates and hotfixes.

But releasing mobile apps requires different processes, steps, and tools. In this chapter, we will explore the various stages of the release management process for mobile applications and cover the following topics:

- Challenges in mobile app release management
- The definition of releasing mobile applications
- Implementing the entire CI/CD process
- Ensuring compliance with app store guidelines and regulations
- Releasing and distributing mobile applications
- Incorporating user feedback with beta testing
- App store submission
- App Store Optimization (ASO)
- Monitoring and reporting on release progress
- Implementing a release train

First, we'll discuss the biggest challenges we face when releasing mobile apps so that we know how to tackle them with the relevant release strategy, process, and tooling.

Challenges in mobile app release management

As an app developer, it is crucial to understand the mobile app release management process to ensure smooth deployment and high user satisfaction.

Having a process in place for releasing apps is essential for businesses, from start-ups to enterprises, as it is the best way to ensure the app's success in the long run. Not only does this help to keep users engaged but it also helps foster a strong relationship between the business and its customers.

Additionally, businesses can reduce the risk of user dissatisfaction and costly technical issues by ensuring that an app remains up to date and bug-free.

As a mobile-first company, customer feedback and ratings on app stores are very important because it gives us an indicator of the app's quality, features, and overall performance – we can't ignore them because this will help us improve our development and release process.

As discussed in the previous chapters, mobile development is unique, and as a result, the release process will be unique and challenging due to the following reasons:

- There is no straightforward process for releasing new features or hotfixes.

- There are no prerequisite tools, services, or platforms to help us release mobile apps smoothly and frequently; mostly, we do this manually, which consumes the team's time and effort, and the releases can be delayed for months.

- Testing on multiple devices, platforms, and configurations can be time-consuming and complex. Because of that, in *Chapter 5*, *Implementing a Robust Mobile App Testing Strategy*, we recommended using test automation and cloud device testing since manual testing can take weeks to be confident about the new release.

- There are specific policies and review procedures for each app store. It can be challenging to navigate these procedures and ensure compliance with app store rules, which may cause delays when launching apps.

- You may need to revert to a previous version when bugs are found after a release has been deployed. It can be difficult to manage several software versions and handle rollbacks efficiently.

- Releasing cross-platform apps is challenging because you manage two apps with different requirements, guides, and processes.

The definition of releasing mobile applications

When a mobile application is released, it becomes accessible to customers who can download, install, and use it on their devices. This involves several stages, including building, testing, and releasing the app on app stores or other distribution platforms. The end goal is to provide customers with a dependable, secure, and functional app that meets their needs and expectations.

Developing a solid release strategy for mobile apps is crucial for ensuring a successful launch and long-term success. Here's a step-by-step guide to defining a release strategy for your mobile app.

Defining a release strategy

Having a **release strategy** for a mobile application is essential to ensure successful release management. This strategy should consider various aspects, such as the frequency of releases, the types of released features, the testing and validation process, the risks associated with each release, and the best methods for mitigating them.

> *Release with confidence and make your app launch successfully with tools and strategies to help publish, manage, and distribute your app worldwide.*

A mobile app release strategy is a well-planned approach to launching, updating, and maintaining a mobile application. It outlines the key steps, milestones, and resources required to ensure a smooth release process while minimizing disruptions and maximizing user satisfaction. A well-defined release strategy can help you manage expectations, allocate resources, and measure success.

Understanding the release management process for mobile apps

Release management for mobile apps involves planning, scheduling, coordinating, and deploying new versions or updates of a mobile application to users. This process is crucial if you wish to regularly update the app with new features, bug fixes, and security patches. But there are different steps we should consider before, during, and after the release process; let's explore them together:

1. Before the release:

    - Plan the release

    - Build and test the app

2. Prepare the release:

    - Manage code signing

    - Prepare `versionCode` and `versionName`

3. Release the app

4. Choose the right release channel:

    - Beta testing

    - App store submission

5. Launch the app:

   - In-app update

   - Monitor the app's performance

6. Post-release:

   - Handle user feedback and reviews

   - Analyze app performance data

   - Plan for future releases

   - Mobile release train

   - App Store Optimization (ASO)

To learn more about each stage, let's take a closer look at each one.

Before the release

This is the initial stage where we should, as a team, define and agree on the release process, including the rollout strategy, the responsibilities, and more.

Planning the release

Once the release strategy has been defined, developing an implementation process is essential. This process should include *scheduling releases*, *managing code changes*, and *ensuring the app meets quality standards*. It should also include steps to ensure the app is tested and validated before release.

Building and testing the app

As mentioned in the previous chapters, we should use a **continuous integration** (**CI**) pipeline to build and test mobile apps and ensure we don't have any blockers or issues that can delay the release process. We can then move on to **continuous delivery and continuous deployment** (**CD**) to release the apps to app stores.

Continuous delivery and deployment (CD)

As mentioned in *Chapter 3*, *Mobile DevOps Fundamentals*, **continuous delivery** automatically delivers the builds that pass the CI checks to production environments (such as *staging*), where they will be tested and reviewed before being released into production.

The goal is to automate development and deployment processes to ensure the rapid, reliable, and budget-friendly delivery of mobile apps.

The process of CI/CD for mobile apps mainly comprises the following steps:

1. Release the build to the QA teams so that they can do additional checks and tests, such as exploratory testing, to ensure that the build meets the expectations.

2. Release the build to beta testers if the company or the team is already participating in the program.

3. If everything is fine after that, the release manager or the person responsible for the release process can approve the build and release it to the relevant app stores or production environments.

4. These steps can be seen in the following figure:

Continuous Delivery

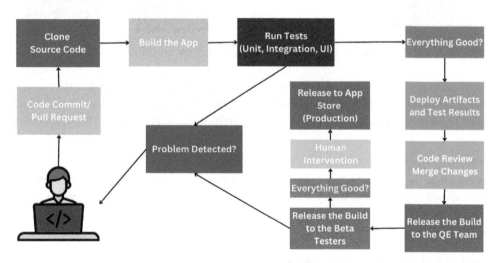

Figure 6.1 – The continuous delivery process

Continuous deployment is often part of the CI/CD pipeline, which means that the code that's deployed to the repository will be automatically deployed to production – or in our case, the mobile apps will be deployed to the relevant app stores. CI/CD pipelines are often referred to as the combination of these practices:

Continuous Deployment

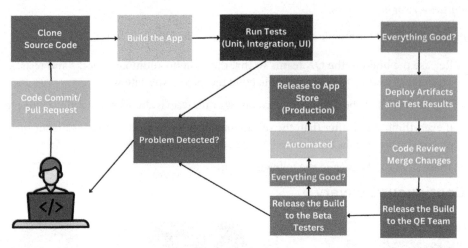

Figure 6.2 – The continuous deployment process

The continuous deployment process automates the process of deploying your app build, preventing human intervention. The only thing that will prevent a new change from being deployed into production is a failed build or test. This is used to speed up app production and get customer feedback faster.

> **Note**
>
> To learn how the GitHub Mobile Team automates its release process with GitHub Actions, go to `https://github.blog/2022-01-12-how-we-ship-github-mobile-every-week/`.

Preparing a release version and tag

We need to perform different steps here based on the application. For example, in **Android applications**, we need to update `versionCode` and `versionName` in the app-level `build.gradle` file.

The next step is to generate a signed APK or app bundle using the **Generate Signed Bundle / APK...** option in the **Build** menu; we will cover code signing and generating bundle files later in this section. This can also be done on the CI server automatically.

Meanwhile, for **iOS applications**, there are different steps, involving updating the version and build numbers in the **General** tab of your app's target settings. Once you've done this, select **Generic iOS Device** as the build target, archive the app from **Product**, then select the **Archive** menu. We will cover how to code-sign and archive the app later in this section.

Once you've done this, the release tag and release notes will be ready in the GitHub repository for the next release.

Preparing the release

Releasing any app to the Apple App Store, Google Play Store, or any other store requires certificates, provisioning profiles, or **Keystores** to identify that the apps have been built by a trusted company or developer.

As a result, we need to manage the code-signing process before building the app for release.

Setting up your developer account

The first step in the process is setting up an *Apple developer account*. This requires you to provide your name, address, and contact details. You'll also need to provide payment information and agree to the *Apple Developer Program License Agreement*. Once your account has been set up, you can access the *Apple Developer Portal*. The same steps must be followed for a Google developer account so that you can release the app to the Google Play Store.

Managing code signing

Code signing is the process of digitally signing an application's executable code, ensuring its integrity and authenticity. This process plays a crucial role in the Android app development life cycle as it helps confirm that the app comes from a trusted source and hasn't been tampered with since it was signed.

Let's explain the required code-signing steps for Android and iOS.

First, let's start with the steps for code signing for Android Apps.

To sign an Android app (`https://developer.android.com/studio/publish/app-signing`), follow these steps:

1. Set up a developer account (`https://play.google.com/console/`).
2. Create a unique private-public key pair using the keytool utility (`https://docs.oracle.com/javase/8/docs/technotes/tools/unix/keytool.html`).
3. Sign the app with their private key and embed the public key into a self-signed certificate.

Android Studio or the *apksigner* tool is used to package and sign the app using the generated key pair.

The Android system verifies the app's signature during installation to ensure its integrity and authenticity.

To generate a private-public key pair and self-signed certificate, follow these steps:

1. Open a Terminal or command prompt.

2. Execute the following command:

    ```
    keytool -genkey -v -keystore my-release-key.jks -keyalg RSA
    -keysize 2048 -validity 10000 -alias my-alias
    ```

3. Provide the required information when prompted, such as your name, organization, and location.

4. Choose a strong password for your keystore and key pair.

    Your key pair and self-signed certificate will be stored in the specified .jks file, as shown in the following screenshot:

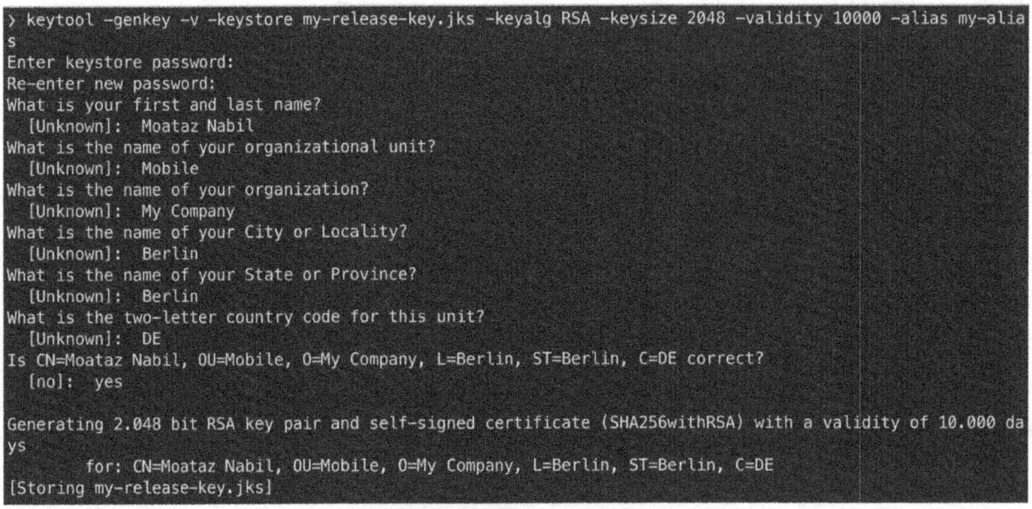

```
> keytool -genkey -v -keystore my-release-key.jks -keyalg RSA -keysize 2048 -validity 10000 -alias my-alia
s
Enter keystore password:
Re-enter new password:
What is your first and last name?
  [Unknown]:  Moataz Nabil
What is the name of your organizational unit?
  [Unknown]:  Mobile
What is the name of your organization?
  [Unknown]:  My Company
What is the name of your City or Locality?
  [Unknown]:  Berlin
What is the name of your State or Province?
  [Unknown]:  Berlin
What is the two-letter country code for this unit?
  [Unknown]:  DE
Is CN=Moataz Nabil, OU=Mobile, O=My Company, L=Berlin, ST=Berlin, C=DE correct?
  [no]:  yes

Generating 2.048 bit RSA key pair and self-signed certificate (SHA256withRSA) with a validity of 10.000 da
ys
        for: CN=Moataz Nabil, OU=Mobile, O=My Company, L=Berlin, ST=Berlin, C=DE
[Storing my-release-key.jks]
```

Figure 6.3 – keytool output

To sign your app in Android Studio, follow these steps:

1. In Android Studio, open the **Build** menu and select **Generate Signed Bundle / APK…**:

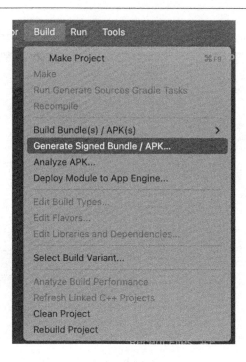

Figure 6.4 – Generate Signed Bundle / APK…

Choose **Android App Bundle** since we know the Google Play Store recently announced that it only supports .aab (the Android App Bundle). Then, click **Next**:

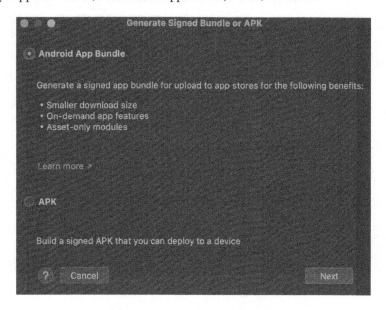

Figure 6.5 – Selecting Android App Bundle or APK

2. Click **Choose existing...** and locate your keystore file (`my-release-key.jks`):

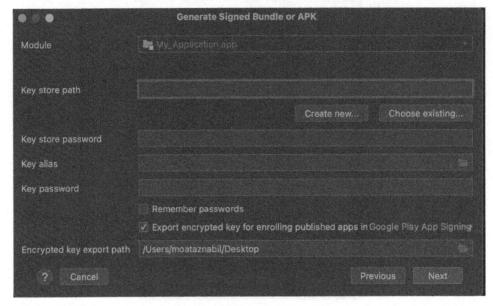

Figure 6.6 – Selecting Key store path

3. Enter the keystore and key pair passwords and the key alias.

4. Choose your **Destination Folder** and **Build Variants** parameters and then click **Finish**:

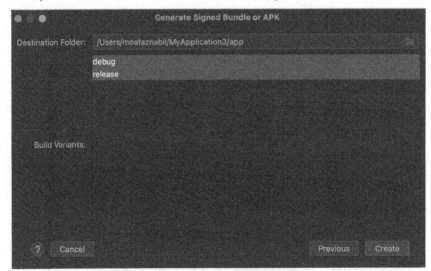

Figure 6.7 – Selecting Build Variants

Android Studio will create a signed App Bundle ready for distribution, as shown in the following screenshot:

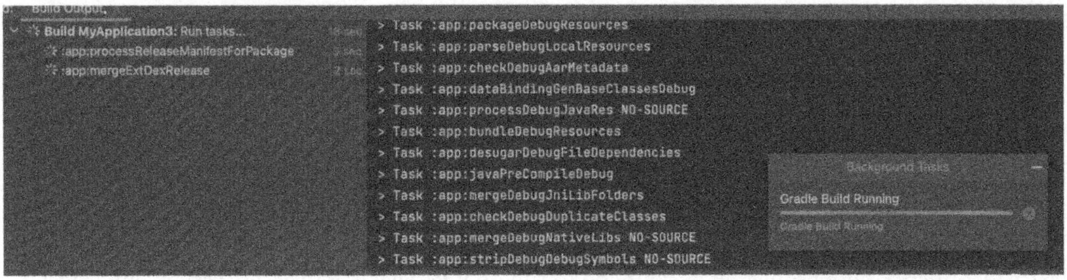

Figure 6.8 – Gradle running the tasks

In the release folder, you can find the generated .aab file, as shown in the following screenshot:

< > release

app-release.aab

Figure 6.9 – The .aab file

> **Note**
>
> Keep your signing key and keystore file secure – they are used to identify and verify your app. You cannot update or maintain your app if you lose your signing key or Keystore file.

Now, let's look at the steps for code signing for iOS apps.

To sign an iOS app, follow these steps:

1. Log in or create an Apple Developer Account (https://developer.apple.com/) if you don't already have one.

2. Go to the Apple Developer Portal and select **Certificates, Identifiers & Profiles** from the dashboard.

Certificates are digital files that are used to verify the identity of the app developer and sign the app code.

There are two types of certificates:

- A **development certificate**, which is used during the app development process

- An **App Store (Distribution) Certificate**, which is used to distribute the apps to the Apple App Store

Identifiers are unique identifiers for your app that are used to associate your app with your developer account, enable certain app features such as push notifications, and create provisioning profiles.

There are three types of identifiers:

- **App ID**: This identifies a specific app
- **Bundle ID**: This identifies the app within a particular app group
- **Team ID**: This identifies the developer or organization

Provisioning profiles are files that contain information about your app, your certificate, and your device identifiers. These profiles allow your app to run on iOS devices and access certain app features, such as push notifications, in-app purchases, and iCloud.

There are two types of provisioning profiles:

- A **Development Provisioning Profile**, which is used during the app development process.
- A **Distribution Provisioning Profile**, which is used to distribute your app on the App Store, as shown in the following screenshot:

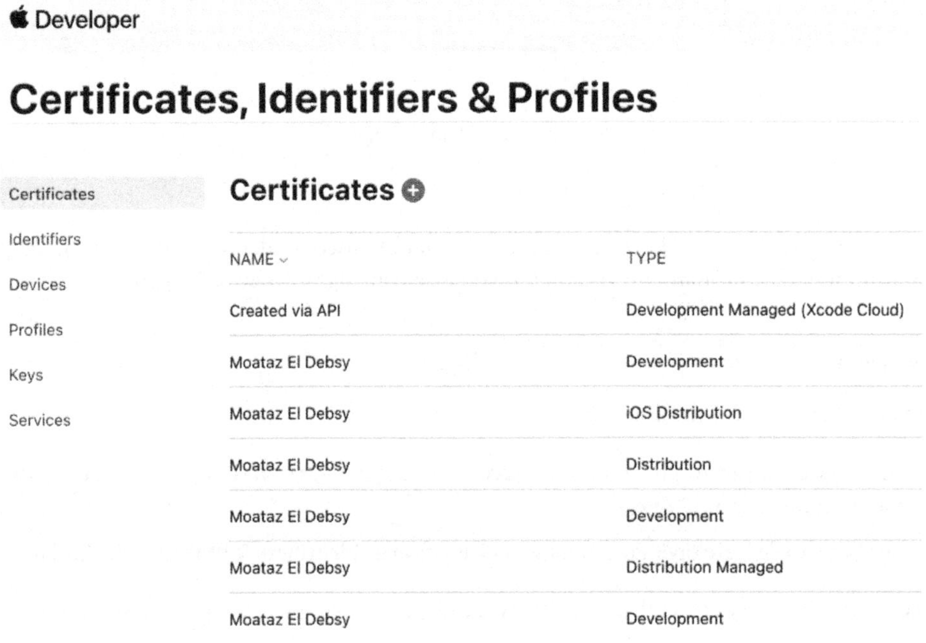

 Developer

Certificates, Identifiers & Profiles

Certificates	**Certificates** ⊕	
Identifiers		
	NAME ⌄	TYPE
Devices		
	Created via API	Development Managed (Xcode Cloud)
Profiles		
	Moataz El Debsy	Development
Keys		
	Moataz El Debsy	iOS Distribution
Services		
	Moataz El Debsy	Distribution
	Moataz El Debsy	Development
	Moataz El Debsy	Distribution Managed
	Moataz El Debsy	Development

Figure 6.10 – Apple Developer certificates

In the Apple Developer portal, open the **Certificates, Identifiers & Profiles** (`https://developer.apple.com/account/resources/certificates/list`) page, then click on the + button to create a new certificate. Choose **iOS App Development** and click **Continue**, as shown in the following screenshot:

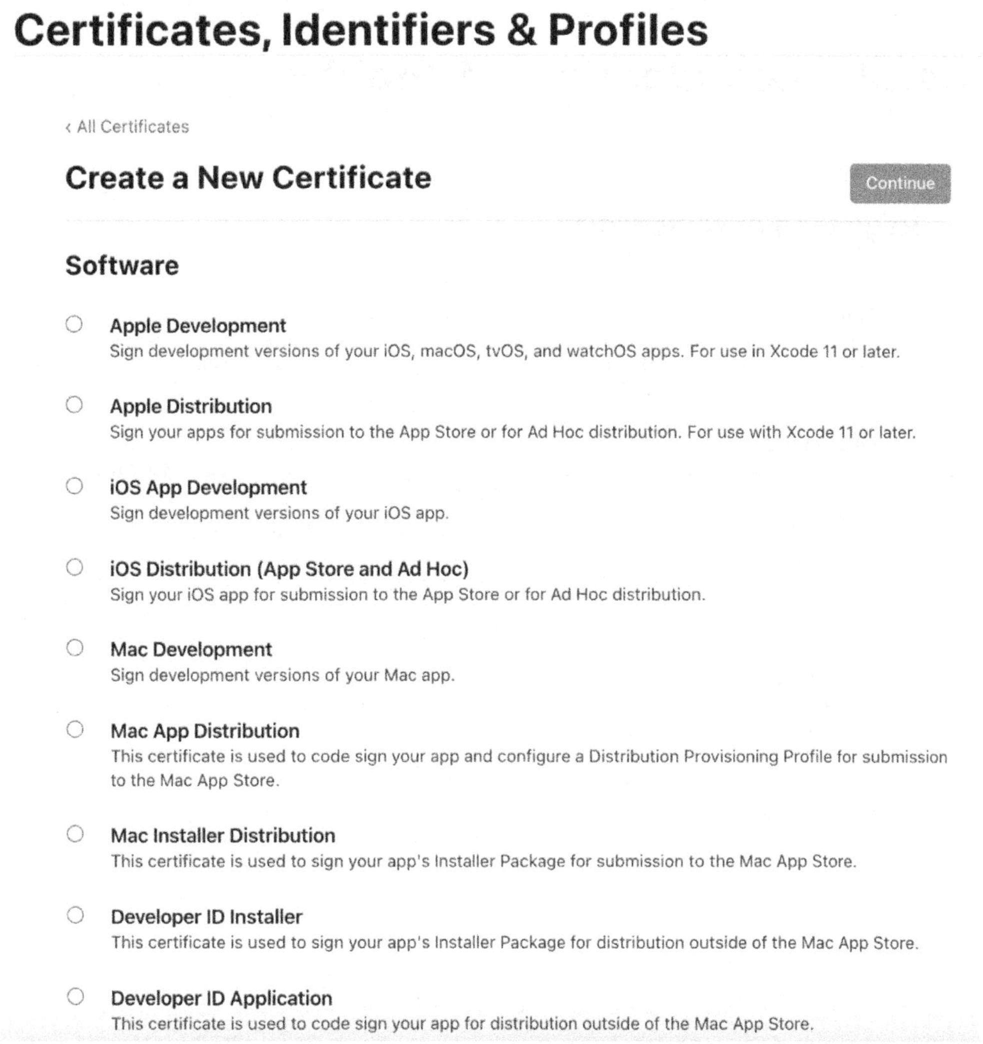

Certificates, Identifiers & Profiles

‹ All Certificates

Create a New Certificate

[Continue]

Software

○ **Apple Development**
Sign development versions of your iOS, macOS, tvOS, and watchOS apps. For use in Xcode 11 or later.

○ **Apple Distribution**
Sign your apps for submission to the App Store or for Ad Hoc distribution. For use with Xcode 11 or later.

○ **iOS App Development**
Sign development versions of your iOS app.

○ **iOS Distribution (App Store and Ad Hoc)**
Sign your iOS app for submission to the App Store or for Ad Hoc distribution.

○ **Mac Development**
Sign development versions of your Mac app.

○ **Mac App Distribution**
This certificate is used to code sign your app and configure a Distribution Provisioning Profile for submission to the Mac App Store.

○ **Mac Installer Distribution**
This certificate is used to sign your app's Installer Package for submission to the Mac App Store.

○ **Developer ID Installer**
This certificate is used to sign your app's Installer Package for distribution outside of the Mac App Store.

○ **Developer ID Application**
This certificate is used to code sign your app for distribution outside of the Mac App Store.

Figure 6.11 – Creating a new Apple Developer certificate

Follow the on-screen instructions to generate a **Certificate Signing Request (CSR)** (`https://developer.apple.com/help/account/create-certificates/create-a-certificate-signing-request`) from your Mac's Keychain Access app. Upload the CSR and download the generated development certificate.

Next, you'll need to create an App ID. This unique identifier links your app to its provisioning profile and certificates. Click **Identifiers** and then the + button. Fill in the necessary details and click **Continue** to register your App ID, as shown in the following screenshot:

 Developer

Certificates, Identifiers & Profiles

‹ All Identifiers

Register a new identifier

◉ **App IDs**
Register an App ID to enable your app, app extensions, or App Clip to access available services and identify your app in a provisioning profile. You can enable app services when you create an App ID or modify these settings later.

○ **Services IDs**
For each website that uses Sign in with Apple, register a services identifier (Services ID), configure your domain and return URL, and create an associated private key.

○ **Pass Type IDs**
Register a pass type identifier (Pass Type ID) for each kind of pass you create (i.e. gift cards). Registering your Pass Type IDs lets you generate Apple-issued certificates which are used to digitally sign and send updates to your passes, and allow your passes to be recognized by Wallet.

○ **Order Type IDs**
Register an order type identifier (Order Type ID) to support signing and distributing order bundles with Wallet and Apple Pay. Registering your order type ID lets you generate certificates to digitally sign and send updates to your orders in Wallet.

○ **Website Push IDs**
Register a Website Push Identifier (Website Push ID). Registering your Website Push IDs lets you generate Apple-issued certificates which are used to digitally sign and send push notifications from your website to macOS.

○ **iCloud Containers**
Registering your iCloud Container lets you use the iCloud Storage APIs to enable your apps to store data and documents in iCloud, keeping your apps up to date automatically.

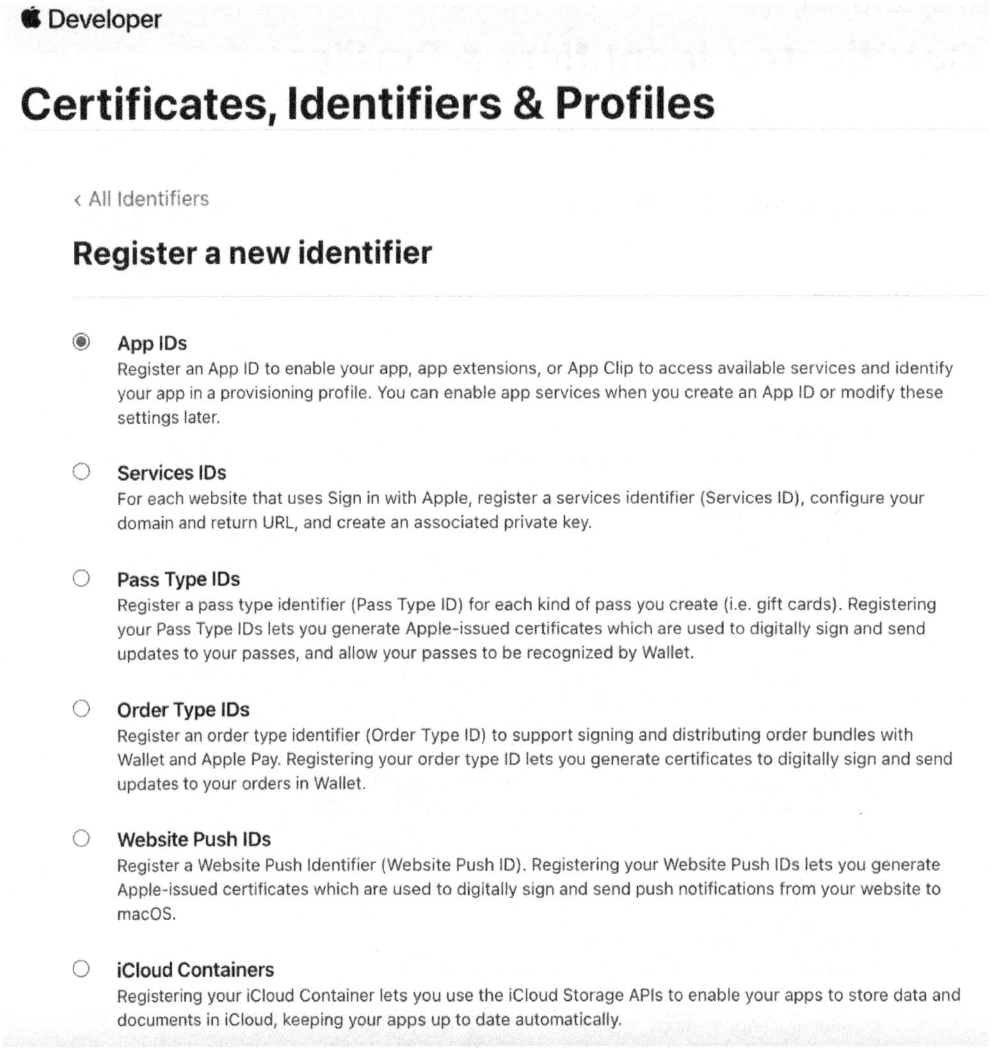

Figure 6.12 – Creating an app identifier

Now, let's create a provisioning profile. Click **Profiles** and then the + button. Choose **iOS App Development** and click **Continue**. Select the App ID you just created, the development certificate, and the devices you want to use for testing. Give your provisioning profile a name and click **Generate**, as shown in the following screenshot:

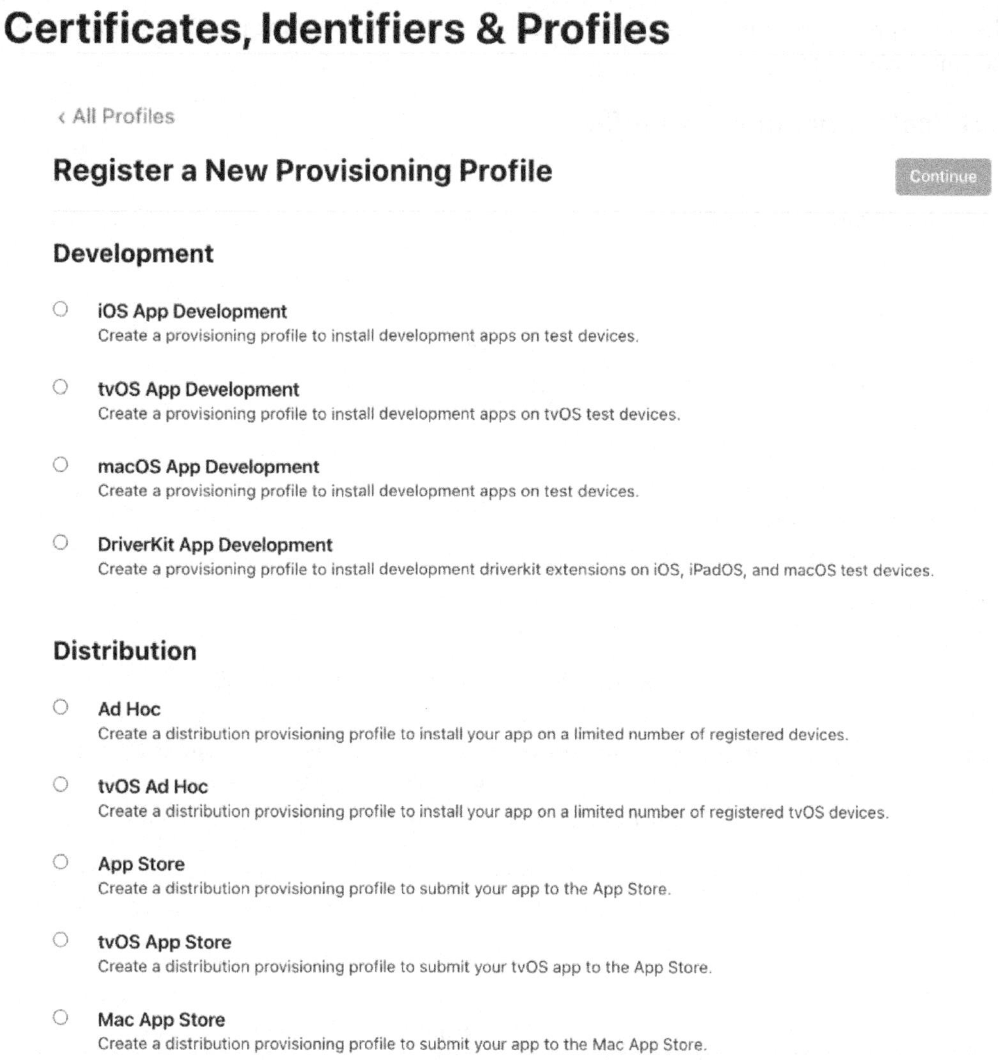

Certificates, Identifiers & Profiles

‹ All Profiles

Register a New Provisioning Profile

Continue

Development

○ **iOS App Development**
Create a provisioning profile to install development apps on test devices.

○ **tvOS App Development**
Create a provisioning profile to install development apps on tvOS test devices.

○ **macOS App Development**
Create a provisioning profile to install development apps on test devices.

○ **DriverKit App Development**
Create a provisioning profile to install development driverkit extensions on iOS, iPadOS, and macOS test devices.

Distribution

○ **Ad Hoc**
Create a distribution provisioning profile to install your app on a limited number of registered devices.

○ **tvOS Ad Hoc**
Create a distribution provisioning profile to install your app on a limited number of registered tvOS devices.

○ **App Store**
Create a distribution provisioning profile to submit your app to the App Store.

○ **tvOS App Store**
Create a distribution provisioning profile to submit your tvOS app to the App Store.

○ **Mac App Store**
Create a distribution provisioning profile to submit your app to the Mac App Store.

Figure 6.13 – Register a New Provisioning Profile

Select the App ID we created previously and configure the provisioning profile, as shown in the following screenshot:

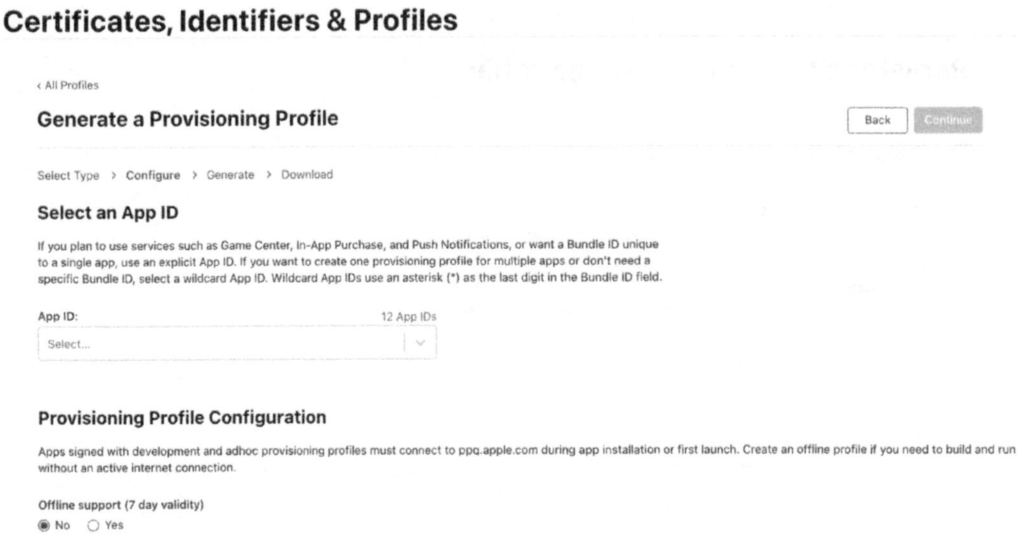

Certificates, Identifiers & Profiles

‹ All Profiles

Generate a Provisioning Profile

Back   Continue

Select Type > **Configure** > Generate > Download

Select an App ID

If you plan to use services such as Game Center, In-App Purchase, and Push Notifications, or want a Bundle ID unique to a single app, use an explicit App ID. If you want to create one provisioning profile for multiple apps or don't need a specific Bundle ID, select a wildcard App ID. Wildcard App IDs use an asterisk (*) as the last digit in the Bundle ID field.

App ID: 12 App IDs

Select...   ⌄

Provisioning Profile Configuration

Apps signed with development and adhoc provisioning profiles must connect to ppq.apple.com during app installation or first launch. Create an offline profile if you need to build and run without an active internet connection.

Offline support (7 day validity)
◉ No   ○ Yes

Figure 6.14 – Generate a Provisioning Profile | Select an App ID

Open your Xcode project and go to the **Signing & Capabilities** tab. Click the **Team** drop-down menu and select your developer account. Xcode should automatically handle the provisioning profile and certificate for you. If not, click **Import Profile** and locate your downloaded provisioning profile.

Once you've set up your account, provisioning profile, App ID, and certificates, you'll need to prepare your app for release. This involves completing tasks such as creating screenshots and setting up the app's metadata.

But before that, you need to upload and save your credentials to your CI provider to sign the app automatically in the release process. For example, **Bitrise** provides a tab in the Workflow Editor where you can upload your provisioning profile and code-signing certificate so that they can be used in the iOS CI/CD pipeline:

Figure 6.15 – Bitrise's iOS Code Signing & Files tab

For Android, you can upload the Keystore file to sign your apps in the CI/CD pipeline:

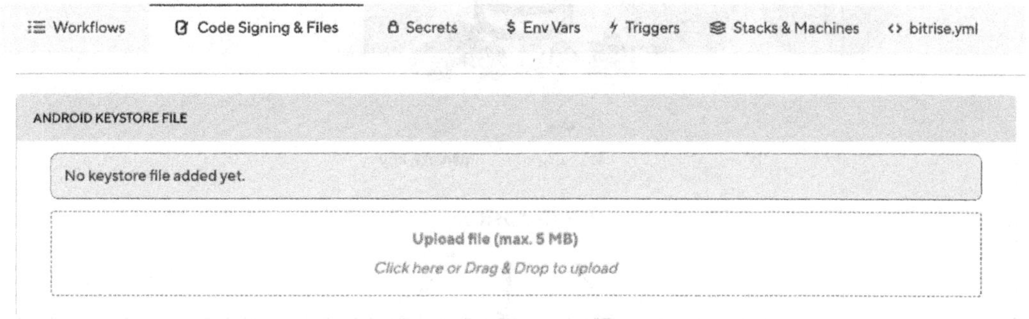

Figure 6.16 – Bitrise's Android Code Signing & Files tab

This should also be the same case with GitHub Actions; you can store the credentials on GitHub Secrets (https://docs.github.com/en/actions/reference/encrypted-secrets) so that they can be quickly passed into GitHub Actions directly. You can also use Codemagic for iOS (https://docs.codemagic.io/yaml-code-signing/signing-ios/) and Android (https://docs.codemagic.io/yaml-code-signing/signing-android/) using the same approach or any other CI provider.

> **Note**
>
> Alternatively, you can connect to an Apple service (such as App Store Connect or the Apple Developer Portal) with the API key to automatically upload iOS apps to the App Store.

Managing certificates and profiles in large mobile teams using fastlane match

In a large and scalable mobile team, it is crucial to manage certificates and profiles in a centralized and secure manner to prevent conflicts and guarantee that all team members are utilizing the latest, uniform files.

Tools such as **fastlane** and **fastlane match** (`https://docs.fastlane.tools/actions/match/`) can be used to manage certificates and profiles in a large team. These tools automatically download the latest versions of developers' signing certificates and provisioning profiles when they build and release apps from a Git repository.

Files should be stored and accessed according to the **Matchfile** in the repository. Once the certificates and profiles have been downloaded, team members can build and release their app using fastlane match, as shown in the following figure:

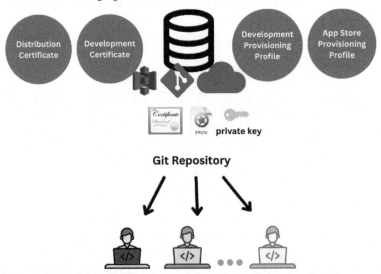

Figure 6.17 – How fastlane match works

Using fastlane match helps eliminate many common issues related to code signing, such as expired certificates or mismatched provisioning profiles. It's a recommended approach to managing code signing securely and collaboratively. In *Chapter 9, Mobile DevOps Best Practices*, we will discuss how to use fastlane in building, testing, and releasing mobile apps.

Releasing the app

The **release candidate** (**RC**) build is ready to go out to our beta testers when the following criteria have been met:

- A *branch* is created for addressing any hotfixes needed for the release candidate
- The *build* is generated with a proper version number and uploaded to TestFlight/Firebase App Distribution, depending on the application's type
- All *unit*, *UI*, and *snapshot tests* have passed
- An issue is created to track the *release process*
- *Release notes* are ready
- The build can be automatically submitted to the App Store or Google Play Store if there are no issues or can be manually approved by the release manager and stakeholders

This workflow or pipeline can be implemented with your CI provider, as discussed in *Chapter 4, Achieving Continuous Integration and Delivery with Mobile DevOps*, but as mentioned previously, it should support integration with different tools and services to make the release process easy.

The team needs to generate an app binary for a given build. Then, it must define a job that contains multiple steps for generating a build, going through the test cases, and then archiving and uploading it to TestFlight for iOS or Firebase App Distribution for Android. You can create a dedicated branch for each version you ship so that you can go back and cherry-pick any changes you want to include, as shown in the following figure:

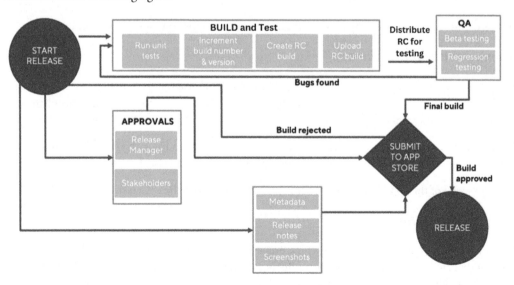

Figure 6.18 – Mobile release cycle

Now, let's learn more about the different release stages, such as beta testing and app store submission.

Beta testing

Mobile app beta testing is a crucial stage in the creation process. Before the official release, it enables developers to test their apps on actual mobile devices and gather user feedback. A limited group of users who are willing to test the release and offer comments on its features, usability, and overall user experience is often used for beta testing.

The beta testing phase of the mobile app development process is crucial because it gives developers a chance to evaluate the usability and functionality of their app before making it available to the general public. However, it can be intimidating to build up an effective beta testing program due to the following reasons:

- **Fear of negative feedback**: When putting an app in the hands of beta testers, there is a fear that they might provide negative feedback or encounter critical bugs that could potentially undermine the confidence of the development team.

- **Lack of resources**: Creating a proper beta testing program requires resources, such as time, money, and personnel. Coordinating with testers, managing feedback, and implementing changes can be resource-intensive, especially for smaller development teams or indie developers.

- **Identifying the right testers**: Finding the right pool of beta testers who are genuinely interested in providing valuable feedback and representing the target audience can be challenging.

- **Time constraints**: The beta testing phase can introduce delays, which might be perceived as a barrier to rapid deployment.

There are different steps to setting up the beta testing program for your apps. Let's take a look.

Defining the scope of the app

The first step in setting up a successful mobile app beta testing program is to define the scope of the app. This should include a clear description of the features of the app, its target users, and the platforms on which it will be available. This is essential to ensure the app is tested in the correct environment.

In addition, developers should consider what metrics they want to track during beta testing. This could include the number of downloads, usage statistics, and user feedback.

Once the scope of the app has been established, it is time to set up the beta testing program.

Preparing for launch

Once the beta testing program has been set up, preparing for the app's launch is essential. This involves ensuring that any issues that were identified during the testing phase are addressed and that the app is ready for public release. Developers should also consider how they will market the app and what steps they will take to ensure a successful launch.

For iOS, developers need to create an App Store Connect account (`https://appstoreconnect.apple.com/login`) and submit their app through the platform. For Android, they need a Google Play Console account (`https://play.google.com/console/about/`) and must submit their app through the platform. This includes providing necessary metadata, such as the app's name, description, keywords, screenshots, app icons, and pricing information.

Developers also need to provide a test account with login credentials, if their app requires authentication, to access content or features of the app store. This allows them to test the apps during the beta testing and app store submission phases.

By allowing a group of users to test the app before it is made available, developers can gain invaluable feedback on the product's performance and make any necessary adjustments or enhancements before the definitive version is released.

Recruiting testers

You can reach out to users in your target audience who have expressed interest in testing apps. You can also post on app-related forums and social media or use a service such as TestFlight to find testers. Here are some effective methods for recruiting testers:

- **Provide clear instructions**: Once you have recruited your testers, provide them with clear instructions on how to install and use the app and how to provide feedback
- **Monitor feedback**: Monitor the responses from the testers and make any necessary changes to the app before releasing it to the public

Beta testing tools

Beta testing is an essential phase in the development of mobile apps. It allows developers to gather valuable feedback from a limited group of users before the app's full release, identify and fix issues, and ensure a smoother launch. There are several tools available for conducting beta testing on mobile apps. Here are some popular ones:

- TestFlight
- Google Play beta testing
- Firebase App Distribution

Let's take a closer look.

TestFlight

TestFlight (`https://developer.apple.com/testflight/`) is an invaluable tool for iOS app developers, allowing them to beta-test their apps before they release them on the app store. It is now an integrated part of the iOS app development ecosystem.

TestFlight makes it simple for developers to invite beta testers to try out their apps. All you need is the tester's email address, and they'll receive an invitation to download the app through TestFlight.

TestFlight's integration with the iOS development environment makes distributing and testing apps for iPhone, iPad, and other Apple devices easy. It is free, making it accessible to developers of all sizes, from individuals to large companies.

Developers can distribute multiple app builds simultaneously, allowing them to test different versions and identify the most successful one.

TestFlight makes it easy for beta testers to provide feedback directly within the app. This ensures that developers receive valuable insights and can make the necessary improvements before launching the app publicly.

Developers can invite up to 10,000 external testers, enabling them to collect a vast amount of feedback and identify potential issues. More information about testing apps with TestFlight can be found at `https://testflight.apple.com/`.

Here are the general steps you must follow to use beta testing with TestFlight:

1. Create a new version in Xcode and ensure that it meets all app store guidelines and requirements, including screenshots and metadata.

2. Upload your app to App Store Connect and select the version you want to distribute to beta testers.

3. Invite beta testers to test your app by sending them an email invitation from App Store Connect. You can invite up to 10,000 testers per app. Once you have invited them, they will receive an email invitation to test your app. They will need to accept the invitation and install TestFlight on their iOS device.

4. After the beta testers have accepted the invitation and installed TestFlight, you can add them to a group in App Store Connect. This allows you to manage the distribution of different app versions to different groups of testers.

5. Once you have added beta testers to a group, you can distribute the app to them by selecting the app version you want to distribute in App Store Connect and selecting the group of testers to which you want to distribute it.

6. Beta testers can provide feedback on the app through the TestFlight app, including screenshots, comments, and ratings.

7. Monitor the app's performance and track issues reported by beta testers, and then fix any issues that are found.

After the beta testing phase is completed and all issues have been resolved, the app is ready to be released to the relevant app store.

Google Play beta testing

Google Play beta testing (`https://support.google.com/googleplay/android-developer/answer/9845334?hl=en&visit_id=638185357369512451-3818777855&rd=1`) is an essential tool for Android app developers, offering a straightforward way to beta-test apps before they're released on the Google Play Store. Its easy setup, seamless integration with the Google Play Store, and support for a large tester base make it a go-to choice for Android app testing.

Google Play beta testing allows developers to distribute their apps to testers via email invitations or by sharing a link. Testers can easily access the app through the Google Play Store, just like any other app.

Testers can provide feedback directly within the app, giving developers essential insights into improving the app before it's released to the public.

Google Play beta testing also supports staged rollouts, allowing developers to release app updates to a percentage of users and gradually increase that percentage over time.

You can test your app with specific groups or open your test to Google Play users with Play Console, as shown in the following screenshot:

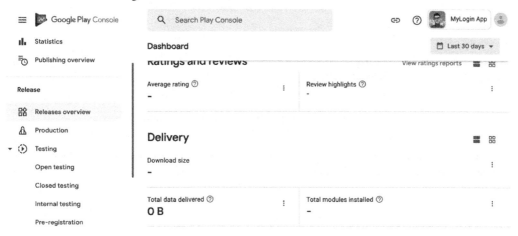

Figure 6.19 – Google Play Console

There are three types of testing with Google Play:

- **Internal testing**: Up to 100 testers can quickly access your app for initial quality assurance checks:

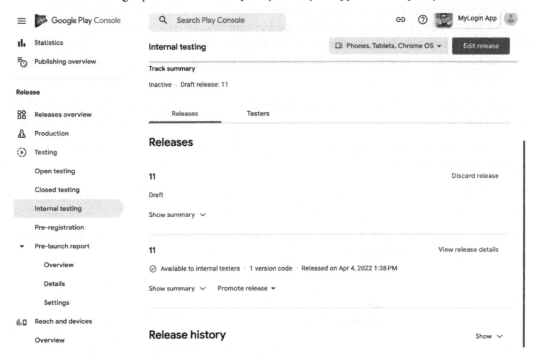

Figure 6.20 – Google Play Console – Internal testing

- **Open testing**: This allows you to run a test with a large group of people and surface the test version of your app on Google Play:

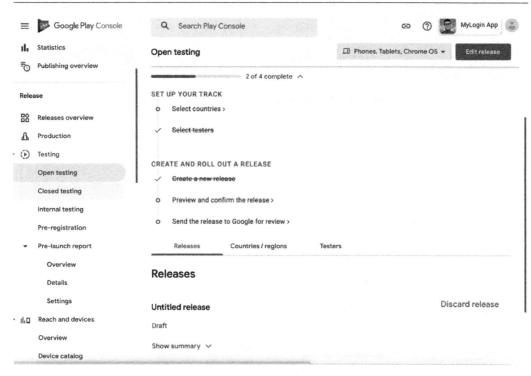

Figure 6.21 – Google Play Console – Open testing

- **Closed testing**: This allows you to gather more targeted feedback from a wider range of testers during pre-release testing:

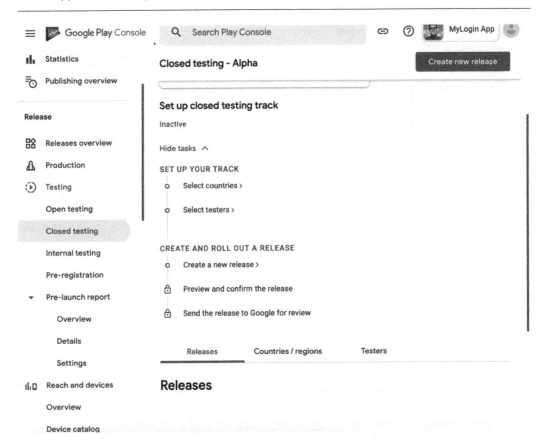

Figure 6.22 – Google Play Console – Closed testing

Here are the general steps to implement beta testing with Google Play Console:

1. Ensure it is ready for testing by creating a beta build and signing it with a Keystore.

2. Create a list of beta testers by adding their Google email addresses to the Google Play Console.

3. Upload the beta build of the app to the Google Play Console, where beta testers can access it.

4. Send out beta testing invites to the testers via email, which will contain a link to download the beta build of the app.

5. Monitor the feedback from beta testers on the Google Play Console and address any reported issues or bugs.

6. Based on the feedback received, we can make changes and improvements to the app before releasing it to the general public.

7. Once it has been tested and all issues have been addressed, it can be released to the public via the Google Play Store.

Firebase App Distribution

Firebase App Distribution (`https://firebase.google.com/docs/app-distribution`) can distribute your apps to trusted testers via a hassle-free process by promptly getting your apps onto testers' devices. By doing this, you can receive feedback early and frequently and align it with your goals for mobile DevOps and CI/CD.

Firebase App Distribution allows developers to distribute and test their apps on both iOS and Android devices, making it a versatile choice for multi-platform app development. However, iOS developers usually prefer to use TestFlight because it's free and integrated more with Apple's services and apps.

Distributing your app to testers is simple with Firebase App Distribution. You can invite testers via email or share a link, giving them quick access to the app.

Firebase App Distribution integrates seamlessly with **Crashlytics** (`https://firebase.google.com/products/crashlytics`), a real-time crash reporting tool. It helps developers identify and fix issues quickly, improving app stability and performance.

Firebase App Distribution supports popular CI/CD tools, allowing developers to automate the process of building, testing, and distributing their apps.

The general steps for using Android beta testing with Firebase App Distribution are as follows:

1. Create a Firebase account and project.
2. Add the Firebase SDK to your project.
3. Create a signed release build of your App Bundle.
4. Use the Firebase CLI, Gradle, or CI server to upload your app's build to Firebase App Distribution.
5. Invite testers by adding their email addresses or by creating tester groups in the Firebase console. You can also import a CSV file with the email addresses of your testers.
6. Once your build has been uploaded and testers have been added, distribute your app to the selected testers. They will receive an email invitation with instructions on how to access and install the beta version of your app.

Once the beta testing stage has been completed, we can move to the final stage, which is submitting the apps to the app stores.

Submitting the app

Before submitting an app for review, developers must ensure it complies with the *App Store Review Guidelines*, which cover a wide range of topics, such as user privacy, content, design, and functionality. Developers should also test their apps extensively on different devices and iOS versions to ensure a smooth user experience.

Submitting the app means uploading it to an app store (such as App Store or Google Play) for review and approval and making it available for users.

Once your app is ready, you'll need to submit it to the relevant app store. This involves uploading your app, providing *screenshots* and other *metadata*, and submitting the app for review. The review process can take up to a week, and your app may only be accepted if it meets the app store's guidelines.

The review process typically takes a few days, but the time frame can vary, depending on the app's complexity and the volume of submissions. During the review process, Apple's team evaluates the app against the App Store Review Guidelines, checking for functionality, performance, design, and content issues.

After the review process, there are several possible outcomes:

- If the app meets all the guidelines, it will be *approved* and published on the Apple App Store. You will receive a notification, and the app will be available for download.

- If the app doesn't meet the guidelines, it will be *rejected*, and you will receive feedback on the specific issues that need to be addressed. Then, you can make the necessary changes and resubmit your app for review.

- If the app's metadata doesn't meet the guidelines, it will be *rejected*, but the binary won't need to be re-reviewed or built again. You can update the metadata and resubmit it for review.

We are now ready for our app to be released. But before that, we need to know which mobile app distribution platforms we can use to make it public.

Mobile app distribution platforms

Mobile app distribution platforms are digital marketplaces where developers can publish, distribute, and sell their mobile applications to users. These platforms are essential for developers to reach a wide audience and gain exposure for their apps. Some of the most popular mobile app distribution platforms include the following:

- **Apple App Store** (`https://www.apple.com/de/app-store/`): The official app store for iOS devices such as iPhones, iPads, and iPod Touches. Developers can submit their apps for review and, if approved, make them available for download.

- **Google Play Store** (`https://play.google.com/store/apps`): The official app store for Android devices, which offers a wide variety of apps, games, and other digital content for users to download. Like the Apple App Store, developers can submit their apps for review and, if approved, make them available for download.

- **Amazon Appstore** (`https://www.amazon.com/mobile-apps/b?ie=UTF8&node=2350149011`): This app store by Amazon is an alternative marketplace for Android apps, featuring a broad selection of apps and games, including some that are exclusive to the platform.

- **Microsoft Store** (`https://apps.microsoft.com/store/apps`): The app store for Windows devices, including devices such as Windows Phone, Surface tablets, and Windows PCs. Developers can distribute both mobile and desktop applications through this platform.

- **Samsung Galaxy Store** (`https://galaxystore.samsung.com/apps`): The app store by Samsung, which offers a variety of apps and games specifically tailored for Samsung devices, including exclusive content and promotions.

- **Huawei AppGallery** (`https://appgallery.huawei.com/`): Huawei's official app store, which offers a selection of apps and games for Huawei and Honor devices. After being cut off from Google services, Huawei has been developing its app store as an alternative to the Google Play Store.

It's important to note that all these app stores have guidelines and policies you should follow when submitting your app:

- App Store (`https://developer.apple.com/app-store/review/`)

- Google Play (`https://play.google.com/console/about/guides/releasewithconfidence/`)

- Amazon Appstore (`https://developer.amazon.com/docs/app-submission/understanding-submission.html`)

- Huawei AppGallery (`https://developer.huawei.com/consumer/en/doc/distribution/app/50104`)

- Microsoft App Store (`https://learn.microsoft.com/en-us/windows/apps/publish/publish-your-app/create-app-submission?pivots=store-installer-msix`)

Ensure your app meets all the requirements and guidelines to complete the review process on time.

App Store submission

Uploading an iOS app to the Apple App Store involves the following steps:

1. You will need to configure your Xcode project to build and archive your app with the necessary provisioning profile and certificates. Make sure that you have the required provisioning profile and certificate for app distribution, not only development.

2. Go to the **App Store Connect** website and log in with your Apple Developer account.

3. Click **My Apps** and select the app you want to submit.

4. In the left sidebar, click on the **App Store** tab, scroll down to the **Metadata** section, and click the **Edit** button. Here, you can add the necessary metadata for your app, including the app's name, subtitle, description, keywords, and category.

5. Scroll down to the **Screenshots & Videos** section and click the **Edit** button. Here, you can add screenshots of your app for each device type and language you support. Ensure your screenshots meet the App Store guidelines, including the correct size and resolution.

6. You can upload screenshots by dragging and dropping them into the **Screenshot** section or by clicking the + button and selecting them from your computer.

7. You will also need to set the price of your app or choose to make it available for free. You can also choose which countries or regions where your app will be available.

8. After you have completed all the necessary steps, you can submit your app to the App Store for review. Ensure you have tested your app thoroughly and meet all of Apple's guidelines and policies.

9. Apple will review your app to ensure it meets all its technical, design, and content requirements. The review process typically takes several days, although it can take longer if there are any issues with your app.

Once your app has been approved, you can release it on the App Store. You can choose to release it immediately or schedule a release date in the future.

Tips for App Store submission

When submitting an app to the App Store, there are a few things you can do to increase your chances of acceptance. First, you should ensure that all required information is included and accurate. This includes screenshots, videos, contact information, a description of the app, and a privacy policy:

*   Make sure the app is compatible with the latest iOS version and devices
*   Use beta testing tools to test your app before submitting it to the App Store
*   Invest in quality design and development services to ensure your app meets the App Store's standards for quality
*   Follow the App Store's guidelines for submitting apps, including providing a complete and accurate description of your app

By following these tips, app developers can increase their chances of having their app accepted by the App Store.

Google Play Store submission

The Google Play Store (`https://play.google.com/store/apps`) is the official app distribution platform for Android devices. Like the Apple App Store, developers can submit their apps to the Play Store for approval and distribution to Android users.

Releasing an Android application can be exciting, but it's essential to understand the process involved to ensure your application's success.

Uploading an Android app to the Google Play Store involves the following steps:

1. In the Google Play Console, navigate to the **All applications** tab, and click on the **Create app** button. Choose a default language and enter a title for your app. This will create a draft listing for your app, which you can update later with more details.

2. Accept the Developer Program Policies and US export laws, then click the **Create app** button:

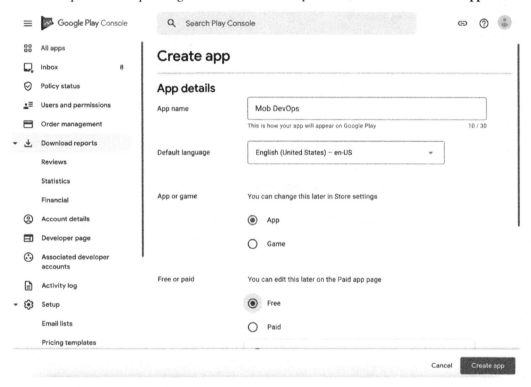

Figure 6.23 – Google Play Console – Create app

3. Be sure to sign your APK or AAB with a secure certificate, create a version code, and update the app's version name

4. Navigate to the **Release overview** section in the Google Play Console, and then to **Production**. Create a new release by selecting the appropriate release track (alpha, beta, or production). Upload your AAB and fill out the necessary details, as shown in the following screenshot:

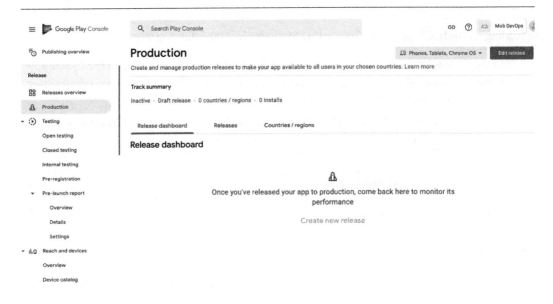

Figure 6.24 – Google Play Console – Release dashboard

5.   Now, you can create a new production release, as shown in the following screenshot:

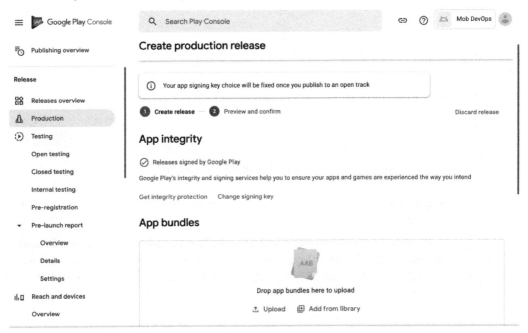

Figure 6.25 – Google Play Console – Create production release

6. If your app has in-app products, subscriptions, or utilizes any other Google Play services, configure them accordingly in the **Monetize** section:

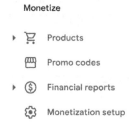

Figure 6.26 – Google Play Console – Monetize

Finally, under **In-app products**, you can add the Google payment details, as shown here:

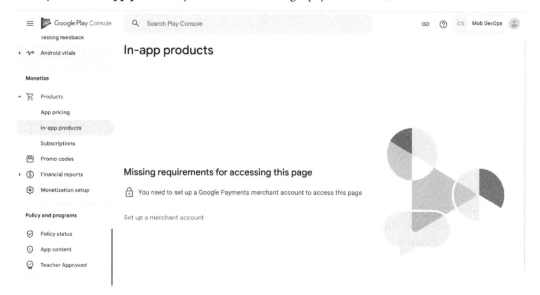

Figure 6.27 – Google Play Console – In-app products

After submission, Google will review your app, which usually takes a few hours to a few days. Once approved, your app will be live on the Google Play Store, and you can start tracking its performance, managing updates, and responding to user feedback.

Additionally, you can upload Android apps to another app store instead of Google Play Store, such as Amazon Appstore, Huawei AppGallery, and Samsung Galaxy Store.

To upload an app to Amazon Appstore, you will need to have an Amazon Developer account (`https://developer.amazon.com/`).

Uploading an Android app to Amazon Appstore involves the following steps:

1. You will need to configure your APK and sign it with a valid certificate. Ensure that your app meets Amazon's technical and design guidelines (`https://developer.amazon.com/docs/app-submission/understanding-submission.html`) and is built with a valid signing certificate:

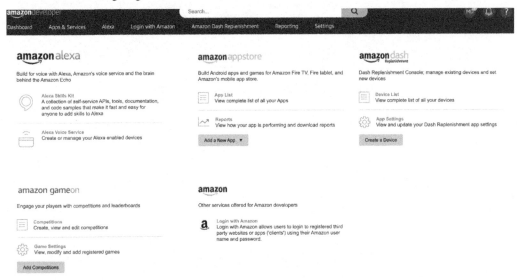

Figure 6.28 – Amazon Developer dashboard

2. Once your app is ready to be uploaded, you will need to provide some information about the app. This includes the app's name, description, keywords, screenshots, and other metadata to help users discover and download your app. Amazon Appstore currently has a staged rollout (`https://developer.amazon.com/docs/app-submission/release-updates-in-staged-rollouts.html`) that lets you gradually introduce new versions of your app to the marketplace in an incremental way.

3. After you have completed all the necessary steps, you can submit your app to Amazon Appstore for review. Ensure you have tested your app thoroughly and meet all of Amazon's guidelines and policies.

4. Amazon will review your app to ensure it meets all of its technical, design, and content requirements. The review process typically takes several hours, although it can take longer if there are any issues with your app.

Once your app has been approved, you can release it on Amazon Appstore. You can choose to release it immediately or schedule a release date in the future.

Completing the CI/CD workflow

To complete the CI/CD workflow that we created in *Chapter 4, Achieving Continuous Integration and Delivery with Mobile DevOps*, you can add the required steps to your pipeline to release the iOS and Android apps to TestFlight, App Store, Firebase App Distribution, Google Play Store, or any other distribution platform.

For example, here's a high-level overview of the workflow of building, testing, and releasing an iOS app to the App Store with Bitrise using steps such as **Xcode Archive & Export for iOS** and **Deploy to App Store Connect**, as shown in the following screenshot:

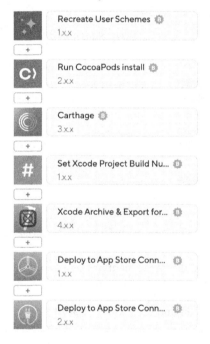

Figure 6.29 – Bitrise iOS CI/CD workflow

Here's a high-level overview of the YAML file for building, testing, and releasing an iOS app to the App Store with Codemagic: `https://github.com/PacktPublishing/Mobile-DevOps-Playbook/blob/main/Chapter-6/codemagic-iOS.yml`.

Additionally, you can perform the same steps with GitHub Actions for building, testing, and releasing an iOS app to the App Store: `https://github.com/PacktPublishing/Mobile-DevOps-Playbook/blob/main/Chapter-6/.github/ios.yml`.

Now, let's examine some examples of building, testing, and releasing Android apps with Bitrise, Codemagic, and GitHub Actions.

We'll start with Bitrise. The following screenshot shows the high-level Android CI/CD workflow for Firebase App Distribution and Google Play:

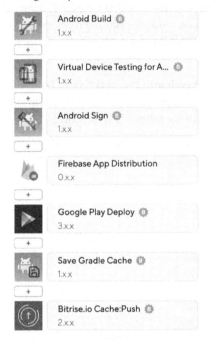

Figure 6.30 – Bitrise Android CI/CD workflow for Firebase App Distribution and Google Play

In terms of Codemagic, you can find the YAML file at `https://github.com/PacktPublishing/Mobile-DevOps-Playbook/blob/main/Chapter-6/codemagic-android.yml`.

Finally, for GitHub Actions, you can find the YAML file at `https://github.com/PacktPublishing/Mobile-DevOps-Playbook/blob/main/Chapter-6/.github/android.yml`.

Additionally, we can upload Android apps to another app store such as Huawei App Gallery for Huawei devices. Here is an example of the workflow for building, testing, and deploying an Android app to Huawei AppGallery with Bitrise:

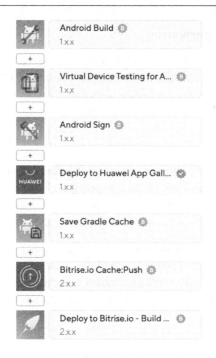

Figure 6.31 – Bitrise Android CI/CD workflow for Huawei App Gallery

Once we've released and deployed an app to the different app stores, we need to wait for the quality team to send us feedback about the releases. If it's approved, it can be released to different stores; otherwise, we will be given reasons for the rejection. In this case, we must fix them and upload another release.

Now, let's look at some common reasons for app rejection and how to avoid them.

When does the App Store reject apps?

Developing an app can be a time-consuming and expensive process. App developers want their apps to be accepted by the App Store, but sometimes, they get rejected.

When an app is rejected, it can be a frustrating experience for the developer. It is important to understand why the app was rejected to prevent it from happening again.

Let's look at the most common reasons (`https://developer.apple.com/app-store/review/#common-app-rejections`) why the App Store rejects apps and what app developers can do to increase their chances of acceptance.

Incomplete or incorrect information

One of the most common reasons for rejection is *incomplete or incorrect information*. For example, the App Store will reject the app if the app developer does not submit all the required screenshots and videos. The app developer should also ensure the app's name, description, and keywords are accurate and up to date and provide complete and accurate information to ensure the app is accepted.

Poor quality

The App Store also rejects apps that do not meet their standards for quality. This includes apps that are difficult to use, have too many bugs, or need to provide a better user experience. Due to this, in *Chapter 5, Implementing a Robust Mobile App Testing Strategy*, we recommended using test automation in DevOps and CI/CD pipelines to act as a gate of quality for mobile apps.

In addition, the App Store has specific design guidelines (`https://developer.apple.com/app-store/review/guidelines/#design`) that must be followed for an app to be accepted. For example, the app should be easy to navigate, have a straightforward user interface, and be free of typos and other errors. It might be rejected if the app's design does not meet the App Store's standards.

Unacceptable content

The App Store also rejects apps that contain illegal content. This includes apps that contain offensive or inappropriate language, content that violates copyright or trademarks, and apps that promote hate or violence. App developers should make sure that their apps do not contain any content that could be deemed offensive or illegal.

As you may have noticed, we discussed the process of releasing mobile apps manually just to understand the flow and the prerequisites for each app.

Now, let's explore different automation tools that can help mobile teams release their apps automatically instead of following the manual process discussed here.

Automating your release pipeline with an automated release tool

At the time of writing, there are different tools on the market to help mobile teams accelerate and automate the mobile app release process. This includes different out-of-the-box solutions such as Runway and the release management add-on from Bitrise.

Runway

Runway.team (`https://www.runway.team/`) is a platform that simplifies the process of shipping your mobile apps. It boasts a user-friendly interface, making it easy for developers to upload and distribute their mobile apps:

Figure 6.32 – Runway dashboard

With a few clicks, you can push your app to different app stores, eliminating the headache of manual submissions. Runway offers integration between different CI/CD platforms, such as Bitrise, Codemagic, GitHub Actions, and more, automating the process of building, testing, and releasing your app. This saves you time and effort and ensures a high-quality product by catching issues early on.

It works with Android and iOS, making it a versatile choice for developers working on multi-platform apps. You can manage your app releases for both platforms in one central location, as shown here for iOS apps:

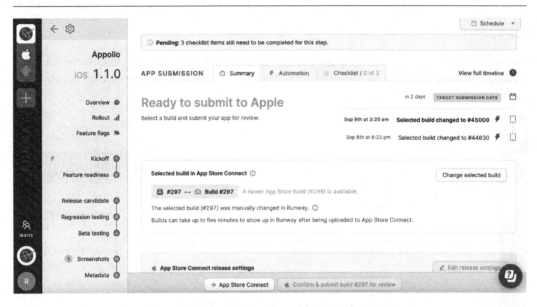

Figure 6.33 – Runway dashboard for iOS submission

You can also do the same for Android apps:

Figure 6.34 – Runway dashboard for Android submission

It lets you set up different release channels (for example, alpha, beta, and production), allowing you to test your app with different user groups before going live:

Figure 6.35 – Runway dashboard for Android rollout summary

Integrations are core to Runway, and it puts a lot of work into making them a seamless, robust, and secure part of the experience:

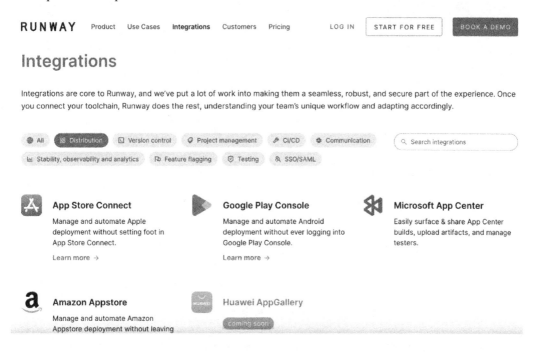

Figure 6.36 – Runway's integration with distribution services

You can take a tour of the platform via its sandbox solutions for iOS (`https://demo.runway.team/dashboard/org/demo/app/appollo-ios`) and Android (`https://demo.runway.team/dashboard/org/demo/app/appollo-android`).

The Bitrise Release Management add-on

In **Bitrise Release Management** (`https://devcenter.bitrise.io/en/release-management.html`), you can see how your app is released. In this way, all team members can understand the progress of upcoming releases, enabling them to coordinate their work more effectively.

With release management, you can automate tasks related to a specific release, such as monitoring feature readiness or submitting your app for App Store review:

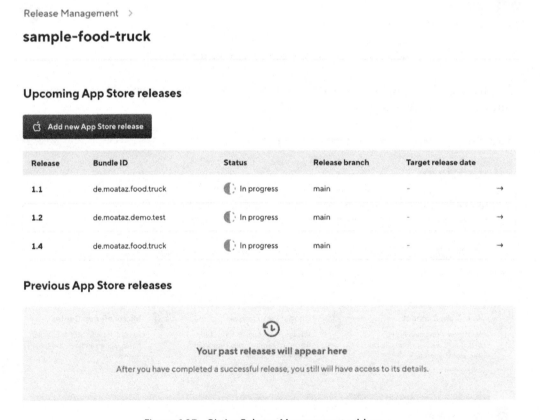

Figure 6.37 – Bitrise Release Management add-on

You can always check the status of the submission process. For example, the following screenshot shows that we submitted the app to TestFlight, and that the next step is submitting the app to the App Store:

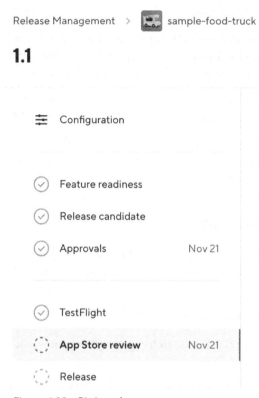

Figure 6.38 – Bitrise release management stages

Additionally, other tools can help you in releasing mobile apps, such as TestFairy (`https://testfairy.com/app-distrubution`) and AppCenter (`https://learn.microsoft.com/en-us/appcenter/distribution/`).

Launching the app

Once the app has been approved by the App Store team, you can notify your users of the new release in a variety of ways and also try to optimize your apps using **ASO**. Let's explore how we can use the in-app update together.

In-app update

Users can update their apps directly through their apps without visiting the app store, and this is a great way to update them with the latest features and bug fixes. In-app updates enable users to update their apps directly within their apps without them having to go to the app store.

By regularly updating your app, you can keep users engaged and reduce the chances of them abandoning your app as a result of bugs or a lack of new features.

There are two types of in-app updates:

- Using **flexible in-app** updates means that the user can continue to use the app while the update is downloading and installing in the background. Once the update is complete, the user is prompted to restart the app so that they can use the updated version.

- An **immediate in-app** update requires the user to update the app before the updated version can be used. Once the user agrees to update, the updated app is downloaded and installed.

In-app updates can be a powerful tool for app developers who are looking to improve the user experience and ensure that more users are using the latest version of the app. Developers can increase user engagement, reduce churn, and stay competitive in the fast-moving mobile app market by implementing in-app updates.

App Store Optimization (ASO)

ASO aims to optimize mobile apps for better visibility and higher ranking in app stores. The process involves researching keywords, writing compelling titles and descriptions, building links, and creating screenshots and videos.

ASO is influenced by the following factors:

- An *app's title* plays a vital role in search engine optimization as it is the first thing users see when they search for your app.

- The *app's description* should clearly explain what it is and why it is useful. It should use keywords throughout but make sure it reads naturally and doesn't sound spammy.

- The app keyword is the term or phrase that users might search for in the app store. Include relevant keywords in the app's description, title, and other metadata to improve the app's visibility.

- You can increase your app's visibility in search engine results by encouraging users to rate and review it and responding to negative feedback.

- Make sure the app icon is eye-catching and reflects the app's purpose when users browse the app store.

- Videos and screenshots can help users understand what the app does. You should use high-quality images and videos to showcase the essential features of your app.

- Optimize the app store metadata for each language if your app is available in multiple languages. App visibility can be improved in different regions by doing this.

- Make sure your app is regularly updated with new features, bug fixes, and performance improvements.

- Conduct A/B testing on app icons, screenshots, and descriptions to find the best-performing combination.

ASO is an ongoing process, and it's essential to monitor and update your app store listing regularly to ensure that it is up to date and reflects any changes to your app.

Iterate and optimize your app store listing based on the data collected.

Following this checklist can improve your app's visibility and conversion rate, leading to increased downloads and user engagement. Different tools on the market can help you with ASO, such as **appfigures** (`https://appfigures.com/aso-tools`). They have interesting insight into the Top Ranked iOS App Store Apps (`https://appfigures.com/top-apps/ios-app-store/united-states/iphone/top-overall`), Google Play Apps (`https://appfigures.com/top-apps/google-play/united-states/top-overall`), and other stores. Additionally, they have different resources and guides about ASO (`https://appfigures.com/resources/guides`).

Post-release

Once a mobile app has been released to different app stores, developers must still perform various maintenance tasks. This includes monitoring app reviews, responding to user inquiries, and updating the app with bug fixes and new features.

Monitoring app performance

As soon as the app is released, it must be closely monitored to ensure it meets the release strategy requirements. As part of this process, you can monitor user feedback and usage analytics, handle user feedback and reviews, and analyze the app and bug reports. By doing so, we can identify potential issues and ensure users have the best experience possible. We will explore mobile app monitoring in *Chapter 7, Establishing Mobile App Monitoring, Observability, and Analytics*.

Planning for future releases

Keeping your mobile application updated and improving it after releasing the current version is essential to maintaining user engagement. To plan for future releases, follow these steps:

1. Update your product roadmap with new features, enhancements, and bug fixes based on feedback and analysis. Your business goals should align with the features that benefit your users the most.

2. Follow the best practices for coding and design when implementing the planned features and enhancements. Make sure all bugs and issues are identified and fixed.

Implementing a release train

The mobile release train is a process that accelerates your release cycles. This approach will help you release more consistently and allows distributed teams to work more aligned around app development.

Once you have CI/CD in place, you can build trains.

During the development phase, your teams have time to review, build, test, and merge features to the main branch that should be part of the train, as shown in the following figure:

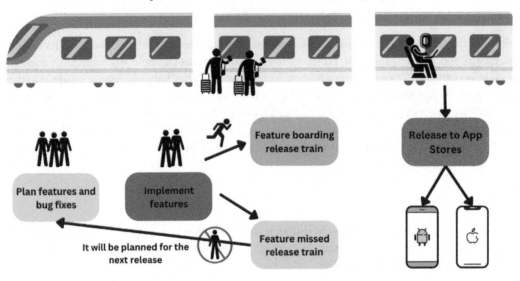

Figure 1.39 – Mobile release train

During the release train, a wide range of stakeholders may be involved, including development teams, quality assurance teams, and product management, as well as multiple iterations and testing phases before the final release is completed.

How to implement the release train

To implement the release train, you must perform the following steps:

1. Adopt a schedule for fixed release trains (for example, 2 weeks or 1 week).
2. Determine who will manage the release (the release manager).
3. Increase release confidence with feature flags and staged rollouts.
4. Identify the scope of the release train. The release schedule includes the features and functionality that will be included in each release.
5. Plan and prioritize features according to a clear process. A wide range of stakeholders, including product managers, developers, and users, should be involved in this process.

Remember, it's an ongoing process since we are in the sustain stage, which requires support from outside for us to stay on track.

Summary

Mobile app release management is a crucial app development process that requires careful planning, testing, and execution. Following the best practices outlined in this chapter can ensure a smooth release process and maximize user satisfaction.

Release management for mobile apps involves the process of planning, scheduling, coordinating, and deploying new versions or updates of a mobile application to users. This process is crucial for regularly updating the app with new features, bug fixes, and security patches. However, there are different steps we should consider before, during, and after the release process. Let's explore them together.

Mobile app release management is essential for businesses to optimize the user experience and maintain high quality. It involves planning and implementing new features/updates and hotfixes.

However, releasing mobile apps requires different processes, steps, and tools. We discovered various stages of the release management process for mobile applications throughout the topics that were covered in this chapter.

In the next chapter, we will continue adding more features to our mobile app and CI/CD pipeline to make sure that we are releasing quickly and frequently to our users.

Part 3: Monitoring, Optimizing, and Securing Mobile DevOps

Mobile DevOps involves monitoring the performance and usage of mobile apps in production environments and using that data to provide feedback to development teams. This can help identify and resolve issues quickly and improve the overall user experience.

This part has the following chapters:

- *Chapter 7, Establishing Mobile App Monitoring, Observability, and Analytics*
- *Chapter 8, Keeping Mobile Apps and DevOps Secure*
- *Chapter 9, Mobile DevOps Best Practices*

7

Establishing Mobile App Monitoring, Observability, and Analytics

In the previous chapter, we learned how to successfully release mobile apps to the relevant app stores. However, this is not the last stage in the CI/CD process. The next stage is to continuously support our customers and trace app usage, performance, crashes, and more. This is where monitoring observability, and analytics for mobile apps, come into play. In this chapter, we will cover the following:

- What is monitoring?
- What is observability?
- The benefits of implementing monitoring and observability for mobile apps
- The differences between monitoring and observability
- What is analytics?
- Factors to consider in monitoring and observability
- Steps to implement monitoring and observability for mobile apps
- Monitoring, observability, and analytics tools for mobile apps
- Key metrics for mobile app monitoring, analytics, and observability
- Implementing continuous monitoring for mobile apps

Mobile apps are complex because they interact with various external systems, such as servers, APIs, and databases. This complexity can make it challenging to identify and diagnose issues when they occur. Monitoring, observability, and analytics can provide real-time feedback on app performance, user behavior, and system interactions. This information can help developers identify potential issues before they impact users and develop effective solutions when issues do occur.

Additionally, to improve your app ratings, user engagement, and revenue, you should establish monitoring and observability practices to identify and address any issues before they negatively affect your users. Ensuring your mobile app performs optimally is essential, providing a seamless user experience.

But first, let's learn more about monitoring, observability, and analytics.

What is monitoring?

Monitoring for mobile apps refers to *continually tracking and analyzing the performance, reliability, and overall stability of mobile applications to ensure a seamless user experience*. It involves collecting data on app crashes, errors, freezes, and other performance issues, which helps developers identify and resolve any problems that might negatively impact the user experience.

The goal of monitoring is to identify and resolve any issues that may affect the quality of the user experience, such as crashes or slow load times.

The following diagram focuses on different key components in monitoring, such as app crashes, error tracking, and app performance:

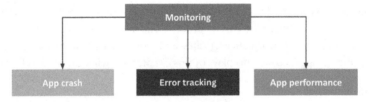

Figure 7.1 – Monitoring components

To ensure optimal application performance and user satisfaction, development teams must prioritize addressing these key components. By analyzing and solving potential issues, teams can guarantee a superior user experience. Let's delve into each component to fully grasp their significance:

- **App crash reporting**: This involves identifying and collecting crash information, including app crash frequency, affected devices, and the specific circumstances leading to a crash. This data facilitates understanding and fixing the root cause.

    "Monitor the symptoms of the crashes, not the crashes only."

- **Tracking errors**: This includes API errors, network errors, or code exceptions that occur during the app's runtime. This information can be used to resolve and diagnose problems in the app's code.

- **App performance monitoring**: This measures how responsive an app is, how long it takes to load, and other performance metrics to ensure a smooth user experience.

What is observability?

Observability for mobile apps refers to *the ability to gain insights into the internal state of an application by analyzing its external outputs, such as logs, metrics, and traces.* It enables developers or the release team to monitor, understand, and troubleshoot the app's behavior and performance.

"Observability is the ability to see what is happening in the production of user devices with our app binary."

Observability is crucial for maintaining a high-quality user experience and ensuring the app's reliability and stability.

Observability focuses on different key aspects, as shown in *Figure 7.2*:

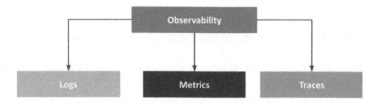

Figure 7.2 – Observability components

As we can see, the goal of observability is to gain insights into how a system operates, detect issues, and troubleshoot problems effectively. Observability focuses on several key aspects, including the following:

- **Logs**: During an app's runtime, logs contain information about user actions, system events, and error messages. Analyzing logs can help developers identify patterns, diagnose problems, and better understand the app.

- **Metrics**: Metrics track the app's health, identifying bottlenecks and optimizing its performance.

- **Traces**: Traces provide a detailed view of individual requests or transactions as they flow through the app's components, such as network calls, API interactions, and database queries.

Implementing monitoring and observability for mobile apps offers numerous benefits that enhance the app's performance, user experience, and overall success. Let's look at some of the key advantages.

Benefits of implementing monitoring and observability for mobile apps

There are several benefits to implementing monitoring and observability for mobile apps. Some of them are as follows:

- Monitoring and observability enable you to identify and resolve performance bottlenecks in your app

- Tracking app performance and user behavior continuously can help you make data-driven decisions to improve the user experience, ultimately leading to higher retention and satisfaction

- You can detect and diagnose issues quickly with monitoring and observability and resolve them before they negatively impact your users

- You can proactively address potential issues with observability by understanding your app's behavior better before they become critical

"Once we have observability in our app, we can alert when things become strange and still seem to work."

- Your app's performance data can be analyzed to optimize resource usage, leading to cost savings and increased efficiency

The differences between monitoring and observability

Monitoring and observability are complementary practices that, when used together, help teams build and maintain high-quality mobile apps. As shown in *Figure 7.3*, monitoring focuses on actively tracking performance and responding to known issues, while observability emphasizes a deeper understanding of app behavior to identify trends, diagnose unknown issues, and optimize performance:

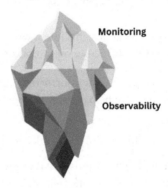

Figure 7.3 – Monitoring versus observability

A monitoring system is reactive, while an observability system is proactive. By combining both practices, teams can create a comprehensive strategy for maintaining and improving their mobile applications.

What is analytics?

In mobile app analytics, the data about app usage, user behavior, and performance is collected, measured, analyzed, and interpreted. Developers, marketers, and product managers can use mobile app analytics to optimize app performance, enhance user engagement, and increase customer loyalty. Analyzing user preferences and pain points enables data-driven decision-making and continuous improvement.

Analytics helps you understand how your users' behavior and app can be optimized to reach your business goals.

Analytics focuses on different key aspects, as shown in *Figure 7.4*:

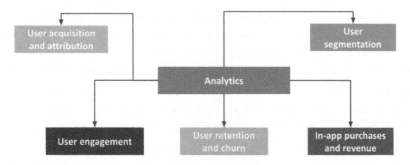

Figure 7.4 – Analytics components

As we can see, analytics encompasses various key aspects:

- **User acquisition and attribution**: Tracking the sources of new users, such as organic search, paid ads, or referrals, helps determine the effectiveness of marketing campaigns and identifies the most valuable channels for user acquisition

- **User engagement**: Monitoring how users interact with the app, including session duration, session frequency, screens visited, and in-app actions performed, provides insights into user preferences and helps identify areas for improvement

- **User retention and churn**: Analyzing user retention rates and churn patterns helps you understand the factors that contribute to user satisfaction or dissatisfaction and enables developers to implement changes that promote long-term user loyalty

- **User segmentation**: Grouping users based on demographics, behavior, and preferences allows personalized marketing campaigns, targeted promotions, and tailored user experiences

- **In-app purchases and revenue**: Tracking in-app purchases, subscription revenue, and advertising revenue helps evaluate the app's monetization strategies and identify opportunities for optimization and growth

Factors to consider in monitoring and observability

To establish a monitoring and observability strategy for mobile apps, we need to consider the following factors:

- Define the key objectives and goals of your monitoring and observability strategy. This determines the metrics to track, such as app performance, user engagement, and error rates, thus reducing downtime, ensuring compliance with regulations, or improving user experience.

- Consider the app's purpose and user expectations to determine the right metrics. For example, if the app is a game, you should track user engagement, such as time spent playing the game, the number of levels completed, and social sharing. On the other hand, if the app is a productivity tool, you should track app performance, such as response time, load time, and error rates.

- Defining the tools and technologies required to achieve these goals is also essential. Once the goals have been defined, the next step is to implement the monitoring and observability tools. Several tools are available for monitoring and observability, including APM, log management, and analytics tools. Choosing the right tools that align with your goals and requirements is essential.

- Identify the key metrics and KPIs that need to be monitored, such as system performance, resource utilization, error rates, and response times. Ensure that these metrics are relevant, actionable, and can be used to track progress toward your objectives.

- Collecting data is only the first step. It is crucial to analyze the data that's been collected and take action based on the insights gained. You can use the data to identify performance bottlenecks, resolve issues, and optimize app performance.

- Determine which data sources are necessary to collect the required metrics. This can include logs, application traces, and system or network metrics.

- Select the appropriate tools and techniques for analyzing and visualizing your data, such as dashboards, anomaly detection, and alerting mechanisms. Ensure these tools can provide actionable insights to support decision-making.

- Set up alerting and notification mechanisms to promptly inform relevant stakeholders of issues or potential problems. Configure the alert thresholds and escalation policies to balance false alarms and missed issues. Alert developers to app crashes and errors in real time, along with detailed information about the cause of the issue.

- Implement in-app feedback. Feedback and suggestions can be provided directly within the app, which can help developers identify improvements.

- Ensure your monitoring and observability strategy is well integrated with other tools in your infrastructure, such as incident management or CI/CD.

- Provide training and documentation for your team members to ensure they can effectively use the monitoring and observability tools and understand the data that's been collected.

Steps to implement monitoring and observability for mobile apps

Let's look at the steps for implementing monitoring and observability:

1. Select suitable tools for your app based on your requirements, budget, and platform support. Some popular choices include the following:

    - **Monitoring tools**: Firebase Crashlytics, Bugsnag, Sentry, Embrace, and Instabug

    - **Analytics tools**: Firebase Analytics, Amplitude, Mixpanel, and Google Analytics for Mobile

- **Observability tools**: Datadog and NewRelic

- **Mobile performance tools**: Emerge

- **Incident management**: PagerDuty, Incident.io, and Grafana Incident

2. For the chosen tools, follow the official documentation to set up the SDKs in your mobile app. This typically involves adding dependencies to your build or dependency files and initializing the SDKs in your app code.

3. Configure the monitoring tools to capture crashes, non-fatal errors, and performance issues. You can also set up custom events, tags, or user properties to provide more context for debugging.

4. Define events and user properties that you want to track while considering aspects such as user engagement, conversion, and retention with the analytics tools.

5. Implement event tracking by adding code to your app to log the defined events and user properties at relevant points. For example, you can log an event when a user completes a purchase or reaches a specific app screen.

6. Regularly monitor the dashboard of your chosen monitoring tool to identify crashes, performance bottlenecks, and other issues.

7. Set up alerts and notifications to stay informed about critical issues that need immediate attention. This can also be integrated with ChatOps if you send these alerts as Slack messages to the Microsoft team or even as SMSs or calls in the case of critical issues.

8. Use the dashboard of your chosen analytics tool to analyze user behavior, such as the number of active users, session duration, and user retention.

9. Create custom reports or use built-in reports to identify trends, patterns, and areas for improvement.

10. Utilize analytics insights to design and implement A/B tests to optimize your app's user experience, engagement, and conversion rates.

11. Analyze the results of A/B tests and make data-driven decisions to improve your app.

Now that we are familiar with how to get started with monitoring and observability for mobile apps, let's discuss the monitoring, observability, and analytics tools for mobile apps in the market and the differences between them.

Monitoring, observability, and analytics tools for mobile apps

Developers can use tools to monitor app performance, receive real-time notifications, and integrate with alerting tools through SDKs. Let's take a look at them together.

Monitoring and observability tools

As mentioned previously, monitoring and observability tools should be integrated with the incident management tools so that it is possible to handle on-call management or responses to incidents.

Observability tools are essential for mobile app development and maintenance. They provide valuable data and metrics that help identify bottlenecks, improve app stability, and enhance the user experience. Popular options include monitoring tools.

Let's discuss different tools that can help us with this.

Firebase Crashlytics

Firebase Crashlytics (`https://firebase.google.com/products/crashlytics`) is an excellent crash reporting tool for mobile app developers that offers *real-time crash reporting, detailed diagnostics, and seamless integration with other Firebase tools*. Its intuitive dashboard and accurate crash reporting make it a reliable choice for developers looking to improve their app's stability.

The following are some of the features of Firebase Crashlytics:

- **Real-time crash reporting**: It monitors your app and automatically captures crash data, providing up-to-date information on any issues.

- **Detailed crash diagnostics**: It dives into the details of each crash and provides rich diagnostics such as stack traces, device information, and user data to help you pinpoint the problem.

- **Crash analytics**: It offers insightful analytics for identifying trends, detecting common issues, and prioritizing bug fixes.

- **Integration with Firebase**: Being part of the Firebase suite, Crashlytics works seamlessly with other Firebase tools, streamlining your app development workflow.

- **Cross-platform support**: It works with Android and iOS apps, making it a versatile choice for mobile app developers.

You can easily add the Crashlytics SDK to your Android app by going to `https://firebase.google.com/docs/crashlytics/get-started?platform=android#add-sdk`; you can follow the same steps for iOS, Flutter, and Unity apps.

Additionally, you can export your Crashlytics data into BigQuery (`https://firebase.google.com/docs/crashlytics/bigquery-export`) for further analysis. You can analyze the data using BigQuery SQL, export it to another cloud provider, and use Google Data Studio to visualize and create custom dashboards.

Additionally, you can analyze any issues from Firebase Crashlytics with App Quality Insights inside Android Studio (`https://developer.android.com/studio/debug/app-quality-insights`).

Xcode Organizer

Xcode Organizer (`https://developer.apple.com/documentation/xcode/analyzing-the-performance-of-your-shipping-app`) is a tool for optimizing mobile app performance within the Apple ecosystem. Its ability to provide detailed performance data, real-time monitoring, and user-centric analysis makes it an invaluable resource for developers striving to deliver exceptional user experiences.

Xcode Organizer helps you manage various aspects of your iOS, macOS, watchOS, and tvOS app development projects. It provides features to organize, archive, and distribute your apps, as shown in the following screenshot:

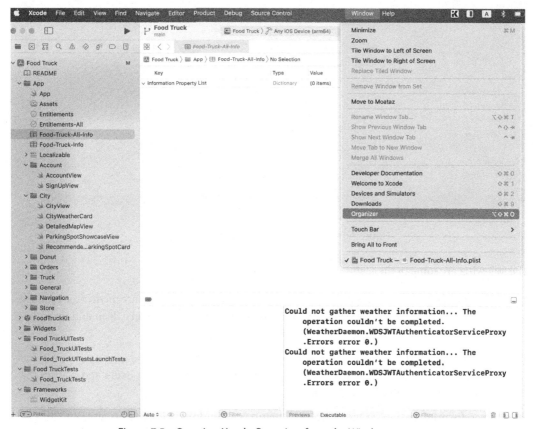

Figure 7.5 – Opening Xcode Organizer from the Window menu

You can check the crashes and the different metrics that are related to specific versions, as shown in the following screenshot:

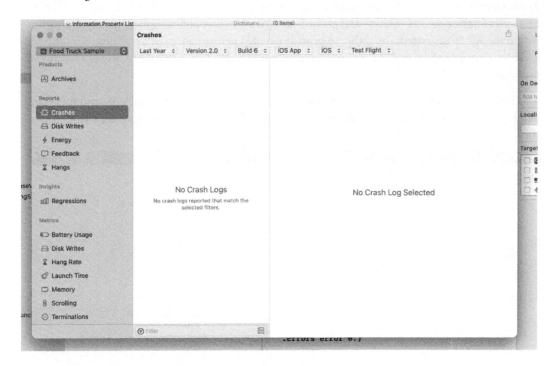

Figure 7.6 – The main screen of Xcode Organizer

The following are some of the features of Xcode Organizer:

- **In-depth performance insights**: This tool provides a wealth of performance metrics for your app, from CPU and memory usage to network activity. It allows you to gain a deep understanding of your app's inner workings.

- **Real-time monitoring**: You can watch how your app performs in real time as users interact with it. This feature is particularly useful for identifying performance issues and crashes that may be impacting the user experience.

- **User-focused analysis**: One of Xcode Organizer's standout features is its ability to analyze performance data based on different user interactions. This is invaluable for making targeted improvements that enhance the most common user scenarios.

- **Comparative analytics**: You can measure your app's performance across different versions or builds. This helps you track the impact of changes you've made and identify areas that require attention.

It is worth noting, however, that this tool is only compatible with apps developed for iOS, macOS, watchOS, and tvOS within the Apple ecosystem. Developers working on cross-platform apps may find this tool less useful.

It's important to keep in mind that the interface and characteristics of Xcode could vary with new updates. To stay informed, it's good practice to refer to the Xcode documentation (`https://developer.apple.com/documentation/xcode`) or relevant resources for the latest information.

Firebase Performance Monitoring

Firebase Performance Monitoring (`https://firebase.google.com/products/performance`) is a tool designed to help you analyze and optimize your app's performance to deliver a smooth user experience. It is a good choice for mobile app developers seeking to analyze and optimize their performance. With real-time performance monitoring, customizable metrics, and seamless integration with other Firebase tools, it's a powerful tool for ensuring a smooth user experience.

The following are some of the features of Firebase Performance Monitoring:

- **Real-time performance monitoring**: It automatically tracks your app's performance metrics in real time, giving you valuable insights into how your app is running

- **Customizable metrics**: It can create custom metrics tailored to your app's specific needs

- **Detailed performance data**: It analyzes granular data on latency, rendering, network usage, and more to pinpoint performance bottlenecks and optimize your app

- **Cross-platform support**: It works seamlessly with Android and iOS apps, making it a versatile choice for mobile app developers

- **Integration with Firebase**: It acts as part of the Firebase suite, which means Performance Monitoring integrates effortlessly with other Firebase tools, streamlining your app development process

- **Performance Data Dashboard**: Performance data is presented in a user-friendly dashboard, making it easy for you to analyze metrics and optimize your app

You can easily add the Performance Monitoring SDK in your Android, Flutter, or iOS apps by following the steps at `https://firebase.google.com/docs/perf-mon`.

Firebase automatically collects data for several common processes in your app when you add the Performance Monitoring SDK, including the following:

- App startup time for Apple and Android apps

- Screen rendering for Apple and Android apps

- Network requests for all types of apps

Here is an example of some information that's been collected from Performance Monitoring: `https://firebase.google.com/support/privacy?authuser=0&hl=en#performance-monitoring-collected-info`.

Instabug

Instabug (`https://www.instabug.com/`) is a powerful, all-in-one platform for mobile app developers looking for comprehensive bug reporting, crash reporting, and performance monitoring tools. Its easy integration, intuitive dashboard, and wide range of features make it an excellent choice for those looking to improve their app's stability and user experience, as shown in the following screenshot:

Figure 7.7 – The Release view

The following are some of the features of Instabug:

- **In-app bug reporting**: It allows users to report bugs directly within your app, complete with annotated screenshots, making it easy to collect valuable feedback:

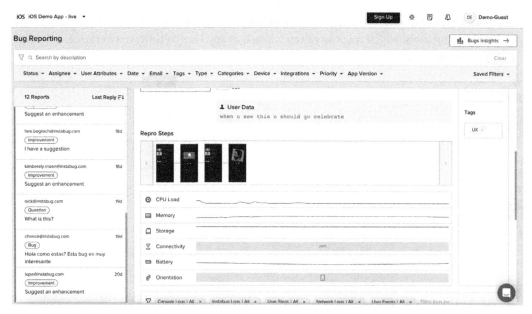

Figure 7.8 – The Bug Reporting view

- **Crash reporting**: It helps in getting real-time crash reports with detailed information such as stack traces and user data, enabling you to identify and fix issues quickly:

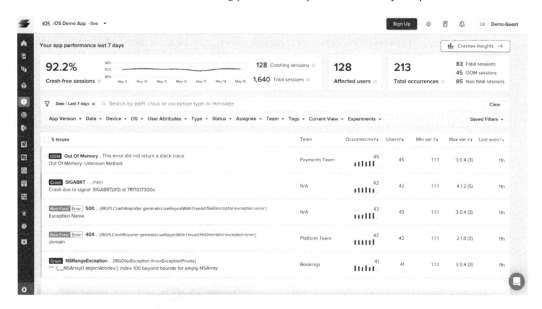

Figure 7.9 – The Crashes view

- **Performance monitoring**: Instabug helps keep an eye on your app's performance via its monitoring tools, which track key metrics such as app launch time, network requests, and UI responsiveness:

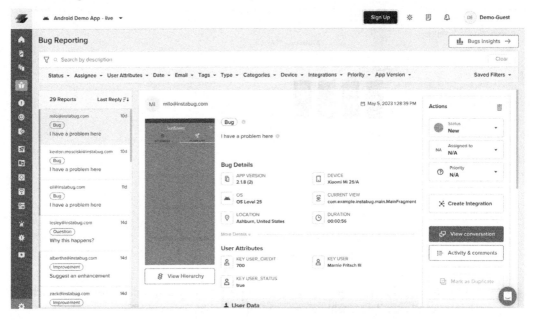

Figure 7.10 – The Bug Reporting detailed view

- **In-app surveys**: This survey collects user feedback effortlessly with customizable in-app surveys, helping you make data-driven decisions to improve your app:

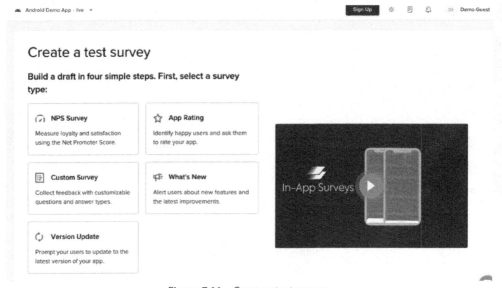

Figure 7.11 – Create a test survey

- **Integrations**: Instabug integrates with popular project management, communication, and issue-tracking tools such as Jira, Slack, and GitHub, streamlining your development workflow.

- **Cross-platform support**: Instabug works seamlessly with Android, Flutter, React Native, Xamarin, Cordova, and iOS apps, catering to various developers:

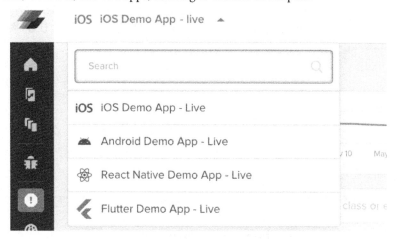

Figure 7.12 – Instabug's supported platforms

Additionally, Instabug provides a sandbox (`https://demo-dashboard.instabug.com/demo`) so that you can tour the product and learn more about its features.

However, note that Instabug's free tier has some limitations, and you may need to upgrade to a paid plan to access advanced features and higher usage limits.

Here's the documentation for adding the SDK to your iOS app: `https://docs.instabug.com/docs/ios-integration`.

Embrace

Embrace (`https://embrace.io/`) is a powerful mobile app performance management platform that offers comprehensive performance monitoring, crash reporting, and user session tracking, as shown in the following screenshot. Its unique replay functionality and detailed insights make it an excellent choice for developers looking to optimize their app's performance and user experience. However, the lack of a free tier and the initial learning curve may be drawbacks for some users:

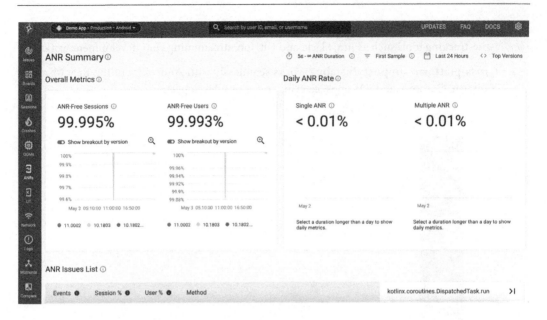

Figure 7.13 – ANR Summary

The following are some of the features of Embrace:

- **Performance monitoring**: Embrace provides detailed insights into your app's performance, covering key metrics such as app startup time, network requests, and user interface responsiveness

- **Crash reporting**: You can get real-time crash reports with rich information, such as stack traces, device data, and user actions, to help you quickly identify and fix issues:

Figure 7.14 – Crash Summary

- **User session tracking**: Embrace enables you to monitor individual user sessions, giving you a complete picture of the user experience, including interactions and issues encountered:

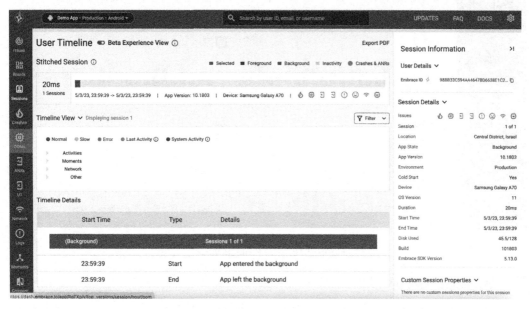

Figure 7.15 – User Timeline

Here's the documentation for adding the SDK to your Android app: `https://embrace.io/docs/android/integration/integration-steps/`.

Sentry

Sentry for mobile apps (`https://sentry.io/for/mobile/`) is a powerful error monitoring and reporting solution that simplifies debugging. Its easy integration, real-time error tracking, and intuitive dashboard make it a valuable tool for catching and fixing issues quickly:

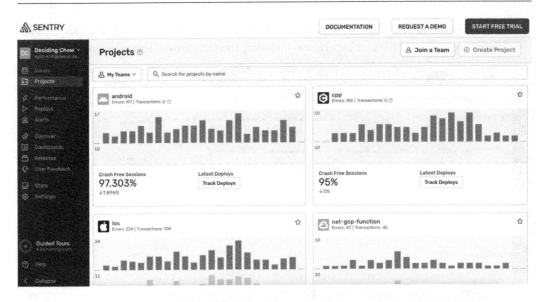

Figure 7.16 – The Projects view

The following are some of the features of Sentry:

- **Real-time error monitoring**: Sentry helps in automatically tracking and capturing errors in your app, providing up-to-date information on any issues.

- **Detailed error diagnostics**: Sentry helps in getting in-depth diagnostics such as stack traces, device information, and user data to help you pinpoint the root cause of errors:

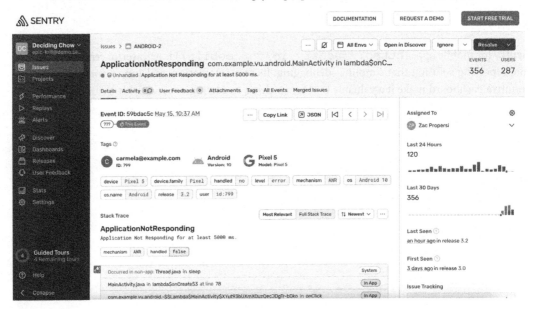

Figure 7.17 – The Issues detailed view

- **Issue grouping**: Sentry intelligently groups similar errors, making identifying trends and prioritizing fixes easier:

Figure 7.18 – The Issues view

- **Integrations**: Sentry integrates with popular project management, communication, and issue-tracking tools such as Jira, Slack, GitHub, and more to streamline your development workflow:

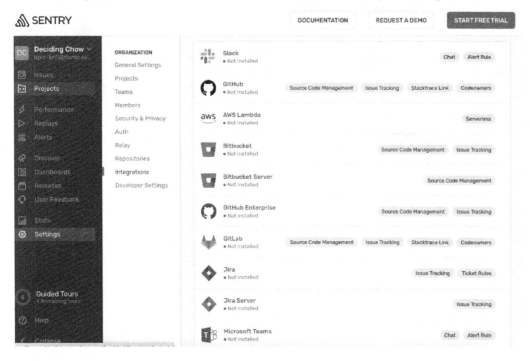

Figure 7.19 – The integration view

- **Cross-platform support**: Sentry works with Android, Flutter, React Native, and iOS apps, making it a versatile choice for developers

- **Real-time error tracking**: Sentry's real-time error monitoring allows you to catch and fix issues quickly, ensuring a smoother user experience

- **Intuitive dashboard**: Sentry's user-friendly dashboard makes monitoring errors and analyzing data easy, helping you stay on top of your app's stability

Here's the documentation for adding the SDK to your Flutter app: `https://docs.sentry.io/platforms/flutter/`. Sentry also provides customers with a sandbox environment (`https://try.sentry-demo.com/organizations/noted-baboon/issues/`) so that they can explore the product with demo apps.

Google Play Console vitals

Google Play Console vitals (`https://developer.android.com/topic/performance/vitals`) is a tool for Android app developers looking to monitor and optimize their app's performance with ease. Its seamless integration, data-driven insights, and free availability make it an excellent choice for tracking app stability, battery usage, and rendering performance:

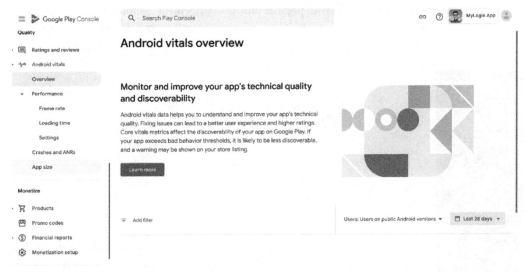

Figure 7.20 – Android vitals overview

The following are some of the features of Android vitals:

- **Android vitals dashboard**: Google Play Console vitals offers a user-friendly dashboard that provides an overview of your app's performance metrics, such as the crash rate, **App Not Responding (ANR)** rate, and more
- **Stability monitoring**: You can track crashes and ANRs in real time to identify and resolve issues that impact your app's stability
- **Rendering performance**: You can monitor your app's rendering performance, including slow rendering and frozen frames, to ensure a smooth user experience
- **Battery usage**: You can keep an eye on excessive wakeups and wake locks to optimize your app's battery usage and minimize the drain on users' devices
- **User feedback**: You can access user reviews and ratings to gain insights into your app's performance and areas for improvement

Note that Google Play Console vitals is only available for Android apps. Hence, iOS app developers should consider alternative performance monitoring solutions. Android Studio's latest version now supports Android vitals without the need for any additional SDKs or configuration (`https://developer.android.com/studio/preview/features#aqi-android-vitals`).

Datadog

Datadog for mobile apps (`https://www.datadoghq.com/dg/real-user-monitoring/mobile-rum/`) is a robust monitoring and analytics platform that offers performance monitoring, detailed error reporting, and powerful analytics. Its flexibility and cross-platform support make it an excellent choice for developers looking for one platform for their mobile app monitoring needs.

The following are some of the features of Datadog:

- **Real-time performance monitoring**: You can monitor your mobile app's performance in real time, including key metrics such as network requests, errors, and latency
- **Detailed error reporting**: Datadog provides detailed information about errors and crashes, including stack traces, device information, and user actions, to help you quickly identify and resolve issues:

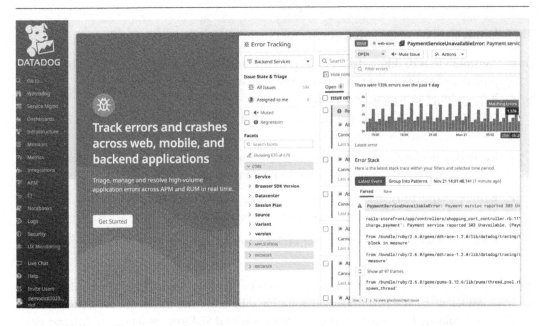

Figure 7.21 – The tracking errors and crashes view

- **Customizable dashboards**: Datadog creates personalized dashboards to visualize and analyze your app's performance data in the way that makes the most sense for your team:

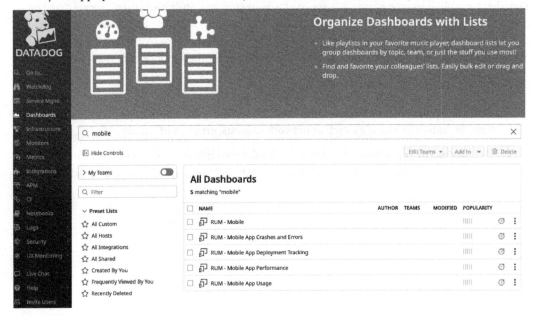

Figure 7.22 – The Dashboards view

- **Log management** (`https://docs.datadoghq.com/logs/log_collection/android/?tab=kotlin`): It automatically collects and analyzes log data from your app to detect anomalies and troubleshoot issues:

Figure 7.23 – Adding a new log

The following screenshot shows how to add the SDK dependency to the Gradle file for your Android app so that you can instrument the performance of your app:

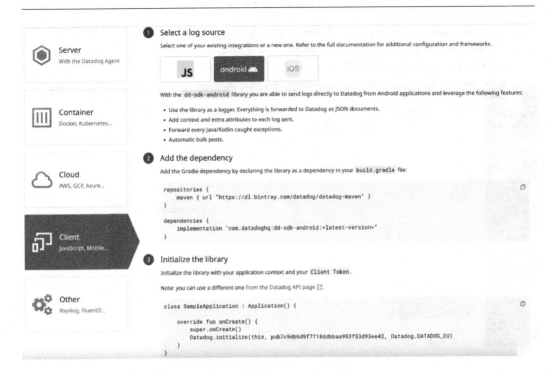

Figure 7.24 – Adding a new Android log

- **Integrations**: Datadog integrates with a wide range of other tools and platforms, allowing you to centralize your data and streamline your development workflow, as shown in the following screenshot:

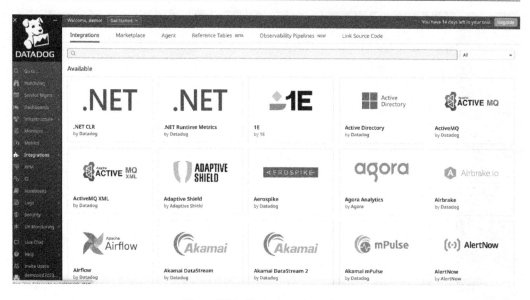

Figure 7.25 - The Integrations view

- **RUM and Session Replay** (https://docs.datadoghq.com/real_user_ monitoring/): Datadog provides real-time visibility into the activity and experience of individual users so that you get the following benefits:

  - Keep track of the performance of your mobile application screens, user actions, network requests, and frontend code

  - Track ongoing bugs and issues over time and versions:

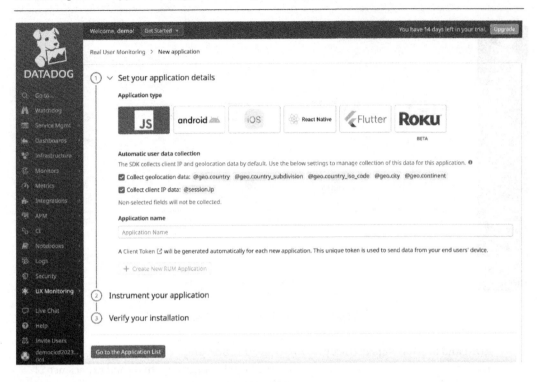

Figure 7.26 – The UX Monitoring view

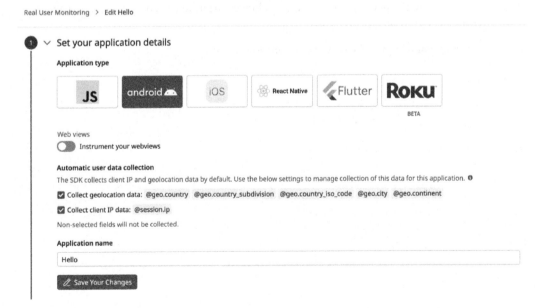

Figure 7.27 – Setting up real user monitoring for Android

You can set up real user monitoring for your application by adding the SDK to the app's dependencies, as demonstrated in the following screenshot:

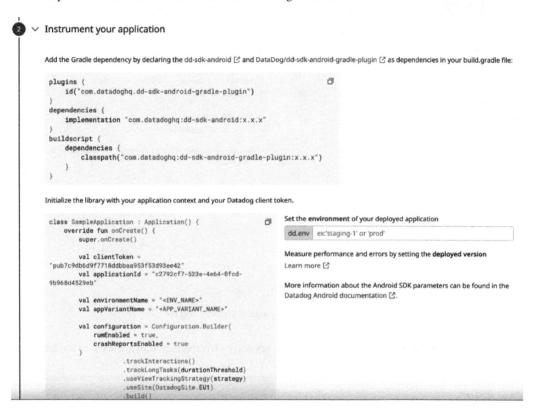

Figure 7.28 – Setting up real user monitoring

- Identify the countries, devices, and operating systems in which your application is used, monitor individual users' journeys, and analyze how users interact with your application (most frequently visited pages, clicks, interactions, and feature usage):

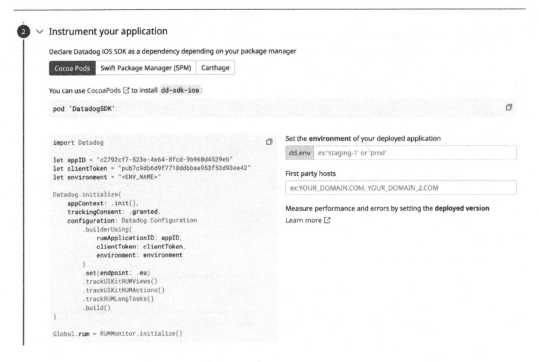

Figure 7.29 – Setting up real user monitoring for iOS

- Get all the information regarding a user session to troubleshoot an issue (session duration, interactions, resources loaded, and errors)

New Relic

New Relic for mobile apps (https://newrelic.com/platform/mobile-monitoring) is a performance monitoring and analytics solution that provides monitoring, detailed crash reporting, and advanced analytics capabilities. Its customizability and cross-platform functionality for Android, iOS, React Native, Capacitor, Cordova, and Flutter make it an excellent choice for developers looking to optimize their app's performance and user experience. However, its complexity and lack of a free tier may be drawbacks for some users.

The following are some of the features of New Relic:

- **Real-time performance monitoring**: New Relic provides real-time monitoring of key performance metrics, such as app load time, network requests, and error rates

- **Crash reporting**: You can get detailed information on crashes, including stack traces, device information, and user actions, to help you quickly identify and resolve issues

- **Customizable dashboards**: You can create personalized dashboards to visualize and analyze your app's performance data in a way that suits your team's needs

- **User interaction tracking**: You can monitor user interactions within your app to gain insights into the user experience and identify areas for improvement

- **Integrations**: New Relic integrates with popular tools and platforms, allowing you to centralize your data and streamline your development workflow, as shown in the following screenshot:

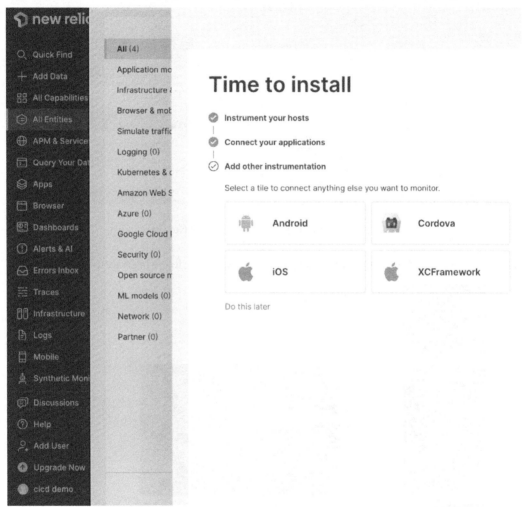

Figure 7.30 – Setting a up mobile app on New Relic

You can get started by choosing which platform you wish to use, such as Android, then continue with the rest of the configuration, as shown in the following screenshot:

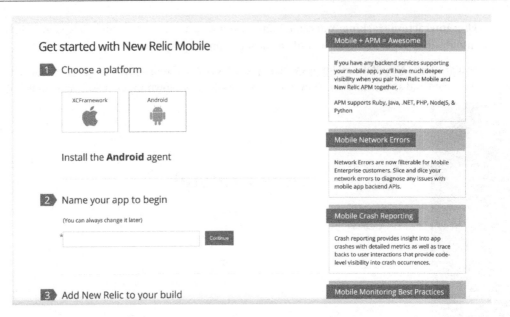

Figure 7.31 – Setting up an Android app on New Relic

After that, you can add the SDK to the Gradle file, as shown in the following screenshot:

Figure 7.32 – Android build configuration

Once you've finished the configuration, you will see a dashboard that displays an overview of the Android app, as shown in the following screenshot:

Figure 7.33 – Android app overview

You can find different examples of how to set up New Relic for Android (https://docs.newrelic.com/docs/mobile-monitoring/new-relic-mobile-android/get-started/introduction-new-relic-mobile-android/), iOS (https://docs.newrelic.com/docs/mobile-monitoring/new-relic-mobile-ios/get-started/introduction-new-relic-mobile-ios/), Flutter (https://docs.newrelic.com/docs/mobile-monitoring/new-relic-mobile-flutter/monitor-your-flutter-application/) and React Native (https://docs.newrelic.com/docs/mobile-monitoring/new-relic-monitoring-react-native/monitor-your-react-native-application/).

Emerge

Emerge (https://www.emergetools.com/) is an innovative mobile app optimization platform designed to help developers reduce app size and improve overall performance.

Its focus on *app size reduction*, *resource optimization*, and *code analysis* makes it a recommended choice for mobile developers looking to minimize their app footprint and enhance the user experience.

The following are some of the key features of Emerge:

- **App size reduction**: Emerge analyzes your mobile app to identify areas for optimization, enabling you to reduce your app's size without compromising functionality:

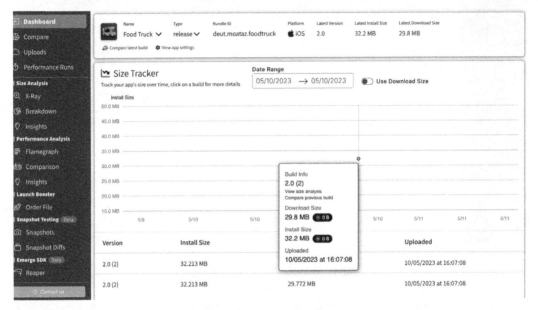

Figure 7.34 – iOS app dashboard

Additionally, you can use Emerge to analyze the app size of, for example, iOS apps, as shown in the following screenshot:

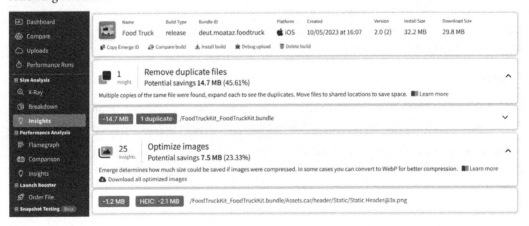

Figure 7.35 – iOS app size analysis

- **Resource optimization**: Emerge helps optimize your app's images, fonts, and other resources to minimize their impact on app size and performance.

- **Code analysis**: You can get insights into your app's code base, identify unused code, and discover opportunities for refactoring and optimization:

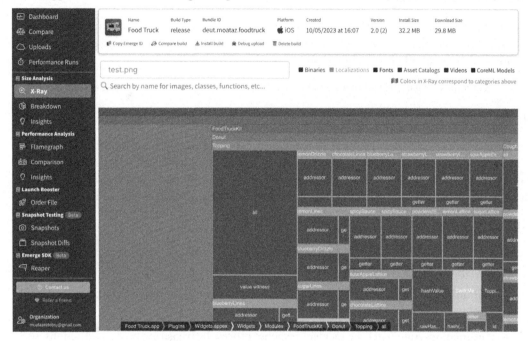

Figure 7.36 – IOS size analysis X-Ray

- **Snapshot Testing (beta)**: You can create snapshots for every upload. These snapshots are automatically compared to pull requests so that you can see what has changed, what has been added, or what has been removed, as shown in the following screenshot:

Figure 7.37 – The Snapshot Testing view

- **CI integration**: With GitHub Actions and Codemagic, you can configure automated comparisons (PR comments/status checks) to appear in your VCS, making it easy for everyone in your organization to be aware of your performance metrics. More details can be found here: `https://docs.emergetools.com/docs/integrate-into-ci`.

- **Automatic alerting**: With Slack Alerts (`https://docs.emergetools.com/docs/slack`), for example, you can receive an alert to a channel when an uploaded build triggers a configurable threshold.

Incident management

Incident management tools for mobile apps play a crucial role in ensuring the smooth operation and stability of your app by helping you detect, analyze, and respond to incidents, such as crashes, performance issues, and other technical problems.

Let's look at some popular incident management tools that are commonly used for mobile app development.

Incident.io

Incident.io (`https://incident.io/`) is a powerful incident management platform that's designed to help teams effectively handle incidents and improve system resilience. Its centralized incident tracking, improved communication, automation features, and postmortem analysis capabilities make it an excellent choice for teams looking to streamline their incident response process.

The following are some of the features of Incident.io:

- **Incident tracking**: Centralizes all incident-related information, making it easy to track and manage incidents from a single platform

- **Communication**: Facilitates team communication and collaboration during incidents with built-in chat features and integration with popular communication tools

- **Automation**: Automates the incident response process by triggering predefined actions, such as alerting responders, creating tickets, and updating stakeholders

- **Postmortem analysis**: Conducts post-incident reviews with comprehensive reports, helping your team learn from incidents and improve system resilience

- **Integration**: Integrates with popular monitoring and ticketing tools, streamlining your incident management workflow

PagerDuty

PagerDuty (`https://www.pagerduty.com/`) is an incident management platform designed to help teams effectively handle incidents and improve system reliability. Its comprehensive incident tracking, flexible alerting, improved communication, automation features, and postmortem analysis capabilities make it an excellent choice for teams looking to streamline their incident response processes.

The following are some of the features of PagerDuty:

- **Incident tracking**: Centralizes all incident-related information, making it easy to track and manage incidents from a single platform

- **Alerting and escalation**: Configures alerting rules and escalation policies to ensure the right team members are notified and engaged during incidents

- **Communication**: Facilitates team communication and collaboration during incidents with built-in chat features and integration with popular communication tools

- **Automation**: Automates the incident response process with predefined actions, such as alerting responders, creating tickets, and updating stakeholders

- **Postmortem analysis**: Conducts post-incident reviews with comprehensive reports, helping your team learn from incidents and improve system resilience

- **Integration**: Integrates with popular monitoring, alerting, and ticketing tools, streamlining your incident management workflow

Additionally, we can optimize a mobile app's performance using profiling tools by following these steps:

1. **Identify the performance issue**: Determine what specific aspect of the app's performance needs to be improved, such as startup time, frame rate, or memory usage.

2. **Choose a profiling tool**: Select a tool appropriate for the platform and the type of performance issue being addressed. Some common profiling tools for mobile apps include XCode Instruments (iOS) (`https://developer.apple.com/documentation/xcode`), Android Profiler (`https://developer.android.com/studio/profile/android-profiler`), and Flutter Profiler (`https://docs.flutter.dev/perf/ui-performance`).

3. **Run the profiling tool**: Use the profiling tool to gather data on the app's performance. This may involve running the app on a device or emulator and performing specific actions or scenarios to simulate real-world usage.

4. **Analyze the results**: Review the data collected by the profiling tool to identify any issues or bottlenecks in the app's performance.

5. **Optimize the app**: Use the insights gained from the profiling tool to optimize the app's performance by fixing any identified issues or improving the efficiency of the app's code and resources.

Analytics tools

Analytics tools for mobile apps play a crucial role in helping the team make data-driven decisions, enhance user experiences, and achieve business goals.

By providing valuable metrics and user insights, these tools empower developers and marketers to optimize their apps continuously and stay competitive in the dynamic mobile app landscape.

Let's look at some popular analytics tools that are used for mobile apps.

Google Analytics for Mobile Apps

Google Analytics for Mobile Apps (`https://developers.google.com/analytics/solutions/mobile`)is like having a personal investigator for your app. This powerful tool helps you gather valuable information about how users interact with your app. Whether you're running a game, a productivity app, or anything in between, this tool provides insights that can help you make better decisions.

The following are some of the features of Google Analytics for Mobile Apps:

- **User base analysis and demographics**: Find out how many users your app has, what their characteristics are, and where they come from

- **User action analysis**: Gain insights into user behavior and interactions within your app

- **In-app purchase revenue measurement**: Track and analyze monetization and payment metrics

- **Customized reports**: Create reports that can benefit your business

- **Visual user journey navigation**: Enhance the user experience through graphical path analysis

- **User group behavior analysis**: Gain deeper insights through data segmentation and analysis

- **Leverage Google Analytics data**: Utilize Google Analytics data across Google products

- **Multi-platform support**: Google Analytics provides analytics data for Android, iOS, and Flutter mobile applications

You can learn how to add the SDK to your Android, iOS, Flutter, and Unity apps at `https://firebase.google.com/docs/analytics`.

Amplitude

Amplitude (`https://amplitude.com/`) is a powerful product analytics platform that provides in-depth insights into user behavior, helping teams make data-driven decisions to optimize their products. Its ease of use, scalability, and integration capabilities make it an excellent choice for businesses looking to drive product growth:

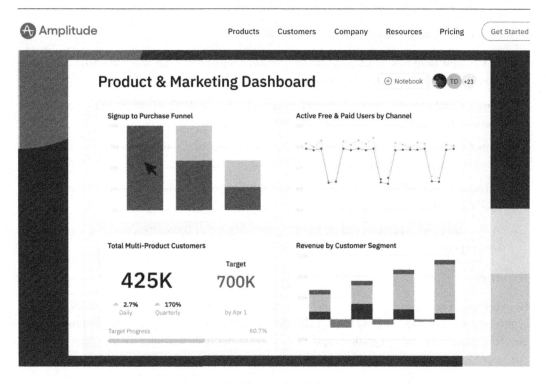

Figure 7.38 – The Amplitude home page

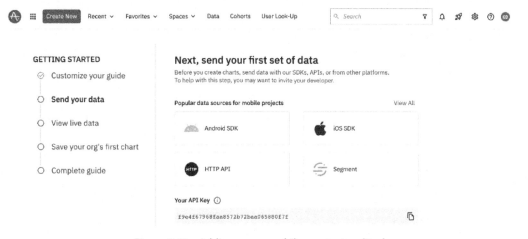

Figure 7.40 – Adding a new mobile app to Amplitude

The following are some of the key features of Amplitude:

- **Behavioral analytics**: Tracks user actions within your product, helping you understand user behavior patterns and identify areas for improvement

- **Funnels and cohorts**: Analyzes user conversion funnels and cohort retention to measure the success of your product features and marketing efforts

- **Real-time analytics**: Monitors your product's performance in real time, allowing you to respond quickly to any issues or changes in user behavior

- **Customizable dashboards**: Creates personalized dashboards to visualize and analyze the data that matters most to your team

- **A/B testing and experimentation**: Runs experiments and A/B tests to optimize your product's user experience and measure the impact of changes

Mixpanel

Mixpanel (`https://mixpanel.com/`) is a product analytics platform that provides in-depth insights into user behavior, helping teams make data-driven decisions to optimize their products. Its ease of use, scalability, and integration capabilities make it an excellent choice for businesses looking to drive product growth:

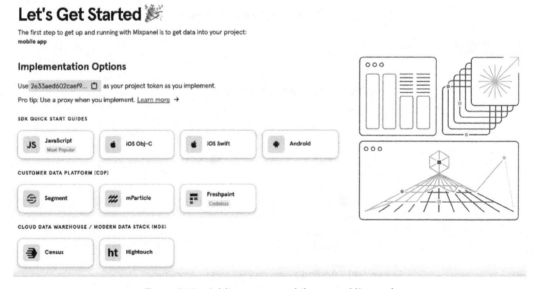

Figure 7.40 – Adding a new mobile app to Mixpanel

The following are some of the features of Mixpanel:

- **Behavioral analytics**: Tracks user actions within your product, allowing you to understand user behavior patterns and identify areas for improvement

- **Funnels and cohorts**: Analyzes user conversion funnels and cohort retention to measure the success of your product features and marketing efforts

- **Real-time analytics**: Monitors your product's performance in real time, enabling you to respond quickly to any issues or changes in user behavior

- **Customizable dashboards**: Creates personalized dashboards to visualize and analyze the data that matters most to your team

- **A/B testing and experimentation**: Runs experiments and A/B tests to optimize your product's user experience and measure the impact of changes

Now that we've explored the different monitoring, observability, incident management, and analytics tools, let's outline the key metrics that we usually consider when using them.

Key metrics for mobile app monitoring, analytics, and observability

In this section, we'll look at a few key metrics for mobile app monitoring, analytics, and observability that you should consider for these purposes.

Monitoring metrics

Some of the key monitoring metrics are as follows:

- **App load time**: The time it takes for your app to initialize and become ready for user interaction upon launch. Faster load times lead to a better user experience.

- **API response time**: The time it takes for your app to receive a response from backend services or third-party APIs. Long response times can make your app feel slow or unresponsive.

- **Frame rate**: The number of frames per second rendered by your app. A low frame rate can indicate performance issues, causing a poor user experience, especially in animation-heavy or game apps.

Observability metrics

Some of the metrics for observability are as follows:

- **Error rate**: The percentage of app requests that result in errors, such as failed API calls or backend issues. A high error rate can affect your app's performance and reliability.

- **Latency**: The time it takes for a request to travel from the user's device to the server and back. High latency can make your app feel slow and unresponsive.

- **Throughput**: The number of requests your app can handle per unit of time. Monitoring throughput can help identify bottlenecks and scalability issues.

Analytics metrics

Analytics metrics for mobile apps refer to the data and measurements that provide insights into user behavior, app performance, and overall success. By leveraging analytics tools and platforms, app developers and marketers can track, analyze, and interpret these metrics to optimize user experiences, enhance app functionality, and drive user engagement and retention.

Some key analytics metrics for mobile apps include the following:

- **Daily active users (DAU)**: This represents the number of unique users who interact with your app daily. DAU is a crucial metric that gauges the level of user engagement with your app.

- **Monthly active users (MAU)**: MAU refers to the number of unique users who interact with your app monthly. This metric provides insights into the overall reach and popularity of your app.

- **Session duration**: This is the average time users spend in your app during a single session. Longer session durations indicate higher user engagement and satisfaction.

- **Session interval**: This metric shows the average time between user sessions, revealing how frequently users return to your app. Shorter intervals typically indicate strong user retention.

- **Retention rate**: The retention rate represents the percentage of users who come back to your app after a specific period, such as days or weeks. A higher retention rate signifies positive, long-term user engagement.

- **Churn rate**: The churn rate indicates the percentage of users who discontinue using your app within a defined time. A high churn rate can highlight issues related to user satisfaction or app functionality.

- **User lifetime value (LTV)**: LTV estimates the revenue generated by a user throughout their entire engagement with your app. Understanding LTV helps you gauge the value of acquiring and retaining users.

- **Conversion rate**: The conversion rate measures the percentage of users who complete a specific desired action, such as making a purchase, signing up, or subscribing. Higher conversion rates indicate better app performance and user satisfaction.

- **Funnel analysis**: Funnel analysis visualizes the user flow through various steps or events in your app, helping you identify drop-off points and opportunities for optimization in the user journey.

- **Custom events**: Custom events track specific user interactions or milestones within your app, providing valuable insights into user behavior and app usage patterns. These events can be tailored to suit your app's unique objectives and requirements.

Implementing continuous monitoring for mobile apps is crucial to ensure their performance and overall quality. Continuous monitoring involves regularly tracking and analyzing the app's behavior, usage, and performance metrics, allowing developers to identify and address issues promptly.

Now, let's look at the recommended practices regarding how to implement continuous monitoring for mobile apps.

Implementing continuous monitoring for mobile apps

Continuous monitoring involves collecting and analyzing data about a mobile app's performance, usage, and security to identify and address any issues or potential improvements. Let's take a look at some of its benefits:

- **Improved reliability**: Continuous monitoring can help identify and fix issues before they impact users, improving the app's reliability and reducing the risk of downtime

- **Better performance**: By collecting data on the app's performance, teams can identify and address bottlenecks or other performance issues, leading to a better user experience

- **Enhanced security**: Continuous monitoring can help identify and address security vulnerabilities or other risks, improving the overall security of the app

- **Faster resolution of issues**: By continuously collecting data on the app's performance, teams can quickly identify and address issues as they arise, reducing the time it takes to resolve problems

Summary

Monitoring and observability are essential for mobile app development. Developers can collect and analyze data by establishing effective practices and using the right tools to ensure their app performs optimally and provides a seamless user experience. Monitoring allows developers to collect data on app performance, user behavior, and system interactions to identify potential issues before they impact users.

Here are the key learning points about monitoring and observability in mobile app development:

- The benefits of implementing monitoring and observability for mobile apps
- Factors to consider in monitoring and observability
- The steps to implement monitoring and observability for mobile apps
- Monitoring, observability, and analytics tools for mobile apps
- Key metrics for mobile app monitoring, analytics, and observability
- Implementing continuous monitoring for mobile apps

As we move forward in our mobile DevOps journey, we will look closer at how security is injected into our CI/CD and mobile DevOps life cycles, which is a crucial step to add to our mobile DevOps life cycle. In the next chapter, we will discuss the importance of security for mobile apps and how we can inject automated security testing into the mobile DevOps and CI/CD pipelines.

8

Keeping Mobile Apps and DevOps Secure

From the previous chapters, we have understood that mobile apps have become a crucial part of our daily lives in the digital age, necessitating ongoing innovation and refinement. Organizations increasingly implement *Mobile DevOps* approaches to accomplish this goal, allowing development, testing, and releasing teams to work together seamlessly.

However, the quick development and rollout of releases can result in mobile app security vulnerabilities. In order to protect your mobile applications and DevOps processes, in this chapter, we will examine the fundamentals of mobile app security, automating security testing, and DevSecOps fundamentals. We will also explore the reasons behind the significance of security in mobile app development and Mobile DevOps, including the following topics:

- Importance of security in mobile development
- Mobile app security threats
- Architecting secure mobile apps
- The traditional way of doing security testing
- Introducing Mobile DevSecOps
- Benefits of Mobile DevSecOps
- Building a culture of security
- Starting your DevSecOps journey
- Automating mobile security testing with mobile continuous automated integration and continuous delivery (CI/CD) and DevOps
- Tips for security automation for Mobile DevOps
- Artificial intelligence and mobile app security

Importance of security in mobile development

It is vital to have security in many areas of life, especially in the age of digital transformation. In business sectors such as automotive, healthcare, financial, retail, and e-commerce, and with embedded and IoT devices, we use sensitive data such as emails, addresses, credit cards, and mobile numbers with different mobile applications.

Mobile app development has experienced exponential growth over the last decade, with millions of apps available on various platforms and app stores. These apps offer various services, from social networking to online banking and everything in between. As more users rely on mobile apps to access services and store sensitive data, the importance of security in mobile app development cannot be overstated.

Security in mobile app development is a critical aspect that developers must prioritize to protect user data, maintain a strong reputation, and comply with regulations. By understanding the importance of security and implementing practical measures, developers can create apps that offer their users a safer and more secure experience.

> *"Security at the expense of usability comes at the expense of security."*
>
> *- Avi Douglen, OWASP Board of Directors*

Hence, it's critical to ensure that security measures are in place to protect user data from unauthorized access.

Did you know?

Over 500K security issues affecting over 300K apps with a combined install base of approximately 250 billion were fixed by developers using Google's App Security Improvements program (`https://developer.android.com/google/play/asi`). According to Google, 1.43 million bad apps were prevented from going into the Play Store in 2022, thanks to improved security features and app review processes (`https://security.googleblog.com/2023/04/how-we-fought-bad-apps-and-bad-actors.html`).

One of the most important businesses that can be affected by security issues is the *fintech* sector and the *digital banking* apps that play a massive role in our everyday activities. Fintech is becoming a big part of our personal and professional lives. Customers are always concerned about safety. If they doubt the app's security, they immediately uninstall it and switch to another service.

Most digital banking apps have robust security features such as **payment blocking**, **biometrics**, and **two-factor authentication** (**2FA**) and only allow users to submit complex passwords. Furthermore, customer data protection and handling are essential, mainly if you operate in the EU, where the *GDPR* rules apply.

What is the GDPR?

The **General Data Protection Regulation (GDPR)** (`https://gdpr.eu/`) is a comprehensive law on data protection implemented on May 25, 2018, in the **European Union** (**EU**). Its main objective is to safeguard the privacy and personal information of individuals by regulating how organizations collect, process, store, and share such data.

The GDPR establishes a set of principles and regulations that organizations must adhere to in order to ensure that the rights of individuals whose data is being collected (known as data subjects) are respected. Failure to comply with these regulations may result in monetary penalties for companies. Therefore, the GDPR helps safeguard your personal information and guarantees that companies handle it appropriately.

The preceding example is only one of many businesses that need to take into account to protect themselves.

In the mobile development process, security can be incorporated at multiple levels. To start, robust authentication protocols should be implemented to ensure that only authorized users can access the application. This can include *biometric authentication*, *fingerprint scanning*, or *password-based authentication*.

Mobile developers should also be aware of the potential risks posed by third-party libraries and APIs. Any additional code added to an application should be thoroughly vetted to ensure it is secure and up to date.

As a result, security is essential to mobile development and should be taken seriously. Following the steps outlined here, developers can ensure their applications are secure and provide users with a safe experience.

Mobile app security threats

Mobile apps face various security threats that can compromise user data and the overall integrity of the application. Here are some common security threats to mobile apps:

- Hackers can gain unauthorized access and extract sensitive user information using reverse engineering, code injection, or bypassing authentication mechanisms.
- Mobile apps often handle personal information, financial details, or login credentials. It is possible for attackers to intercept or steal data during transit or storage if proper security measures are not implemented, resulting in data breaches and privacy violations.
- There are many ways in which mobile devices can be compromised or infected with malware. These malicious programs can compromise the device's security, steal data, or perform unauthorized actions.
- Attackers can access user data through physical device compromises, filesystem vulnerabilities, or insecure server configurations if an app doesn't encrypt or protect user data.

- Weak or ineffective authentication mechanisms can lead to unauthorized access to user accounts. Additionally, insufficient authorization controls may allow attackers to perform actions beyond their privileges, such as accessing sensitive functionalities or manipulating user data.

- Poor coding practices or unpatched vulnerabilities in an app's code can introduce security weaknesses. Attackers can exploit this vulnerability to execute arbitrary code, escalate their privileges, or gain unauthorized access to the device.

- Attackers can flood mobile app servers with overwhelming requests, causing service disruptions and rendering the app inaccessible to legitimate users.

A mobile app developer must mitigate these threats by following secure coding practices, encrypting sensitive data, implementing robust authentication mechanisms, and educating users about the best security practices.

Mobile developers should put security first when architecting and developing mobile apps. Let's look into that next.

Architecting secure mobile apps

Architecting secure mobile apps is crucial in today's widespread mobile device usage. Neglecting mobile app security can lead to various mistakes that put user data and privacy at risk. To ensure secure mobile applications, developers should follow these best practices:

- Identify the security objectives for your app by considering factors such as protecting user data, ensuring secure communication, and preventing unauthorized access. Assess potential threats and vulnerabilities specific to your app and industry.

- Implement strong encryption techniques to protect sensitive data stored on the device.

- Employ multi-factor authentication and the latest authentication frameworks, such as *OAuth 2.0*, to manage user access securely.

- Use *SSL/TLS* for data transmission and validate certificates to establish encrypted communication between the app and backend servers.

- Safeguard sensitive data using up-to-date cryptographic algorithms and techniques such as *SHA-256*.

- Implement secure methods to store sensitive information, such as using environment variables or secure storage solutions.

- Validate user input on both the client and server sides to prevent injection attacks and other security vulnerabilities.

- Conduct security testing, including static and dynamic analysis, penetration testing, and vulnerability assessments, to identify and resolve potential security flaws.

- Regularly update third-party libraries and frameworks to avoid any vulnerabilities present in outdated versions.

- Integrate security measures throughout the development life cycle, from design and coding to testing and deployment.

- Ensure that developers are trained in secure coding practices and are knowledgeable about common mobile app security risks and mitigation techniques.

- Continuously monitor the app for security incidents and promptly address any issues. Stay updated on industry best practices and new security developments to ensure ongoing protection.

Let's look at how the mobile development and security teams typically perform security testing and why it may not be the best practice for Mobile DevOps.

The traditional way of doing security testing

Traditional security practices often involve security measures being applied in the later stages of development, leading to potential vulnerabilities being overlooked as shown in the following diagram. DevSecOps aims to address these issues by embedding security throughout the entire development process.

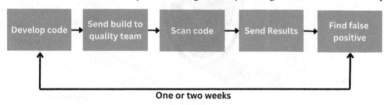

Figure 8.1 – The traditional security testing process

With these practices, we usually have the following characteristics:

- The process is too slow; as shown in *Figure 8.1*, it takes a long time, from 1 to 2 weeks, and might be extended to 1 month to ensure the app is secure before releasing it.

- Teams work in silos with no collaboration between the mobile development, testing, and security teams.

The emergence of DevOps has led to the growth of DevSecOps, as traditional methods no longer fit well with the changing landscape. These factors have contributed to the need for a new approach.

Let's examine DevSecOps and go over its benefits and how to implement it.

Introduction to mobile DevSecOps

Mobile DevSecOps brings together software development, security, and operations engineering disciplines to ensure mobile applications are secure, robust, and maintained.

The term DevSecOps refers to *"injecting security into the mobile CI/CD pipelines at an early stage of development. Security is integrated as a shared responsibility across culture, automation, and platform design throughout the entire Mobile DevOps life cycle."*

A shift in team culture is necessary to turn security testing from being a blocker to becoming an enabler. Mobile DevSecOps combines with DevOps and is focused on continuously delivering mobile apps and security as shown in the following diagram.

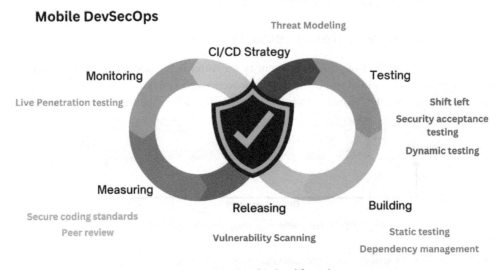

Figure 8.2 – DevSecOps life cycle

Mobile DevSecOps encompasses many development activities, as shown in *Figure 8.2*, such as **threat modeling**, **code scanning**, **vulnerability scanning**, **secure code review**, and secure coding practices; these activities ensure that mobile applications are secure, reliable, and maintainable.

Here are some principles of DevSecOps for mobile apps:

- The most fundamental aspect of DevSecOps is integrating security measures right from the beginning of the mobile app development process. This is a shift from the traditional approach, where security checks are typically the last step. In DevSecOps, security is considered at every stage of the development process, from planning and coding to testing and releasing.

- Everyone is responsible for ensuring that security is incorporated into every aspect of software development, including developers, testers, DevOps engineers, security professionals, and business stakeholders.

- By using tools and technologies to automatically check for potential security vulnerabilities during the coding process, you can identify and address issues faster and more efficiently than waiting for a manual review. This can include techniques such as **static application security testing (SAST)**, **dynamic application security testing (DAST)**, and penetration testing.

- The security measures should not be a one-time thing. The DevSecOps approach emphasizes continuous security, meaning that even after the app has been released, it should be continuously monitored and updated to address any new security threats that might emerge.

- DevSecOps encourages a culture where the developers, security teams, and testing teams work together, sharing responsibility for the application's security. This is often called the *shift-left* approach, where security considerations are brought to the forefront of the development process.

- Identifying potential threats before they become an issue. This might include data breaches, insecure APIs, or malware attacks for mobile apps.

- Developers should be trained in secure coding practices. This means writing code with security in mind.

- Finally, a robust DevSecOps approach should include plans for responding to and recovering from security incidents. This might include patch management, disaster recovery planning, and a dedicated incident response team.

DevSecOps is a process that combines the principles of DevOps and security to ensure that organizations develop and release mobile applications faster and more securely.

Benefits of Mobile DevSecOps

Mobile DevSecOps offers a proactive and collaborative approach to mobile app development that ensures security is an integral part of the process. It helps build more robust and secure mobile applications while reducing the risk of security breaches and enhancing overall development efficiency.

First, it helps reduce the risk of security vulnerabilities in mobile applications. By implementing security measures throughout development, Mobile DevSecOps helps identify and mitigate security issues before they become significant problems.

Secondly, Mobile DevSecOps helps speed up the delivery of secure, reliable, and maintainable mobile applications. By automating processes and implementing continuous delivery, Mobile DevSecOps helps mobile teams deliver applications faster and with better quality. Additionally, here are some other benefits of DevSecOps:

- DevSecOps can help identify and address any issues that could cause the application to slow down or become unreliable. This can help ensure that the application continues to perform optimally.

- Mobile DevSecOps can help reduce the costs associated with manual security checks and audits by automating security processes. This can help companies save money and focus their resources on other aspects of development.

- Mobile DevSecOps can help improve the overall user experience by ensuring that applications are secure and reliable. This can boost user engagement and satisfaction with the application.

For businesses looking to stay ahead of the competition, mobile DevSecOps is a must.

Organizations can ensure their mobile DevOps processes are secure by following the best practices outlined here. This will help to protect user data, ensure secure mobile application development, and reduce the risk of malicious attacks.

Before implementing DevSecOps, it's crucial to have a security mindset and a team that believes in it. Let's talk about how to establish a culture of security as the first step.

Building a culture of security

For DevSecOps to work effectively, the team must first build a culture of collaboration between developer and security teams. You'll need to do the following:

- Implement a security-first approach
- Build a security-focused mindset across teams
- Adopt a DevSecOps approach along with shifting security left (collaboration between development and security teams) and using a **CI/CD** pipeline is invaluable for preventing security incidents
- Ensure developers have the right tools
- Involve your security strategy in your mobile testing strategy
- Provide trusted security guidance (Reinforce Your Mobile App Security with OWASP MASVS Recommendations) – we will discuss this later in this chapter
- Build dashboards to show the security health of your mobile apps
- Train developers and QA engineers in secure coding practices
- Engage non-technical team members in security awareness
- Leverage external resources and partnerships for security expertise if needed

Let's dive deep into DevSecOps and begin our implementation.

Starting your DevSecOps journey

As we mentioned at the start of this book, the implementation of DevOps and DevSecOps is not solely dependent on tools but also involves various steps and other factors that must be taken into account.

The following are some steps to inject security into the DevOps process for mobile apps.

Identifying your goals and objectives

The first step in starting your DevSecOps journey is identifying your goals and objectives. What do you want to achieve with DevSecOps? Do you want to improve the speed of deployment? Are you looking to reduce the number of security issues in your mobile apps? Whatever your goals and objectives, set clear and measurable metrics to ensure that you can track and measure your success. But always ensure that the goal is to *maintain security without slowing down development and delivery*.

Building the right team

Having the right team is essential to achieving your DevSecOps objectives. You'll need to have a team that understands the principles of DevOps and security and is experienced in mobile development. You'll also need to ensure that your team is equipped with the right tools and processes to ensure your DevSecOps journey is successful.

Leverage security as a shared responsibility

The *DevSecOps Manifesto* (`https://www.devsecops.org/`) highlights the need for collaboration among all team members involved in the software development process. Security should not be the sole responsibility of a dedicated security team; instead, developers, operations, and other stakeholders must work together to identify and address security concerns throughout the software life cycle.

Shift security left

According to *Chapter 5, Implementing a Robust Mobile App Testing Strategy*, shifting testing to the left is highly recommended to ensure different testing types are executed at each stage of the DevOps cycle. In the same way, DevSecOps ensures security is checked at every stage of the DevOps cycle to ensure no vulnerabilities or security issues exist.

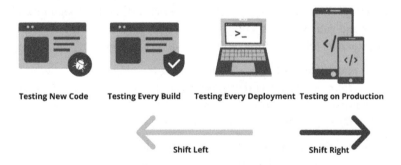

Figure 8.3 – Shift left security testing

Shifting security left means integrating security practices early in the development process rather than waiting until later. This approach enables teams to identify and address security vulnerabilities before they become critical in production.

We can shift security to the left and keep mobile DevOps secure with the following practices:

- Establish a secure development process; this should be established and enforced across the entire mobile DevOps team. The process should include secure coding practices, secure testing, and secure deployment of mobile apps.

- Incorporate security requirements during the planning and design phases.

- Implement secure coding practices and use security-focused tools during development.

- Conduct security reviews and testing, such as static and dynamic analysis, as part of the **continuous integration (CI)** process.

- This allows the security team to work closely with the development and testing teams so that the results can be returned quickly, and testing can occur whenever necessary.

Establishing a secure development life cycle

Once your team is in place, *establishing a secure development life cycle* is the next step. This involves setting up processes and procedures to ensure security is built into every step of the development process. This includes setting up automated testing, code reviews, penetration testing, security scanning, and more. The following are the recommended steps to establish a secure development life cycle:

- **Automated security testing**: Integrate automated security testing tools into your CI/CD pipeline. This includes static and dynamic analysis tools, dependency checkers, and vulnerability scanners. Perform regular security tests to catch vulnerabilities early and reduce the time between discovering and fixing issues.

- **Secure code review**: Incorporate security-focused code reviews into your development process. Use peer reviews and automated tools to identify and address potential security issues in your code.

- **Threat modeling**: Conduct threat modeling exercises during the design phase to identify potential risks and vulnerabilities and develop strategies to mitigate them. Regularly update threat models for app, infrastructure, or threat landscape changes.

- **Vulnerability management**: Establish a process for tracking, prioritizing, and addressing vulnerabilities discovered during development, testing, or in production. Create a clear communication channel for reporting security issues and ensure all team members understand the process and the importance of promptly addressing vulnerabilities.

- **Continuous monitoring and auditing**: Monitor the mobile app for security events, performance issues, and suspicious activity. Use monitoring tools, log analysis, and intrusion detection systems to detect potential security incidents or vulnerabilities in real time.

- **Incident response plan**: Develop an incident response plan to effectively and efficiently handle security incidents, such as data breaches or cyberattacks. Regularly review and update the plan and conduct drills to ensure all team members are prepared to respond in case of an incident.

- **Collaborate with security teams**: Encourage close collaboration between development, operations, and security teams. Break down silos and promote a shared responsibility for security, ensuring that all team members understand their role in protecting the app and user data.

- **Continuous Improvement**: Regularly review and improve your security practices, tools, and processes. Stay informed of the latest security trends and best practices and update your DevSecOps strategy as needed.

Choosing the right security toolset

Security toolsets are chosen based on various factors, including your specific security needs, the size and complexity of your organization, budget constraints, and technology stacks.

Here are some general considerations to help you select the appropriate security toolset.

OWASP Security testing guide (MASTG)

The **OWASP Mobile Application Security (MAS)** (`https://mas.owasp.org/`) project defines the industry standard for mobile application security and provides a security standard for mobile apps in two parts:

- **OWASP Mobile Application Security Verification Standard (MASVS)** is the go-to standard for ensuring mobile app security in the industry. It is beneficial for mobile software architects and developers who want to create secure mobile apps, as well as security testers who want to ensure that their test results are complete and consistent.

- **OWASP Mobile Application Security Testing Guide (MASTG)** covers the processes, techniques, and tools used during a mobile app security test, as well as a comprehensive set of test cases enabling testers to provide consistent and complete results. You can find the checklist at `https://github.com/OWASP/owasp-mastg/releases/latest/download/OWASP_MAS_Checklist.xlsx`.

- The OWASP Mobile Top 10 is a list of the most significant security risks for mobile apps that developers can use to identify and resolve critical security issues. According to the OWASP website (`https://owasp.org/www-project-mobile-top-10/`), the 2023 Top 10 is currently under development and includes the following risks:

  - **M1: Improper Platform Usage**

  Misusing platform features, such as Android intents or iOS Touch ID, or not following security best practices for the platform

  - **M2: Insecure Data Storage**

  Storing sensitive data insecurely on the user's device, potentially exposing it to unauthorized access or data leakage

- **M3: Insecure Communication**

Failing to protect data transmitted between the app and backend services or third-party APIs, potentially exposing it to interception or man-in-the-middle attacks

- **M4: Insecure Authentication**

Implementing weak or ineffective authentication mechanisms, allowing unauthorized users to access the app or impersonate other users

- **M5: Insufficient Cryptography**

Using weak or outdated cryptographic algorithms, keys, or protocols, or implementing them incorrectly, potentially exposing sensitive data to decryption

- **M6: Insecure Authorization**

Failing to implement proper access controls or authorization checks on the server side, allowing users to perform actions or access data they should not be authorized for

- **M7: Client Code Quality**

Writing insecure or poorly maintained code that may lead to vulnerabilities, such as buffer overflows or memory leaks

- **M8: Code Tampering**

Failing to protect the app from tampering or modification, potentially allowing attackers to modify the app's behavior or inject malicious code

- **M9: Reverse Engineering**

Failing to protect the app's source code or intellectual property from reverse engineering or decompilation, potentially allowing attackers to discover vulnerabilities or extract sensitive information

- **M10: Extraneous Functionality**

Including hidden or unused functionality in the app, potentially introducing security risks or exposing sensitive information

Additionally, when the team starts thinking about implementing security testing, they should explore different methods including the following:

- **Static Application Security Testing** (**SAST**): This involves analyzing the source code of an application without executing it to find vulnerabilities

- **Dynamic Application Security Testing** (**DAST**): Analyzing a running application for vulnerabilities involves examining it in real time

- **Interactive Application Security** (**IAST**): This is a process that involves the monitoring of the performance of an application through software instrumentation, whether actively or passively

Let's examine SAST and DAST in more detail.

SAST

SAST scans the source code of an application to detect any potential security issues. It is a proactive approach that identifies risks before they become issues. This allows developers to address problems before they become exploitable.

Furthermore, SAST enables developers to avoid manually checking every line of code, a time-saving and cost-effective approach to security testing.

By utilizing SAST, developers can reduce the risk of their applications being vulnerable to security breaches, resulting in a more secure and reliable application.

DAST

DAST analyzes your application's source code, mobile applications, and other components to identify and report any security vulnerabilities. This type of testing is often used to protect against malicious attacks, data breaches, and other forms of malicious activity. It can help your application stay secure and up to date.

DAST can be a great tool to help reduce the risk of data breaches, as it can detect and alert you to any potential security flaws before they become a problem. It can also help you ensure your application is up to date with the latest security patches and updates. Additionally, DAST can give you insights into how your application interacts with others and help you identify any risks or vulnerabilities in the broader environment.

Additionally, DAST can provide valuable insights into your application's security and performance, so you can make informed decisions about improving your application's security posture.

Now that we've learned how to get started with DevSecOps and the difference between static and dynamic testing, let's examine how to automate security testing with CI/CD and mobile DevOps.

Automating mobile security testing with mobile CI/CD and DevOps

Automating mobile security testing within a CI/CD and DevOps environment can help improve the efficiency, speed, and reliability of security testing processes.

Here's an overview of how you can automate mobile security testing in such a setup:

1. Research and choose appropriate tools that can integrate into your CI/CD pipeline. Some popular tools for mobile security testing include **NowSecure**, **Guardsquare**, **Snyk**, **Oversecured**, and **Mobile Security Framework (MobSF)**. Ensure that the tools chosen support automation and can be easily integrated into your development and deployment processes.

2. Integrate the mobile security testing process into your CI/CD pipeline. Typically, this involves adding security testing stages to your pipeline, such as pre-commit hooks, build stages, and post-deployment verification.

3. Leverage mobile emulators and simulators that replicate various device configurations and environments. This allows you to perform automated testing on various devices without requiring physical devices for every test.

4. Utilize static code analysis tools to scan your mobile app's source code for security vulnerabilities. These tools can identify common coding flaws, insecure coding practices, and potential security weaknesses. Integrating code analysis tools into your CI/CD pipeline helps catch security issues early in development.

5. Configure your CI/CD pipeline to execute automated security tests during the build and deployment stages. These tests should be triggered whenever new code is committed, during the build process, and after deployment to ensure continuous security validation.

6. Configure your automation framework to generate security reports after each testing cycle. These reports should provide details on the identified vulnerabilities, their severity, and recommendations for remediation.

Let's examine some tools you can use to automate security testing.

Tools to automate security testing

There are several tools available to automate security testing, making the process more efficient and thorough. Keep in mind that the landscape of security tools is constantly evolving, so newer tools might have emerged since then.

Here are some popular security testing tools.

NowSecure

NowSecure (`https://www.nowsecure.com/`) offers a robust and accessible platform for mobile app security testing. With its user-friendly interface, comprehensive testing capabilities, and extensive platform support, it is an excellent choice for organizations seeking to bolster the security of their mobile applications as shown in the following screenshot.

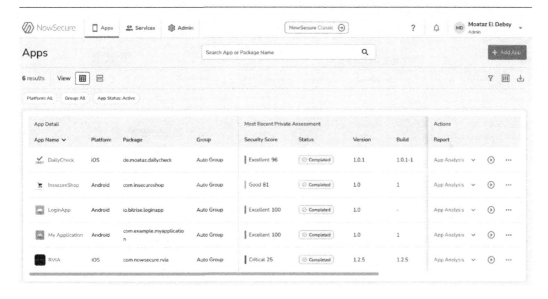

Figure 8.4 – NowSecure dashboard

NowSecure offers the following features:

- It provides a clean and intuitive user interface, making it accessible even to those with limited technical expertise. The tool offers step-by-step guidance, allowing users to quickly navigate through the testing process.

- It covers a wide range of security testing aspects, including vulnerability scanning, behavioral analysis, and penetration testing. Its robust feature set ensures that various security loopholes can be identified and patched effectively.

- It supports testing on multiple platforms, including iOS and Android, allowing developers and security professionals to evaluate the security posture of their apps across different operating systems as shown in the following screenshot.

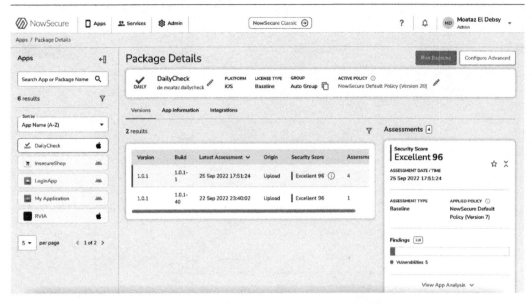

Figure 8.5 – NowSecure – Package or App Details

- It offers automated scanning and testing capabilities, which significantly reduces the time and effort required to identify potential security risks. This feature is particularly beneficial for organizations with large app portfolios.

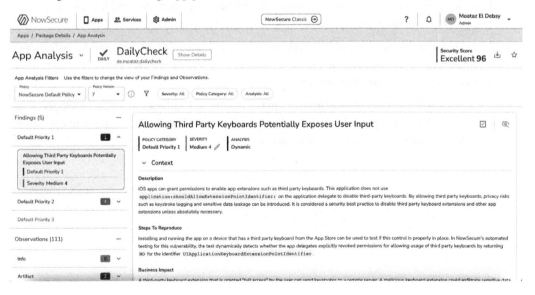

Figure 8.6 – App Analysis

- It generates comprehensive reports that highlight vulnerabilities, along with detailed explanations and recommendations for remediation. These reports make it easier for developers to prioritize and address security issues efficiently.

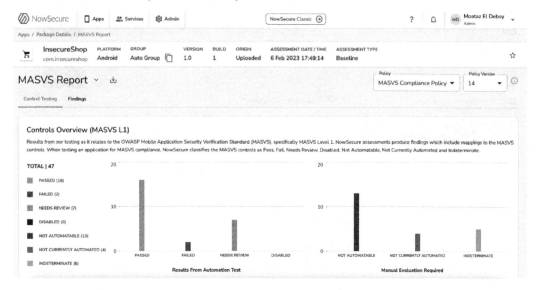

Figure 8.7 – NowSecure MASVS Report

Additionally, Nowsecure gives you security scanning results based on MASVS categories as shown in the following screenshot.

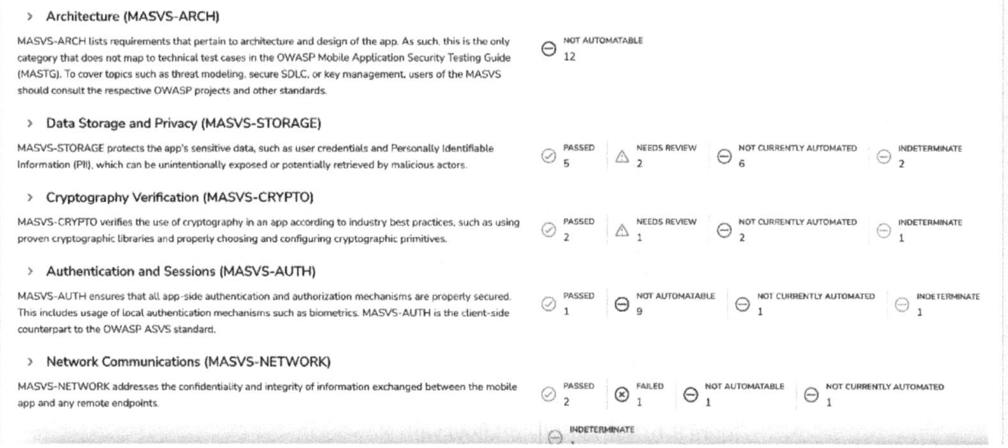

Figure 8.8 – The security scanning results based on the MASVS category

- It can be integrated into CI/CD pipelines such as Bitrise. Typically, this involves adding security testing stages to your pipeline, such as pre-commit hooks, build stages, and post-deployment verification. You just need to have a NowSecure account, an access token, and a group ID:

Figure 8.9 – Secret management on Bitrise

Then, you can add the NowSecure integration step into the CI/CD workflow or pipeline to execute the security testing, as shown in the following screenshot.

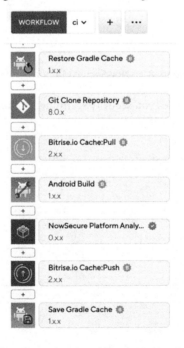

Figure 8.10 – Android workflow with NowSecure

The NowSecure integration step is required to add the NowSecure API token and the group ID as shown in the following screenshot.

Figure 8.11 – Configuration of NowSecure

NowSecure also can be run with GitHub Actions (`https://github.com/nowsecure/nowsecure-action`) with the following YAML file (`https://github.com/PacktPublishing/Mobile-DevOps-Playbook/blob/main/Chapter-8/android.yml`).

Additionally, NowSecure supports GitLab, Azure DevOps, and CircleCI (`https://www.nowsecure.com/solutions/by-need/mobile-devsecops/`).

Guardsquare

Guardsquare (`https://www.guardsquare.com/`) is a powerful mobile app protection suite that offers advanced code obfuscation and anti-tampering measures to secure mobile applications against reverse engineering and tampering. With its robust feature set, multi-platform support, and optimized performance, Guardsquare is a good choice for developers and organizations seeking to protect their app's code and intellectual property.

Guardsquare offers the following features:

- It offers powerful code obfuscation techniques that transform the structure and logic of the application's code, making it significantly more challenging for attackers to reverse-engineer or understand the inner workings of the app. This helps protect intellectual property, prevent unauthorized access, and deter malicious activities.

- It incorporates anti-tampering mechanisms to detect and prevent runtime modification of the app, safeguarding against attacks aimed at altering or bypassing security measures. These measures ensure the integrity of the app's code and protect against unauthorized modifications.

- Guardsquare's code obfuscation techniques are designed to have minimal impact on the app's performance. The optimization process helps maintain the app's functionality and responsiveness, ensuring a seamless user experience.

- It supports a wide range of platforms, including Android, iOS, and Xamarin, making it a versatile solution for securing mobile apps across different operating systems.

The following different products are available from Guardsquare:

- **DexGuard** (https://www.guardsquare.com/dexguard): This provides comprehensive mobile app protection.

- **iXGuard** (https://www.guardsquare.com/ixguard): It ensures the highest level of protection for your mobile apps. The solution offers comprehensive security measures for your iOS apps and SDKs, including multiple layers of code hardening and **runtime application self-protection** (**RASP**).

- **AppSweep** (https://www.guardsquare.com/appsweep-mobile-application-security-testing): This lets you find and fix security issues in your Android app's code and dependencies in accordance with security standards such as OWASP as shown in the following screenshot:

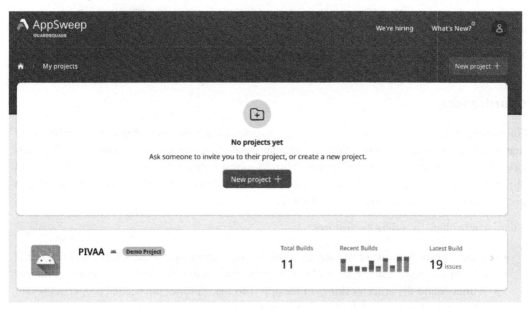

Figure 8.12 – AppSweep projects dashboard

It also gives you release analysis details for the app as shown in the following screenshot.

Figure 8.13 – Release analytics

You can also find the recent build details with the scanning and analysis results and you can also compare between two builds as shown in the following screenshot.

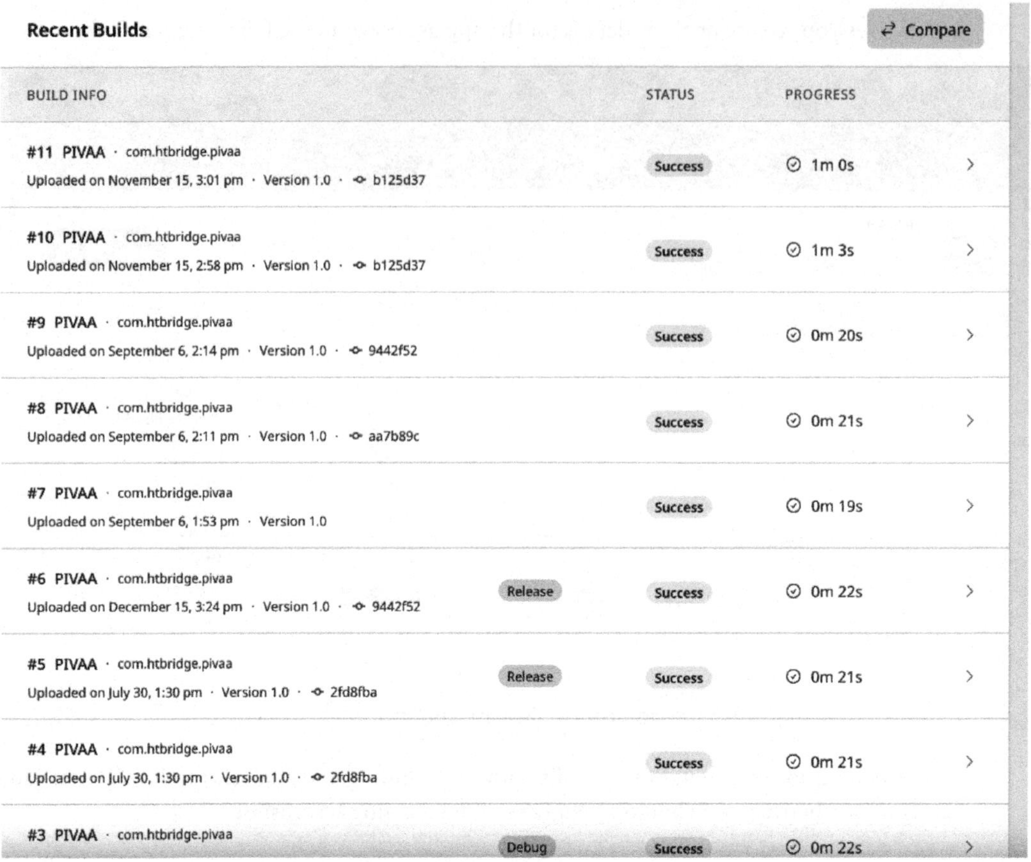

Figure 8.14 – Recent builds

The scanning results on AppSweep are mapped to the OWASP MASVS as shown in the following screenshot.

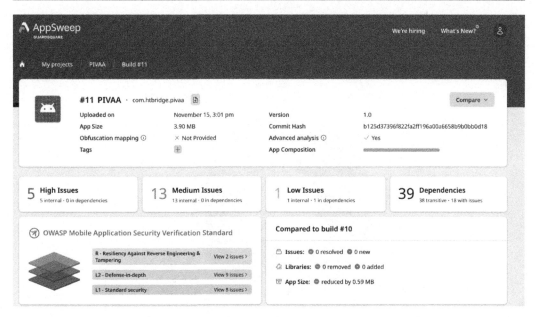

Figure 8.15 – The scanning results mapped to the OWASP MASVS

And it can give you a detailed view of the security issues that are found in the app and group them into different categories, such as Application Security, Insecure communication and more as shown in the following screenshot.

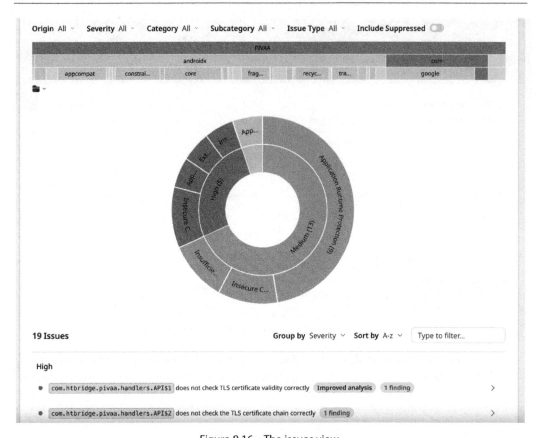

Figure 8.16 – The issues view

Finally, in the issue details section, you can find recommendations on what to change in the code based on the OWASP guide.

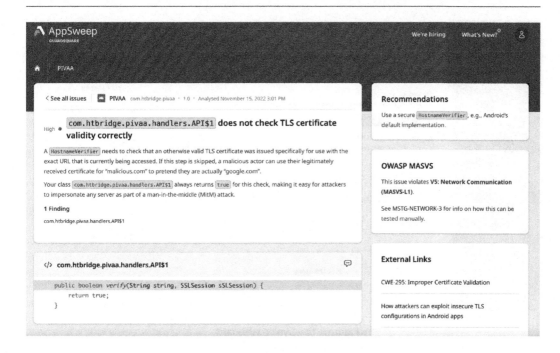

Figure 8.17 – The issue details with a recommendation

- **ThreatCast** (https://www.guardsquare.com/threatcast-mobile-threat-defense): This monitors mobile apps in real time and continuously improves your security implementation.

Snyk

Snyk (https://snyk.io/learn/application-security/mobile-application-security/) is a valuable platform for mobile app security, particularly in the area of vulnerability management and code remediation. With its comprehensive vulnerability detection, easy integration, continuous monitoring, recommendations, and language/platform support, Snyk.io simplifies the process of identifying and addressing security weaknesses in mobile app code.

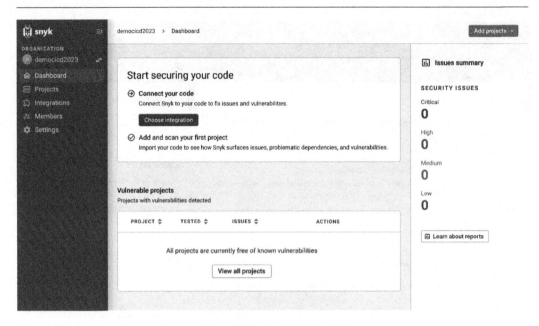

Figure 8.18 – Synk dashboard

The following are some of the features of Snyk:

- It offers an extensive vulnerability database and scanning capabilities that help identify security weaknesses within mobile app code. It detects common vulnerabilities and provides detailed insights into the specific lines of code where issues are making it easier for developers to import and scan their projects easily to understand and address the problems as shown in the following screenshot.

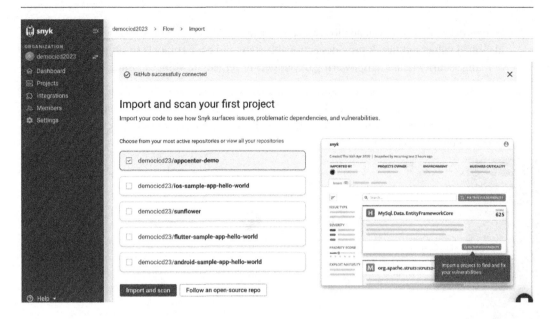

Figure 8.19 – Import projects from GitHub

- It integrates seamlessly with popular development tools and workflows, including CI/CD pipelines and source code repositories using the Snyk CLI (`https://github.com/snyk/cli`). This allows developers to incorporate security checks into their existing development processes, ensuring that vulnerabilities are identified early in the development life cycle as shown in the following figure:

```
Organization:     democicd2023
Package manager:  gradle
Target file:      build.gradle
Project name:     MyApplication
Open source:      no
Project path:     /Users/moataznabil/AndroidStudioProjects/MyApplication
Licenses:         enabled

✓ Tested /Users/moataznabil/AndroidStudioProjects/MyApplication for known issues, no vulnerable pat
hs found.

Tip: This project has multiple sub-projects (1), use --all-sub-projects flag to scan all sub-projec
ts.

Next steps:
- Run `snyk monitor` to be notified about new related vulnerabilities.
- Run `snyk test` as part of your CI/test.
```

Figure 8.20 – Snyk CLI

- It offers detailed fix recommendations and remediation guidance to assist developers in addressing identified vulnerabilities. It provides actionable steps and code snippets to simplify the process of fixing security issues, empowering developers to remediate vulnerabilities effectively.

- It supports a wide range of programming languages and platforms, including popular mobile app development frameworks such as iOS and Android. This versatility ensures developers can leverage the platform regardless of their preferred language or platform choice, as shown in the following screenshot.

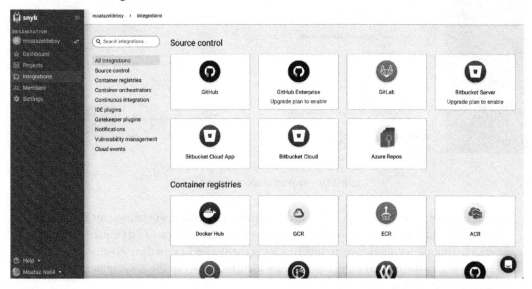

Figure 8.21 – Snyk integrations

It is possible to seamlessly integrate Snyk with your current tools and workflows. This integration will allow you to efficiently secure your projects during all stages of development.

- **Snyk Code** (https://snyk.io/product/snyk-code/)

Figure 8.22 – App details with different scan options

To use Snyk with an Android app, follow these general steps:

1. Start by installing the Snyk **Command-Line Interface** (**CLI**) on your development machine. You can find instructions for installation in the Snyk documentation specific to your operating system.

2. Open a terminal or command prompt and navigate to the root directory of your Android app project.

3. Run the `snyk auth` Snyk login command in the terminal and follow the prompts to authenticate with your Snyk account. This step is necessary to associate your app with your Snyk account, as shown in the following screenshot:

```
> snyk auth

Now redirecting you to our auth page, go ahead and log in,
and once the auth is complete, return to this prompt and you'll
be ready to start using snyk.

If you can't wait use this url:
https://app.snyk.io/login?token=
aign=CLI_V1_PLUGIN&utm_campaign_content=1.1155.0&os=darwin&docker=false

/ Waiting...
```

Figure 8.23 - Run the Synk command

4. Use the Snyk `test` command to analyze your Android app's dependencies for known vulnerabilities as shown in the following screenshot. Run the following command in your project's directory: `snyk test`.

Figure 8.24 – snyk test and monitor commands

Snyk will scan your app's dependencies and provide a report on any vulnerabilities it finds. It will also suggest the following steps to remediate the issues:

- If Snyk identifies any vulnerabilities, recommendations will be provided in the scan report for how to fix them. This typically involves updating the affected dependencies to newer versions that include security patches.

- You can configure Snyk to run as part of your CI pipeline (`https://docs.snyk.io/integrations/ci-cd-integrations`) or set up scheduled scans.

Oversecured

Oversecured (`https://oversecured.com/`) is a robust platform for mobile app security testing and vulnerability remediation. With its advanced security testing capabilities, real-time feedback, integrated remediation, and support for multiple platforms, it offers a comprehensive solution to enhance the security posture of mobile applications, as shown in the following screenshot.

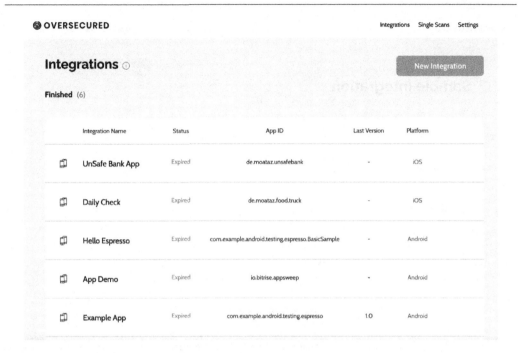

Figure 8.25 – Oversecured dashboard

The following is a brief overview of Oversecured's features:

- It offers a wide range of advanced security testing techniques, including SAST, DAST, and IAST.

- It provides real-time feedback and actionable guidance to developers during the testing process. It highlights vulnerabilities, explains the potential risks, and suggests specific remediation steps, empowering developers to fix security issues efficiently.

- It offers integrated remediation capabilities, enabling developers to address identified vulnerabilities directly within the platform. This streamlined workflow helps accelerate the vulnerability fixing process and ensures that security issues are remediated promptly.

- It supports mobile platforms such as Android and iOS. This flexibility makes it suitable for developers working with diverse technology stacks as shown in the following screenshot:

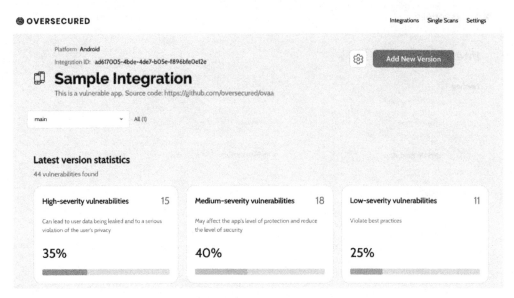

Figure 8.26 – App view

- It provides collaboration features that allow developers, security teams, and other stakeholders to work together seamlessly. It also generates reports with detailed vulnerability information, supporting documentation, and progress tracking, facilitating communication and accountability as shown in the following screenshot.

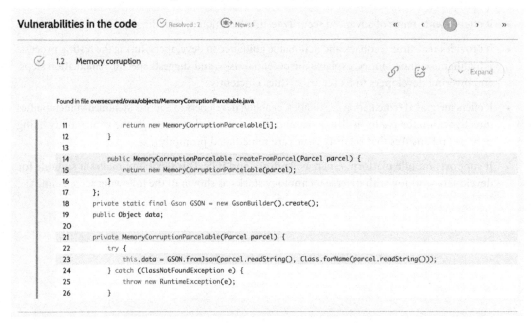

Figure 8.27 – Vulnerabilities in the code view

Oversecured supported different CI/CD tools (`https://oversecured.com/docs/ci-cd/`) with the public API. Regardless of which CI/CD tool you use, you will need to do the following:

- Get an Integration ID in the list of active Integrations

- Generate an API token

The following tools are currently supported:

- Bitrise

- Jenkins

- CircleCI

- Travis CI

MobSF

MobSF (`https://github.com/MobSF/Mobile-Security-Framework-MobSF`) is an open source automated framework for pen testing, malware analysis, and security assessment of mobile applications (Android/iOS). All you need to do is to upload your iOS or Android app as shown in the following screenshot:

Figure 8.28 – MobSF landing page

After that, MobSF will start the analysis process by scanning the `.apk` or `.ipa` file, as shown in the following screenshot.

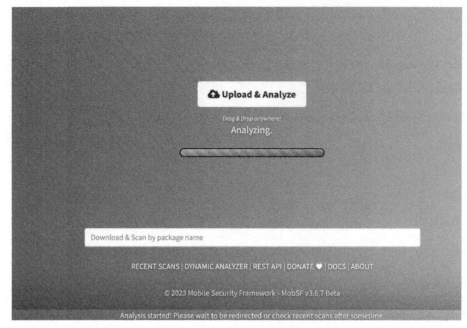

Figure 8.29 – Analyzing the app

Then, the scan results and report will be displayed, displaying details including the security score and analysis results as shown in the following screenshot.

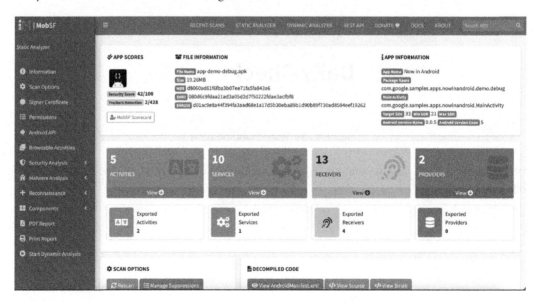

Figure 8.30 – The scan results

The following screenshot shows an example of the certificate analysis inside the app.

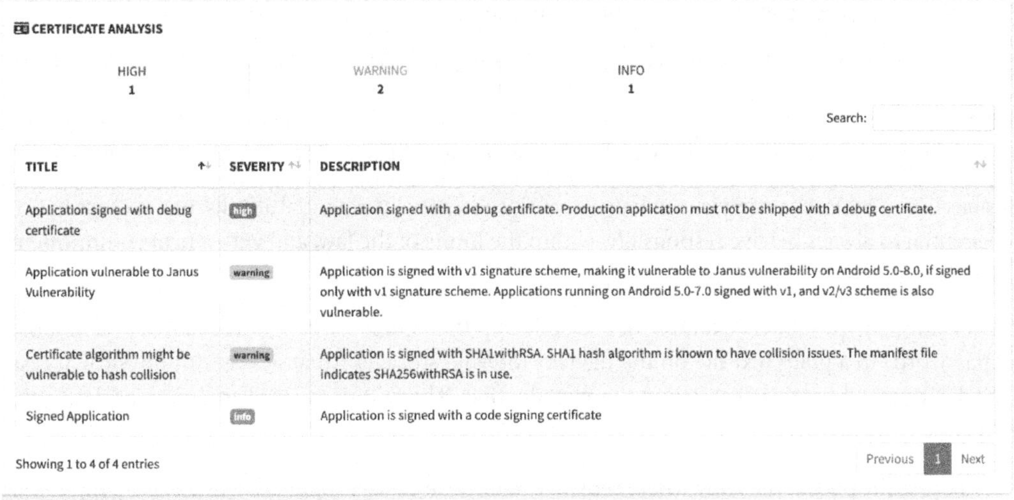

TITLE	SEVERITY	DESCRIPTION
Application signed with debug certificate	high	Application signed with a debug certificate. Production application must not be shipped with a debug certificate.
Application vulnerable to Janus Vulnerability	warning	Application is signed with v1 signature scheme, making it vulnerable to Janus vulnerability on Android 5.0-8.0, if signed only with v1 signature scheme. Applications running on Android 5.0-7.0 signed with v1, and v2/v3 scheme is also vulnerable.
Certificate algorithm might be vulnerable to hash collision	warning	Application is signed with SHA1withRSA. SHA1 hash algorithm is known to have collision issues. The manifest file indicates SHA256withRSA is in use.
Signed Application	info	Application is signed with a code signing certificate

Figure 8.31 – The certificate analysis view in the app

You can also run your Android or iOS static analysis tests on the cloud using MobSF and Amazon Web Services with Docker.

You can install the prebuilt Docker image by running the following command (consult the MobSF documentation at `https://mobsf.github.io/docs/#/docker` for more info):

```
docker pull opensecurity/mobile-security-framework-mobsf
docker run -it --rm -p 8000:8000 opensecurity/mobile-security-framework-mobsf:latest
```

Docker will start to pull the image and build the container and it will run on port `8000`.

MobSF is an open-source project, but some companies may choose to use a licensed automated security tool instead. This is because licensed tools typically include training, support, and access to security experts.

GitHub Advanced Security

GitHub Advanced Security (`https://docs.github.com/en/get-started/learning-about-github/about-github-advanced-security`) can help address different security issues and vulnerabilities including:

- Dependency scanning
- Securing your code in real time by enabling developers to fix vulnerabilities as they code in their native workflow

- Enabling crowd-sourced intelligence from millions of developers and researchers
- Facilitating easy collaboration among team members no matter where they are
- Shipping secure software in an automated way that speeds you up instead of slowing you down

It is crucial to recognize the potential security issues that can arise from exploiting weaknesses in mobile apps, which emphasizes the importance of responsible and ethical conduct within the security team.

The objective of ethical hacking is to enhance security and prevent potential attacks, not to cause harm. It is essential to always behave responsibly, within the limits of the law, and with a firm commitment to ethical conduct.

Let's consider a hypothetical example of a mobile app that stores user login credentials (username and password) in a plain text file on the device's internal storage. An attacker with physical access to the device could potentially retrieve these credentials. The following steps are how we investigate and fix this vulnerability:

1. Locate the part of the code where sensitive data, such as user login credentials, is being stored on the device.
2. Verify that the data is indeed being stored in an insecure manner, such as plain text files or unencrypted databases.
3. To fix this vulnerability, sensitive data should be stored in an encrypted format.
4. Integrating security scanning tools such as SAST and DAST into your security process can greatly enhance your ability to identify and mitigate vulnerabilities. Integrate these automated tests into your CI pipeline. Run the tests whenever new code is pushed to the repository to ensure that security remains intact as the app evolves.
5. Regularly run your automated security tests as part of your app's testing regimen. Keep the test regimen up to date with any changes to the app's security mechanisms or code base.
6. Consider periodic manual penetration testing by security professionals. They can provide insights into potential vulnerabilities that automated tests might miss.

Tips for security automation for mobile DevOps

The following are some tips to avoid slowing down the build and affecting developer productivity after implementing DevSecOps by injecting security checks and scanning:

- It is important that the CI build is not slowed down. However, certain security tools may take time to scan the mobile app, which can impact the CI build time and cause developers to be idle for a period.

- If necessary, split the tests up to reduce the scanning execution time if the tests take a long time. Running automated security tests on different mobile devices in parallel can reduce the overall execution time, without affecting the running time of the CI build. This process avoids running the tests sequentially on a single device.

- If a critical vulnerability or security issue could potentially harm end users or the system, block the build or release it with security testing (I suggest prioritizing and focusing on the critical cases that have high priority and severity). Development and security teams should collaborate to determine whether to block a build or release, taking into account the potential impacts and risks to the system and the timeframe for fixing it.

Summary

In this chapter, our focus was on safeguarding your mobile applications and DevOps processes. We explored the fundamentals of mobile app security, automating security testing, and the basics of DevSecOps.

After reading this chapter, you will have gained valuable insights and essential skills that will greatly benefit your mobile app development journey and you understand the importance of security in the realm of mobile app development and Mobile DevOps.

You learned about the introduction of mobile DevSecOps and how it can significantly enhance the security of your mobile apps. Understanding the various mobile app security threats and architectural considerations empowers you to build secure mobile applications from the ground up.

A crucial aspect of ensuring mobile app security is employing comprehensive testing methods and tools. You are now familiar with techniques such as static and dynamic analysis, penetration testing, and API security testing. By incorporating these security measures into your development pipeline, you can efficiently detect and mitigate vulnerabilities early in the process.

Your skill set now extends to automating security within the Mobile DevOps process. Practical tips on CI/CD, containerization, and automated code analysis have equipped you to streamline security practices throughout your app development life cycle.

By understanding and implementing the concepts discussed in this chapter, organizations can ensure that their mobile apps are secure and resilient in the face of evolving threats.

Moving on to the next chapter, we will discuss the mobile DevOps best practices for accelerating the whole process and increasing developer productivity.

9

Mobile DevOps Best Practices

As discussed in the previous chapters, it is essential to use the mobile DevOps process in order to develop and release quality mobile applications frequently and quickly to your customers. It is possible to speed up the development and distribution of mobile applications by combining the best practices of developers, test engineers, release experts, and other stakeholders. As a result of the shorter delivery times, quality and user experience will also be improved.

Throughout this chapter, we will explore a range of essential topics that will empower mobile app developers and DevOps teams to implement efficient and effective **continuous integration/continuous delivery (CI/CD)** pipelines; we will delve into the fundamental practices that drive successful mobile app development.

In this chapter, we will cover the following topics:

- Best practices for CI/CD in mobile app development
- Managing mobile app versions and releases
- Managing mobile app infrastructure
- The A/B testing and feature flags
- Remote and dependency caching for mobile apps
- Execution of CI builds and tests in parallel
- Automating build, test, and release with fastlane
- Mock APIs
- ChatOps for mobile DevOps collaboration

Best practices for CI/CD in mobile app development

Keeping your mobile DevOps processes effective, efficient, and aligned with your overall strategy for developing mobile apps requires you and your team to review and refine them regularly. There is no silver bullet, so we should always refine our mobile DevOps processes based on team and business growth.

There are various practices that can be added to mobile DevOps processes to optimize CI/CD pipelines, code review processes, development speed, and so on.

We discussed, in the previous chapters, the different stages when implementing CI/CD pipelines or workflows for mobile apps.

Here are some best practices to ensure a successful CI/CD pipeline for mobile apps:

- **Automate as much as possible**: Automate building, testing, code analysis, releasing, and other tasks to reduce manual intervention, minimize errors, and accelerate the development process.

- **Implement a testing strategy:** Use a mix of unit tests, integration tests, UI tests, and end-to-end tests to ensure high-quality code. Test various devices, screen sizes, and operating systems using emulators or real devices.

- **Optimize build and test times:** Use caching, parallelization, and incremental builds to reduce build times. Parallelize test execution and prioritize critical tests to speed up test runs.

- **Adopt a well-defined branching strategy**: When dealing with large or complex code, it's helpful to use a branching strategy such as GitFlow or trunk-based development. This can maintain a tidy commit history and make integration and deployment easier.

- **Enforce good commit practices**: This includes atomic commits, descriptive commit messages, and frequent code reviews to maintain code quality and ensure easy traceability of changes. This helps ensure the code's quality and correctness and can improve collaboration among team members. There are different tools that can be used to improve and automate the code review process, such as the following:

  - **What The Diff** (`https://whatthediff.ai/`): This is an AI-powered code that acts as a review assistant. Its purpose is to assist your team in writing better pull request descriptions, and it can even help to speed up the reviewing and merging process. Additionally, it can keep your non-technical team members informed and involved.

  - **Danger** (`https://github.com/danger/danger`): This is an incredible tool that can help your team automate code review conventions. By adding another logical step to the process, Danger can assist with linting those routine tasks during your daily code review.

  - **MergeQueue** (`https://mergequeue.com/`): A faster way to automate merge workflows, manage queues in large teams, and never worry about build failures again.

- **Keep an eye on essential CI/CD metrics**: It is important to monitor the CI/CD metrics such as build times, test execution times, deployment frequency, and code quality. These metrics will be discussed further in this chapter to help identify bottlenecks and areas for improvement.

- **Incorporate security measures into your CI/CD pipeline**: To ensure safety in your CI/CD pipeline, it is important to include security measures. This can be done by utilizing both static and dynamic code analysis tools, scanning dependencies for any vulnerabilities, and enforcing access control through the principle of least privilege.

- **Prepare a well-defined rollback strategy**: It is important to have a clear and defined plan in place for rolling back to a previous stable version in the event of any issues during deployment. This may require submitting a new update to the app store for mobile applications.

- **Establish clear communication channels**: It is important to establish clear communication channels among team members in order to keep everyone informed about the project's progress and any potential issues that may arise.

- **Collaborate with cross-functional teams**: Work together with cross-functional teams to ensure all aspects of the development and deployment processes are taken into consideration. This involves collaborating with designers, developers, testers, and operations teams.

In addition, we should keep an eye on the performance of our CI builds and CI servers overall as we improve our mobile DevOps processes and CI/CD implementation. Let's look at a few metrics to track the CI/CD.

Key metrics to track for CI/CD in mobile app development

Tracking key metrics in your CI/CD pipeline can help you measure the effectiveness of your development and deployment process, identify bottlenecks, and optimize the pipeline.

Here are some essential metrics to track for CI/CD in mobile app development:

- **Build success rate**: Measure the time taken for each build, including compilation, packaging, and any other build-related tasks. Tracking this metric can help you identify inefficiencies and improve build performance – for example, you have the option to incorporate caching steps to decrease the build time of the app in case the app modules haven't undergone any changes from the previous build. This will prevent the app from being built from scratch and start the process from where it last left off. We will discuss caching later in this chapter.

- **Deployment frequency**: Track how often you deploy new releases or updates to your mobile app. High deployment frequency indicates a mature CI/CD process and faster delivery of features and bug fixes to users.

- **Lead time for changes**: Measure the time a code change takes from commit to production. Shorter lead times can indicate an efficient pipeline and faster value delivery to users; we will discuss different tools that help in the code commit process later in this chapter.

- **Change failure rate**: Monitor the percentage of changes that results in failures or require rollbacks. A low change failure rate indicates that your testing and release processes effectively catch issues before they reach production.

- **Mean time to recovery** (**MTTR**): Measure the average time it takes to fix issues or recover from a failure in production. A short MTTR indicates that your team effectively identifies and addresses problems quickly.

- **Test execution time**: Monitor the time taken to execute your test suite. Long test execution times can slow down the development process. Identifying slow tests or optimizing test parallelization can reduce execution time. We will discuss parallelization later in this chapter.

- **Test coverage**: Track the percentage of your code base covered by tests to ensure that you have adequate testing in place to catch issues and maintain high code quality.

- **Test pass/fail rate**: Monitor the percentage of tests that pass or fail in each build. A high pass rate indicates a stable code base, while a high failure rate may indicate issues with the code or testing process. Flaky tests produce inconsistent results, passing in some runs and failing in others without any apparent reason. Address flaky tests as soon as possible to avoid false negatives and maintain confidence in your test suite. Here is an example of how Slack teams handle the flaky tests art scale: `https://slack.engineering/handling-flaky-tests-at-scale-auto-detection-suppression/`.

- **Code quality metrics**: Track metrics related to code quality, such as code complexity, code duplication, and adherence to coding standards. These metrics can help you maintain a clean and maintainable code base.

Tracking key metrics for CI/CD in mobile app development is crucial for evaluating the efficiency of the development and deployment process. By monitoring these metrics, teams can identify bottlenecks, optimize their pipeline, and ensure a smooth and reliable delivery of features and updates to users.

These metrics provide valuable insights into the overall health and effectiveness of the CI/CD pipeline, enabling teams to make data-driven improvements and maintain a stable and high-quality code base.

With a well-monitored CI/CD pipeline and a clear understanding of key metrics, let's explore together the essential strategies for managing mobile app versions and releases.

Managing mobile app versions and releases

Managing versions and releases of a mobile app can be a complicated task, but there are some best practices that can help simplify it:

- **Follow semantic versioning**: It's essential to adopt a clear and consistent version numbering system. Semantic versioning (`https://semver.org/`) is a widely recognized standard used by developers. A version number consists of three parts: **MAJOR.MINOR.PATCH**. **MAJOR** version changes indicate breaking changes, **MINOR** version changes introduce new features, and **PATCH** version changes address bugs and issues.

- **Comprehensive release notes**: Provide thorough release notes for each release, including new features, bug fixes, known issues, and additional instructions or requirements.

- **Streamlined branching strategy**: Adopt a clear and well-defined branching strategy, such as **GitFlow** or **trunk-based development**, to avoid confusion and maintain a clean commit history. This will help ensure a smooth integration and deployment process.

Now, let's examine the two strategies for organizing and managing source code in version control systems: *monorepo* and *multi-repo*.

Monorepo

A **monorepo** (`https://monorepo.tools/`) is a single repository containing multiple distinct projects with well-defined relationships. This approach is designed to make it easier to manage and develop large, complex software systems by providing a single, unified source of truth for all the code and resources required by the project.

There's a difference between a *monolith* and a *monorepo*; a good monorepo is the opposite of a monolith, as shown in the following figure:

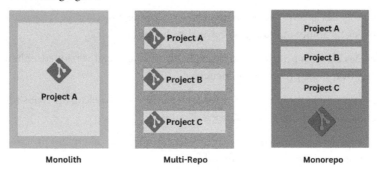

Figure 9.1 – Monolith versus multi-repo versus monorepo

A monorepo offers several benefits for project development:

- Firstly, storing all code in a single repository makes it easier to understand how different system pieces fit together and depend on one another. This also simplifies dependency management, reducing complexity in the development process and facilitating seamless building and deployment of changes.

- A monorepo enhances collaboration between developers by providing a centralized location for all relevant code and resources. This improves communication, minimizes conflicts, and enables smoother collaboration on the project.

However, there are some challenges associated with monorepos:

- They can become large in size, making it more difficult to clone and work with the repository due to increased disk space requirements and longer cloning times

- They can be more complex, particularly for large and complex projects, as changes impact the entire repository

Security enforcement may pose difficulties as well, as all code is stored in a single location and accessible to multiple developers. This can be particularly challenging for sensitive projects, necessitating careful authorization processes.

Multi-repo

Multi-repo is a development approach where each component of a project is stored in its own separate repository. It promotes modularity and allows teams to work independently on specific components. While it offers flexibility, coordinating changes across repositories can be challenging.

Here are some characteristics and challenges associated with multi-repo:

- In a multi-repo approach, each project, library, or module has its own separate repository. This keeps the code base for each project isolated and independent.

- Each repository has its own version control history, allowing projects to be versioned independently. This provides flexibility in managing release cycles and updates.

- Dependencies between projects must be explicitly managed and versioned, enhancing visibility and control over inter-project dependencies.

- Each repository contains only the code for a specific project, keeping the repository size smaller and potentially improving performance.

- The multi-repo approach allows for a more decentralized development process, as each team can manage its repositories independently.

- Managing dependencies, versions, and configurations across multiple repositories can be more complex and time-consuming compared to a monorepo.

- Making changes across multiple projects can be challenging, as it may require coordinating commits and releases across multiple repositories.

As a result, the choice between monorepo and multi-repo depends on factors such as team size, project complexity, development processes, and tooling preferences. Some organizations prefer the simplicity and unified approach of a monorepo, while others prefer a multi-repo setup's independence and decentralized nature.

Since mobile applications rely on backend services, databases, and configuration management, the team should consider automating the release and managing of these to prevent any issues. Let's examine the concepts behind managing mobile app infrastructure

Managing mobile app infrastructure

Managing mobile app infrastructure is a critical aspect of successful app development and deployment. It involves overseeing the underlying systems, servers, databases, and cloud resources that support the app's functionality and user experience.

Efficient infrastructure management ensures scalability, reliability, and performance. Tasks include provisioning and configuring servers, setting up databases, monitoring resource utilization, and implementing security measures. Embracing modern **infrastructure-as-code** (**IaC**) practices allows teams to automate infrastructure provisioning and configuration, making it easier to maintain consistency and deploy changes seamlessly.

A well-managed mobile app infrastructure is vital for delivering a smooth and reliable user experience while efficiently handling increasing user demands and scaling with the growth of the app. Let's discuss how to manage the infrastructure of mobile apps.

IaC for mobile apps

IaC is a powerful approach that allows you to define and manage your app's infrastructure using code, bringing benefits such as reproducibility and scalability. While IaC is commonly associated with server-based infrastructure, it can also be applied to mobile apps, as shown in the following figure:

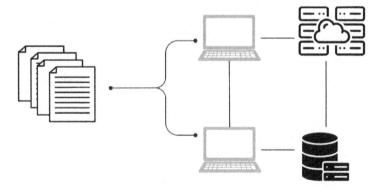

Figure 9.2 – IaC

Here's how you can utilize IaC for mobile apps in more detail:

- IaC enables you to create reproducible environments easily. You can spin up identical infrastructure setups for different environments such as development, testing, staging, and production. By using the same infrastructure code, you ensure consistency across environments, reducing the chances of configuration drift and environment-related issues.

- Define the infrastructure components required to support your mobile app. This may include server resources, databases, storage services, **content delivery networks** (**CDNs**), and other necessary resources. Determine the configuration settings, dependencies, and relationships between these components.

- Select an IaC tool that supports mobile app infrastructure provisioning. Popular options include Terraform and AWS CloudFormation. These tools allow you to describe and manage your IaC and support various cloud providers and services.

- Store your infrastructure code in a version control system (e.g., Git) to track changes, enable collaboration, and maintain a history of infrastructure modifications.

- Utilize IaC to define auto-scaling capabilities for your mobile app's infrastructure. This allows your app to automatically scale resources up or down based on demand, ensuring optimal performance and cost efficiency. Specify scaling policies and thresholds within your infrastructure code.

- With IaC, you can manage configuration settings and variables as code, making it easier to maintain consistency and avoid manual errors. For example, you can define environment-specific configuration values (e.g., API endpoints and database credentials) within your infrastructure code and use them consistently across different environments.

- With IaC, you can version and track these changes, ensuring transparency and simplifying deployment. Instead of manually modifying resources, you modify the infrastructure code and apply the changes, and the IaC tool handles the updates.

- Apply testing principles to your infrastructure code. Write automated tests to validate the correctness and integrity of your infrastructure definitions. This helps catch potential issues before provisioning or modifying the infrastructure.

- Integrate your infrastructure code into your CI/CD pipeline. This allows you to automate the provisioning and updating of your mobile app's infrastructure alongside your application code, ensuring consistent and reliable deployments.

After IaC, let's explore configuration management for mobile apps and how to use it.

Configuration management for mobile apps

Manage configuration settings and variables for different environments to ensure consistency and avoid manual errors with the following steps:

- Identify the configuration settings and variables your mobile app requires. These can include API endpoints, database connection strings, feature flags, logging levels, credentials, and any other values that may vary across environments.

- Separate the configuration settings from your application code. Hardcoding configuration values directly into the code can make it challenging to update them when moving between environments. Instead, abstract the configuration values into separate configuration files or externalize them through environment variables.

- Use configuration files specific to each environment. For example, you can have separate configuration files for development, testing, staging, and production environments. These files can be JSON, XML, YAML, or properties files. Each file contains the corresponding values for that environment.

- Leverage environment variables to store configuration values. Environment variables are set at the system level and can be accessed by your mobile app during runtime. This approach provides flexibility and allows for easy configuration changes without modifying files.

- Use a centralized configuration management solution to store and manage your configuration settings. Solutions include AWS Secrets Manager secrets, Parameter Store parameters, or HashiCorp Vault for configuration values. They allow you to store different configurations for each environment and provide APIs for retrieving values at runtime.

- Automate the deployment of configuration settings to different environments as part of your CI/CD pipeline. This ensures that the correct configuration values are deployed with your mobile app, reducing the risk of human error during manual configuration updates.

- Store your configuration files or scripts in version control to track changes, maintain a history, and enable collaboration. This allows you to revert to previous configurations if needed and provides an audit trail of configuration modifications.

- Avoid storing sensitive information directly in configuration files or environment variables. Instead, use secure storage mechanisms provided by your chosen configuration management solution or encrypt the sensitive values before storing them.

- Include configuration testing as part of your automated testing strategy. Write tests that validate the correctness and integrity of your configuration settings. This helps catch configuration-related issues early in development and ensures that the app behaves as expected in different environments.

- Establish a change management process for modifying configuration settings. Implement approval workflows to ensure that changes are reviewed and approved by the appropriate stakeholders before being applied to production environments. This helps maintain control and prevent unauthorized or unplanned changes.

Optimize your build process to reduce build times, as long as it can slow the development cycle and increase developer waiting times. Use techniques such as caching, parallelization, and incremental builds to speed up the process. In the next section, we'll dive into remote and dependency caching for mobile apps and explore the benefits.

Remote and dependency caching

Building and releasing mobile apps often involves downloading dependencies and assets to the CI servers or the local machines to be able to build the apps, which can be time-consuming and data-intensive. However, with the advent of remote and dependency caching solutions, developers now have a powerful tool to enhance their productivity.

Remote and dependency caching for mobile apps refers to *storing and retrieving frequently used dependencies and assets from a remote server*. Instead of downloading these resources every time an app is built, developers can leverage caching to significantly reduce the time and bandwidth required for the build process. This optimization technique can significantly streamline app development workflows, resulting in faster build times, improved iteration cycles, and reduced data consumption.

Here are some benefits of remote and dependency caching:

- It eliminates the need to download the same resources repeatedly, enabling developers to save valuable time during the build process. This acceleration can be particularly noticeable when working on large-scale projects with numerous dependencies.

- Caching facilitates collaboration among team members by ensuring that everyone has access to the same set of dependencies and assets. This helps avoid versioning conflicts and ensures consistent development environments across the team.

- Developers can rapidly iterate on their apps without waiting for resource downloads, enabling quicker testing and debugging cycles.

- Some caching solutions provide offline support, allowing developers to continue working on their projects even when an internet connection is unavailable. This feature is particularly useful for developers on the go or in areas with intermittent connectivity.

But depending on the caching solution chosen, developers may need to monitor and manage the cache to prevent it from growing too large or becoming cluttered with outdated resources. Efficient cache management strategies are crucial to maintain optimal performance.

When it comes to remote and dependency caching for mobile apps, several tools and platforms offer similar functionality, including the following:

- **Gradle's build cache** (https://docs.gradle.org/current/userguide/build_cache.html): Gradle is a popular build automation system that provides a build cache feature that can be leveraged to cache dependencies and resources. It integrates seamlessly with Gradle-based Android projects and is well suited to large-scale builds.

- **npm's cache** (`https://docs.npmjs.com/cli/v8/commands/npm-cache`): For JavaScript-based mobile apps such as React Native, the npm package manager includes a caching mechanism that allows for efficient dependency resolution and retrieval. npm's cache significantly reduces the time required to fetch and install frequently used packages.

- **Bazel** (`https://bazel.build/`): Bazel is an open source build automation tool developed by Google. It is designed to provide fast, reproducible, and scalable builds across various programming languages and platforms. `Bazel.build` utilizes a sophisticated dependency graph and caching mechanism to intelligently determine what needs to be rebuilt, significantly reducing build times and improving developer productivity. You can read examples of how Reddit uses Bazel with the iOS app (`https://www.reddit.com/r/RedditEng/comments/syz5dw/ios_and_bazel_at_reddit_a_journey/`) and how Square uses Bazel with Apple Silicon (`https://developer.squareup.com/blog/getting-squares-ios-build-ready-for-apple-silicon-with-bazel/`).

- **Tuist** (`https://tuist.io/`): Tuist is a command-line tool that simplifies the process of setting up and maintaining iOS projects using a declarative approach. Tuist caching (`https://docs.tuist.io/building-at-scale/caching`) optimizes build times by storing and reusing previously built dependencies, assets, and intermediate build artifacts. This caching mechanism can greatly reduce the time required to build and iterate on iOS projects.

- **BuildBuddy** (`https://www.buildbuddy.io/`): BuildBuddy is a cloud-based build execution platform that helps developers offload and distribute their builds to remote machines. It offers a user-friendly interface, extensive build insights, and collaboration features to streamline the development workflow. By utilizing BuildBuddy, teams can reduce build times, save infrastructure costs, and enhance developer efficiency. Here is an example of how to use Remote Build Execution with GitHub Actions: `https://www.buildbuddy.io/docs/rbe-github-actions`.

- **XCRemoteCache** (`https://github.com/spotify/XCRemoteCache`): XCRemoteCache is a remote cache tool for Xcode projects. It reuses target artifacts generated on a remote machine, served from a simple REST server.

- **Carthage cache**: Carthage, a dependency manager for iOS apps, offers a caching feature to speed up dependency retrieval and build times. It provides compatibility with Xcode and simplifies sharing dependencies across team members. Additionally, you can use Rome (`https://github.com/tmspzz/Rome`), the shared cache for frameworks built with Carthage that allows developers on Apple platforms to use Amazon's S3, a local folder, or your own custom engine.

You can also use the Cocoapods cache (`https://cocoapods.org/pods/Cache`) or the **Swift Package Manager** (**SPM**) (`https://github.com/apple/swift-package-manager`) cache if you are using it in your iOS apps.

Remote and dependency caching for mobile apps is a game-changer in mobile app development and mobile DevOps, offering tangible benefits in terms of time savings, bandwidth conservation, collaboration, and iteration efficiency.

Mobile CI/CD systems use caching to transfer data between isolated builds. As CI builds run in ephemeral, isolated virtual machines, a typical CI workflow must take extra steps to bootstrap the local environment ordinarily available to the developer.

Caching these operations will make your CI workflows faster since installing CLI tools and downloading third-party dependencies take time, as shown in the following figure:

Figure 9.3 – Caching between the CI builds machines

While there may be some initial setup complexities and considerations around cache management, the overall advantages make caching a valuable addition to any developer's toolkit.

Here's an example of how you can use GitHub Actions to set up a simple Gradle cache pipeline for an Android app build to speed up build times:

1. Inside the `.github/workflows` directory, create a YAML file – for example, `android_build.yml`.

2. Add the following `android_build.yml` file: `https://github.com/PacktPublishing/Mobile-DevOps-Playbook/blob/main/Chapter-9/.github/android_build.yml`. The workflow caches the Gradle dependencies based on the contents of your Gradle files.

3. Depending on your app's complexity and needs, you might want to add more steps, such as running tests, deploying artifacts, or integrating with other services.

Let's look at an example of how to use caching in the CI/CD workflow on Bitrise.

Bitrise offers features known as **Cache Pull Step** and **Cache Push Step**, which enable you to cache and retrieve particular directories or files between builds, based on the app dependencies in your apps.

To set up caching for your iOS project, you need to add these steps to your Bitrise workflow: `https://github.com/PacktPublishing/Mobile-DevOps-Playbook/blob/main/Chapter-9/bitrise.yml`.

You can learn more about Bitrise dependencies and caching at the following link: `https://devcenter.bitrise.io/en/dependencies-and-caching.html`.

Finally, by comparing and selecting the most suitable caching solution based on your project's requirements, you can optimize your app development process and unlock greater productivity.

It is important to always search for the appropriate caching solution for both your mobile app and CI provider.

Execution of CI builds and tests in parallel

Leveraging parallel execution for CI builds and tests in mobile app development can significantly enhance developer productivity, shorten feedback loops, and improve overall efficiency. Consider the capabilities of tools such as Fastlane, Firebase Test Lab, and CI tools to achieve optimal parallelization and accelerate your mobile app development process.

Some of the benefits of parallel execution for mobile app CI builds are as follows:

- **Faster feedback**: Parallel execution reduces the time required to build steps and test suites, providing quicker feedback on code changes. This enables developers to iterate faster and catch issues early in the development cycle.

- **Improved efficiency**: By utilizing parallel execution, you can fully utilize available resources and distribute the workload across multiple agents or devices. This improves resource efficiency and maximizes the utilization of your CI infrastructure.

- **Scalability**: Parallel execution allows your CI pipeline to scale seamlessly as your mobile app project grows. It enables you to handle larger code bases, increased test suites, and support for multiple platforms and configurations without sacrificing speed or performance.

- **Time and cost savings**: By reducing build and test times through parallel execution, you save valuable developer time and potentially reduce costs associated with maintaining CI infrastructure.

Most of the CI/CD tools support parallel builds or splitting the CI pipeline or workflow into small patches or tasks to run in parallel to save the build time. For example, with GitHub Actions, you can use Matrix (`https://docs.github.com/en/actions/using-jobs/using-a-matrix-for-your-jobs`) to test your code in multiple versions of a language or on multiple operating systems.

With Bitrise, you can use Build Pipelines (`https://bitrise.io/why/features/pipeline`), which helps you organize your entire mobile CI/CD build process and allows you to set up advanced configurations with multiple tasks and tests running in parallel and/or sequentially.

In parallel execution, multiple UI tests are executed simultaneously on different devices or simulators, as shown in the following figure:

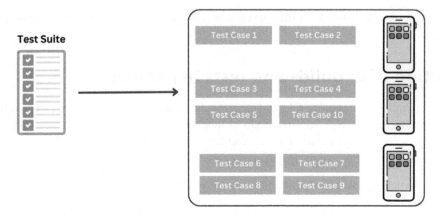

Figure 9.4 – Parallel UI tests execution

Parallel execution for mobile app UI testing helps improve the speed and quality of your testing process, leading to more reliable and robust mobile applications.

Here are some benefits of parallel execution for mobile app UI testing:

- By running UI tests in parallel, you can significantly reduce the overall execution time. Instead of executing tests sequentially, parallel execution allows multiple tests concurrently on different devices or simulators. This helps save time and improves the efficiency of your testing process.

- With parallel execution, you can execute tests on multiple devices or simulators simultaneously. This allows you to cover a broader range of device configurations, operating systems, and screen sizes in less time. It helps ensure your app is tested on various devices and increases the likelihood of catching device-specific issues.

- Parallel execution provides scalability for your UI testing process. As your test suite grows, executing tests in parallel allows you to handle more tests without significantly increasing execution time. You can easily add more devices or simulators to your testing infrastructure and distribute the test workload across them.

- Parallel execution makes efficient use of available resources. By utilizing multiple devices or simulators concurrently, you can maximize the utilization of your testing infrastructure. This helps optimize resource allocation and ensures tests are executed without unnecessary wait times.

- Parallel execution is well suited for integration into CI/CD pipelines. You can achieve faster feedback cycles and builds by executing tests in parallel. It allows you to integrate UI testing seamlessly into your CI/CD workflows and ensure that your app remains stable and functional with each code change.

It is possible to run parallel Android and iOS tests using Flank (`https://flank.github.io/flank/`), which is compatible with the gcloud CLI. Flank provides extra features to accelerate velocity and increase quality.

One useful practice for mobile teams to safely release features quickly is to implement feature flags. Let's discuss this concept and how it can be utilized.

A/B testing and feature flags

A/B testing and feature flags are powerful techniques used in mobile app development to experiment, validate, and roll out new features or variations to a subset of users. Let's delve into how A/B testing and feature flags can benefit mobile apps and the tools available for implementing them.

A/B testing for mobile apps

A/B testing involves presenting different versions of an app or specific features to different user groups to evaluate their impact on user experience, engagement, or **key performance indicators** (**KPIs**).

Here's how it works:

1. **Experimentation**: A/B testing tools enable developers to define experiments, create alternative variations (A and B), and assign users randomly to each variation. For example, you might test different app layouts, navigation structures, or button placements.

2. **Measurement**: Metrics and analytics are essential for evaluating the success of A/B tests. By monitoring user interactions, conversions, or other relevant KPIs, you can assess which variation performs better and drives the desired user behavior.

3. **Analysis and iteration**: Analyzing the test results helps you make data-driven decisions. You can refine and iterate on the tested features or versions based on the insights gained to improve the app's performance and user experience, as shown in the following figure:

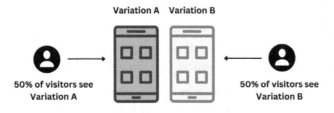

Figure 9.5 – How A/B testing works

Feature flags for mobile apps

Feature flags, or toggles, enable developers to control the visibility and behavior of specific features or code sections within an app. Feature flags provide flexibility, allowing developers to roll out new features gradually, test them in production, or enable/disable them dynamically.

Here's how feature flags work:

- Feature flag libraries or SDKs are integrated into the app's code base to enable runtime control over feature availability. Flags can be configured to turn features on or off based on predefined conditions, such as user segments, device types, or app versions.

- Feature flags enable developers to conduct targeted tests by selecting features for specific user groups. This helps assess feature performance, gather feedback, and make data-driven decisions before releasing the features to a broader audience, as shown in the following figure:

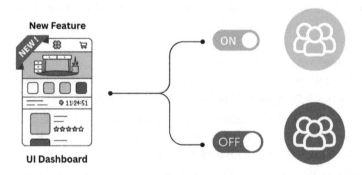

Figure 9.6 – How feature flags work

Here are some of the most popular tools for flagging features in mobile apps:

- **LaunchDarkly** (`https://launchdarkly.com`) is a feature management platform that provides robust feature flagging capabilities. It allows you to control feature availability, target specific user segments, and easily manage flags through a web-based dashboard.

- **ConfigCat** (`https://configcat.com/`) offers a feature flag and configuration management platform that supports mobile app development. It allows you to create feature flags, control their visibility, and dynamically update configurations without requiring app updates.

- **Flagsmith** (`https://flagsmith.com/`) is an open source feature flagging and remote configuration platform. It provides a range of features, including A/B testing, targeting rules, and integration with various development frameworks for mobile app implementation.

- **Firebase Remote Config** (`https://firebase.google.com/products/remote-config`) is a cloud-based service that allows developers to dynamically configure and customize their applications without requiring a new release or an app update. It enables developers to remotely control and personalize various aspects of their app, such as text, images, colors, and behavior, allowing for targeted content delivery and A/B testing.

- **Optimizely** (`https://www.optimizely.com`) is a powerful experimentation and personalization platform that enables businesses to make data-driven decisions and enhance their digital experiences.

Some of the benefits of A/B testing and feature flags for mobile apps are as follows:

- They help you make informed decisions based on real user data, improving the chances of successful feature launches and updates.

- By gradually rolling out features or enabling them for specific user segments, you mitigate risks associated with bugs, performance issues, or negative user reactions. This ensures a smoother and safer deployment process.

- They allow for quick iteration and refinement of features based on user feedback and measurable results. This iterative process enhances the development cycle and speeds up feature delivery.

- Feature flags enable personalized experiences by tailoring app features to specific user groups or individual users. This customization enhances user satisfaction and engagement.

A/B testing and feature flags offer mobile app developers valuable techniques for experimentation, validation, and controlled rollouts. Consider using tools such as Firebase Remote Config, Optimizely, LaunchDarkly, ConfigCat, or Flagsmith to implement these strategies and unlock the benefits of data-driven decision-making and flexible feature management in your mobile app development process.

Next, we will examine the use of mock APIs for mobile UI testing, which can save you time and effort by allowing you to test your app's UI without setting up a real API or waiting for network responses. It can also help you test the app's behavior in different scenarios and conditions that may be difficult to set up with a real API.

Mock APIs

Mock APIs are vital in simplifying mobile app development by decoupling backend dependencies, speeding up development cycles, and enhancing testability.

When selecting a mock API solution, consider its integration with your development workflow, customization options, documentation, and community support. By leveraging mock APIs, mobile app developers can streamline development, improve app quality, and iterate more efficiently.

A mock API for mobile UI testing is a simulated API that allows you to test the UI of your mobile app without having to connect to a real API. It can be helpful in a number of different situations, such as when the real API is not yet available, when you want to test the app's behavior in different scenarios that may not be possible to set up with a real API, or when you want to test the app's performance without being slowed down by network latency.

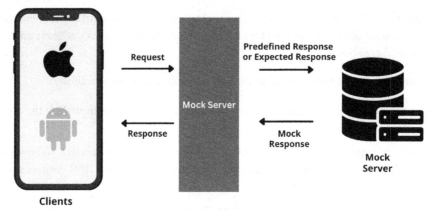

Figure 9.7 – How a mock server works

You can create a mock API for mobile UI testing using several tools, such as **WireMock** (`https://wiremock.org/`), the open source tool that allows you to create a mock API by defining the HTTP requests and responses it should return. It can be run as a standalone server, or it can be used as a Java library in your test code.

Here's an example of setting up a simple mock API endpoint that returns a JSON response: `https://github.com/PacktPublishing/Mobile-DevOps-Playbook/blob/main/Chapter-9/mockTest.kt`.

Here's an example of how you can incorporate the WireMock server into your Android test setup: `https://github.com/PacktPublishing/Mobile-DevOps-Playbook/blob/main/Chapter-9/MyApiTest.kt`.

Run the Android tests. The requests made to the specified API endpoint on the local mock server (e.g., `http://localhost:8080/api/endpoint` or `http://mock-server.com/api/endpoint`) will be intercepted by WireMock, which will respond with the configured mock response.

Building, testing, and releasing with fastlane

fastlane (`https://fastlane.tools/`) is a powerful automation tool specifically designed to streamline the process of building, testing, and releasing mobile apps. It provides different features and integrations to automate repetitive tasks, saving mobile developers valuable time and effort.

Let's dive into the key aspects of using fastlane for building, testing, and releasing mobile apps:

- fastlane simplifies the build configuration process. You can define your build settings, such as code signing, provisioning profiles, and build flavors, in a readable manner using fastlane's configuration files (Fastfile) (`https://docs.fastlane.tools/advanced/Fastfile/`). This eliminates the need for manual configuration and reduces the chances of errors.

- fastlane integrates with popular testing frameworks such as XCTest and Espresso, enabling you to run unit, UI, and other custom tests as part of your build process. It can also handle test reporting and generate comprehensive test result reports.

- fastlane seamlessly integrates with popular CI/CD platforms such as GitHub Actions, Codemagic, and Bitrise. It provides dedicated plugins and integrations that facilitate the smooth incorporation of fastlane into your CI workflows. This ensures the consistent and automated building, testing, and releasing of your mobile apps as part of your CI pipeline.

- fastlane simplifies releasing your app to app stores. With its App Store Connect and Google Play plugins, you can automate the entire release process, including versioning, code signing, metadata management, and uploading your app bundles or APKs.

- fastlane's extensibility allows you to extend its functionality by creating custom actions or utilizing numerous existing plugins. fastlane's plugin ecosystem (`https://docs.fastlane.tools/plugins/available-plugins/`) provides a wide range of pre-built plugins that integrate with third-party services such as Slack, Firebase App Distribution, Sentry, BrowserStack, and more. These plugins enable you to incorporate additional functionality, such as crash reporting, beta testing, or analytics, into your fastlane workflows.

- fastlane has a vibrant and active community that actively contributes to its development. Regular updates, new features, and bug fixes are released, ensuring you have access to the latest improvements and enhancements

Getting started with fastlane is relatively straightforward. Here's a step-by-step guide to help get you up and running with fastlane:

1. Ensure you have Ruby installed on your system. You can check this by running `ruby -v` in your Terminal. If Ruby is not installed, you can install it using a package manager such as **Homebrew** (for macOS) or **Chocolatey** (for Windows).

2. Install fastlane by running `gem install fastlane` in your Terminal. This command will fetch and install the latest version of fastlane.

3. Navigate to your mobile app project's directory using the Terminal.

4. Run `fastlane init` in the project directory. This command initializes fastlane and creates a new fastlane folder with configuration files.

5. fastlane uses a Fastfile to define and manage automation tasks. Open the Fastfile located in the fastlane directory using a text editor.

6. fastlane provides a wide range of built-in actions that cover common tasks. For example, you can use the scan action to run tests, and the delivery action to upload your app to the App Store.

7. fastlane allows you to store sensitive information, such as code-signing certificates and API keys, securely. Create a new `.env file` in the fastlane directory and add the necessary environment variables for your project.

8. Update the `Appfile` located in the fastlane directory with relevant information, such as your app's bundle identifier and Apple Developer account details.

9. To execute a specific lane, run `fastlane <lane_name>` in the terminal. For example, fastlane beta will execute the beta lane defined in your Fastfile.

Here's an example of a Fastfile for an iOS app that includes lanes for building, testing, and releasing the app to TestFlight and the App Store (`https://github.com/PacktPublishing/Mobile-DevOps-Playbook/blob/main/Chapter-9/fastlane/Fastfile%20`).

Here is a basic example of how to use fastlane with GitHub Actions to automate your iOS app deployment process:

1. Create a `.github/workflows` directory in your GitHub repository if it doesn't exist. Inside this directory, create a YAML file (e.g., `iOS-fastlane.yml`).

2. Configure a GitHub Actions workflow such as this example: `https://github.com/PacktPublishing/Mobile-DevOps-Playbook/blob/main/Chapter-9/.github/iOS-fastlane.yml`.

3. Replace `./path/to/your/project` with the actual path to your iOS project directory, and replace `your_lane` with the fastlane lane you want to run (e.g., beta, release, etc.).

Now, whenever you push changes to the `main` branch, the GitHub Actions workflow will be triggered, and it will execute the defined steps, which include setting up the environment, installing dependencies, and running your fastlane lane.

This is a basic example, and you might need to adapt it to your specific project setup and requirements.

Make sure to review the fastlane and GitHub Actions documentation (`https://docs.fastlane.tools/best-practices/continuous-integration/github/`) for more advanced configurations and options.

When using Bitrise, Codemagic, or any other CI providers, the process is similar. You will need to replace the pipeline steps with the fastlane commands and ensure that the necessary prerequisites for fastlane are installed on the VMs.

Remember that fastlane is highly customizable, so feel free to adapt it to your specific project requirements. Don't hesitate to refer to the official fastlane documentation (`https://docs.fastlane.tools`) for more detailed information and examples.

The next section will explore ChatOps and how to include chat tools in team conversations in order to accelerate the mobile DevOps life cycle.

ChatOps for mobile DevOps collaboration

In today's fast-paced world of software development, effective collaboration and communication are key to achieving seamless mobile DevOps. With the rise of remote work and distributed teams, having a reliable and feature-rich platform that fosters real-time interaction is crucial.

ChatOps is a collaborative approach that brings together development, operations, and other teams by using chat platforms as the central hub for communication and automation. It enables seamless collaboration and integrates various tools, making it easier to manage the software development and deployment processes, as shown in the following figure:

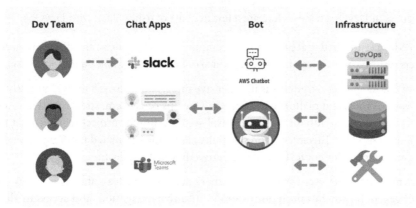

Figure 9.8 – How ChatOps works

Collaborating on mobile DevOps projects can be made more efficient and transparent by implementing ChatOps. This will improve communication and enable faster decision-making within the development team.

The benefits that can be derived from ChatOps are as follows:

- Communication and the deployment of bots for automated tasks improve the agility of cross-functional teams, resulting in a shorter time to resolution.

- ChatOps allows us to combine skilled workers across various fields into a team without affecting organizational structures.

- Automation: Integrating bots is one of the most important achievements. They are our helpers that perform tasks according to programmed commands. In this way, bots can be assigned functions such as the search and deployment of code, and server reset, drastically reducing the time spent on an issue.

Together, let's explore various tools and services that can aid in implementing ChatOps for our mobile DevOps processes.

Slack

Slack (`https://slack.com/`) is a popular communication tool known for its versatility and integration capabilities. Slack proves to be a powerful tool for ChatOps in mobile DevOps collaboration. Utilizing Slack for DevOps, also known as **SlackOps**, is the practice of utilizing the popular team collaboration tool Slack to streamline and enhance communication, collaboration, and automation within DevOps processes. DevOps is an approach that combines software **development** (**Dev**) and IT **operations** (**Ops**) to foster a culture of collaboration, CI/CD, and automation. SlackOps takes advantage of Slack's real-time messaging, channels, integrations, and bots to improve the efficiency and effectiveness of DevOps teams. Here are a few benefits of using Slack with DevOps:

- It provides a centralized space for teams to communicate, share ideas, and discuss project updates. It offers real-time messaging and voice and video calling, allowing quick and efficient collaboration.

- One of Slack's greatest strengths is its extensive integration ecosystem. It seamlessly connects with various tools and platforms used in the DevOps ecosystem, such as GitHub Actions for CI/CD pipelines, GitHub for version control systems, Jira for project management tools, and monitoring services. This integration capability allows for automated notifications and updates, reducing the need for context-switching across different applications.

- Slack's mobile app delivers a smooth user experience, enabling team members to stay connected and engaged. It provides push notifications, intuitive navigation, and access to all essential features, ensuring uninterrupted collaboration regardless of location.

Mobile DevOps teams can use Slack to simplify workflows, automate the release process, share the test results, and stay productive.

AWS Chatbot

AWS Chatbot (`https://aws.amazon.com/chatbot/`), a service provided by **Amazon Web Services** (**AWS**), aims to streamline these processes by integrating them with popular chat platforms. It can integrate with popular messaging services such as Slack, Microsoft Teams, and Amazon Chime. You need to choose the messaging service you want to use and connect AWS Chatbot to it. This will enable you to receive notifications and alerts from AWS services in your messaging service.

To begin, it's important to create an AWS Chatbot within your AWS account. This can easily be done by accessing the AWS Management Console and selecting the AWS Chatbot service. From there, you can create a new chatbot and customize its settings according to your needs. Keep in mind that AWS Chatbot offers several advantages, including the following:

- Integrates seamlessly with popular chat platforms such as Slack, Microsoft Teams, and Amazon Chime. This integration lets teams receive real-time notifications, alerts, and updates directly in their preferred chat environment, reducing context switching and keeping everyone informed.

- Teams can define custom workflows for ChatOps, automating repetitive tasks and facilitating collaboration. By using chat commands, team members can perform actions on AWS resources, retrieve information, initiate deployments, and execute predefined scripts. This capability empowers teams to efficiently manage their infrastructure without leaving the chat environment.

In conclusion, adopting mobile DevOps best practices is a crucial step toward achieving streamlined and high-quality mobile application development. By combining the expertise of developers, test engineers, release specialists, and other stakeholders, organizations can accelerate the development and deployment process, resulting in faster delivery times and improved user experiences.

Summary

In this chapter, we focused on the best practices of mobile DevOps to accelerate the development and release process of high-quality mobile applications. By combining the expertise of developers, test engineers, release experts, and other stakeholders, organizations can streamline the mobile app development process and deliver frequent updates to customers, thereby enhancing both speed and quality.

In this chapter, you gained essential skills in the best practices for CI/CD, mobile app versioning, IaC, configuration management, A/B testing, remote and dependency caching, parallel CI builds, fastlane automation, API mocking, and ChatOps collaboration. These skills will empower you to excel in mobile app development and streamline your processes effectively.

In the next chapter, we'll discuss how platform engineering and **developer experience** (**DevX**) can increase productivity.

Part 4:
Moving Beyond Mobile DevOps and the Future of DevOps

The future of Mobile DevOps is likely to involve a continued focus on improving the speed and quality of mobile app development. This will likely involve the use of newer technologies and practices that help to improve the speed and quality of mobile app development.

This part has the following chapters:

- *Chapter 10, Improving Productivity with Developer Experience and Platform Engineering*
- *Chapter 11, Predicting the Future of Mobile DevOps*

10
Improving Productivity with Developer Experience and Platform Engineering

Mobile developers are the cornerstone of many companies and organizations, and having a dedicated team to understand their needs and provide the best possible experience is critical to success and improving their productivity, especially while the team is scaling and the company is growing. This is where **developer experience (DX)**, **internal developer platform (IDP)**, and **platform engineering (PE)** teams come in.

In this chapter, we will cover the following topics:

- The concepts of DX and IDP
- The importance of having a DX and IDP team
- The relationship between Mobile DevOps and DX teams
- The concepts, benefits, and principles of PE
- The difference between DevOps engineering, site reliability engineering, and PE

In today's mobile app development landscape, delivering high-quality, innovative, and user-friendly apps is not just about coding, testing, and releasing the app. Mobile DevOps teams need to manage a complex set of activities, as we discussed in the previous chapters, including **Continuous Integration and Delivery (CI/CD)**, release orchestration, monitoring, and analytics. Investing in DX can help Mobile DevOps teams to streamline and automate these activities, leading to improved app quality, faster **time-to-market (TTM)**, and better team productivity.

It's not only about tooling, processes, and activities; the developer's happiness and productivity should be the most important goal of the DX team.

Let's take a deeper dive into DX and learn more about what it means.

What is DX?

DX describes the overall experience that mobile developers have with tools or platforms. In order to increase developer adoption, engagement, and retention, DX focuses on creating positive experiences for mobile developers.

It has become increasingly important to have a DX team for companies working with mobile developers at scale and remotely. This ensures mobile developers have access to up-to-date tools and resources and also provides the organization with valuable feedback and insights that can be used to enhance mobile apps and services and make mobile developers happier.

DX is an approach to thinking about engineering excellence and maximizing engineering performance by increasing the capacity and performance of individuals and the team as a whole.

Organizations can take several steps in order to involve DX in their Mobile DevOps culture. This can include providing access to the necessary tools and processes, creating an open and collaborative environment, and encouraging a culture of continuous learning and improvement.

Additionally, organizations can focus on providing resources and support to mobile developers, as well as recognizing their achievements, in order to further establish a positive DX.

Ensuring a good DX in the Mobile DevOps culture is essential for organizations in order to reap the numerous benefits that it can bring, such as a *reduced TTM, improved collaboration between teams,* and *the ability to attract and retain top talent.*

Organizations should focus on providing access to the right tools and processes, creating an open and collaborative environment, promoting a culture of continuous learning and improvement, and providing resources and support to mobile developers in order to accomplish this.

What does a DX team do?

The DX team's role is based on three pillars: understanding developer needs, creating user-centric solutions, and improving developer interactions. As described in the following figure, the goal of the DX team is to improve the productivity, efficiency, and satisfaction of developers who use their platform:

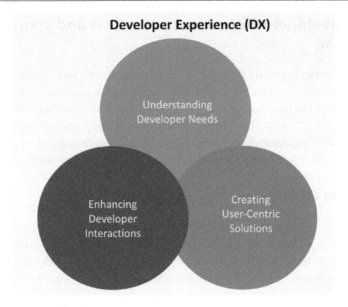

Figure 10.1 – The focus of DX

The DX team represents and advocates for developers within the company, prioritizing their needs and experience. It provides technical support and develops tools and interfaces that simplify the development process and improve application performance.

Understanding developer needs

The main purpose of a DX team is to understand the needs of mobile developers in order to ensure that the organization is creating the best possible experience for its mobile developers.

This involves examining the current tools and services being used by mobile developers and comprehending the problems they face when using them. By having a clear and comprehensive understanding of the needs of mobile developers, the DX team can come up with tailored solutions and services that meet those needs.

Creating user-centric solutions by organizing the workflow

Once the needs of mobile developers are identified, the DX team can start to create user-centric solutions. This means the team will design software and services that are tailored to the needs of mobile developers and look for ways to make the experience more intuitive and enjoyable. By designing services and software that are tailored to the needs of mobile developers, the team can ensure that mobile developers have the best possible experience when working with the organization.

Enhancing developer interactions with clear and standardized communication

The DX team also works to ensure that mobile developers have a positive interaction with the organization. This can include providing mobile developers with the resources they need to succeed, as well as ensuring that mobile developers have a good experience when working with the organization's products and services. Furthermore, the team will look for ways to create a more positive and productive relationship between the organization and its mobile developers, such as doing regular surveys asking them for their feedback regarding the process, tools, and company objectives.

DX and Mobile DevOps

The DX team can offer an *invaluable understanding of the needs of mobile developers*, which can help to ensure that all team members are on the same page. It can also act as a *bridge between mobile developers, product managers, and executives, helping to ensure that everyone's needs are met*. This can help to create an environment where all team members are working together in order to develop successful mobile apps.

DX encompasses all aspects of a developer's interaction with a mobile development platform or ecosystem. Here are some key responsibilities of the DX team:

- **Onboarding support**: Providing mobile developers with the appropriate materials, training, and business documentation to assist with the onboarding process of newcomers or joiners. This will enable them to get involved quickly and not waste time and effort learning about the business or the code.

- **Documentation**: Comprehensive and clear documentation is essential for mobile developers to understand how to use libraries, APIs, SDKs, frameworks, and other tools and processes. Documentation should be easy to find, read, and understand, with examples and explanations for common use cases.

- **Tools and SDKs**: The tools, libraries, APIs, and SDKs provided by a platform should be intuitive and easy to use, with clear documentation and examples. The tools should help mobile developers automate repetitive tasks, speed up development and release, and provide insights into code quality and performance.

- **Testing**: Testing and debugging tools should be easy to use, comprehensive, and reliable. Mobile developers should be able to identify and resolve issues quickly and debug code efficiently.

- **Performance and scalability**: The DX team should focus on the performance of mobile apps, and also the scalability of backend services.

- **Security and compliance**: The DX team should provide strong security and compliance guidance, such as data encryption, access controls, and auditing. It should comply with industry standards and regulations, and provide clear guidelines for secure development practices to mobile developers across the company.

Learn more about how the mobile DX team at Slack keeps mobile developers in flow at `https://slack.engineering/Mobile-developer-experience-at-slack/`.

After exploring the concept behind DX, let's talk about the relationship between an IDP and Mobile DevOps.

What is an IDP?

An IDP (`https://internaldeveloperplatform.org/`) is all about how to best equip your mobile development team with the tools and resources they need to work efficiently and effectively.

In my opinion, as depicted in the following screenshot, an IDP is a subset of DX, which is a collection of tools and technologies that binds DX together. IDPs enhance developer productivity, improve DX, reduce manual operations, lower costs, and lower maintenance overhead for teams. They enable developer self-service while keeping the cognitive load low:

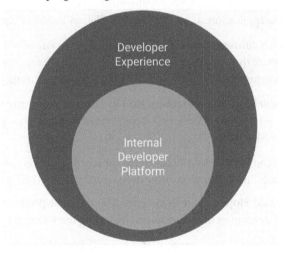

Figure 10.2 – DX versus IDP

As we discussed in the first chapter, Mobile DevOps is a set of practices that enables organizations to build, test, release, and monitor mobile applications in a secure and cost-effective way. To ensure maximum developer productivity, it is important to invest in the right tools, processes, and practices.

This includes investing in automation tools, setting up an agile development environment, and providing access to the latest technologies. They should also utilize techniques such as CI/CD to automate development and release cycles as much as possible.

For Mobile DevOps, it is important to ensure that you have the right tools and processes in place. This includes an automated testing framework, as well as a mobile device lab that allows mobile developers to quickly test and push out updates to their applications.

> **Note**
>
> Learn more about the Netflix journey in developer productivity at `https://www.droidcon.com/2022/06/28/netflix-gradle-a-journey-in-developer-productivity/`, how Uber does developer productivity engineering at `https://www.youtube.com/watch?v=YdmzVzxz9DI`, and how DoorDash does developer productivity engineering at `https://www.youtube.com/watch?v=MN9U-JmRFJA`.

The IDP and DX can solve a number of pain points faced by organizations.

An IDP reduces cognitive load across the organization and allows mobile developers to self-serve without abstracting context or obscuring the underlying technology, including the following:

- **Mobile CI/CD infrastructure orchestration and release management**: Managing the tools and processes that enable these stages to occur. This includes tools for building and testing the application and tools for automating the deployment process, as well as managing the release of new versions of the application, as we discussed in *Chapter 6, Mobile App Release Management*.

- **Mobile application configuration**: The settings and preferences that can be customized by the user to customize the app's appearance and behavior. Among these options are language selection, theme customization, notification settings, privacy settings, and user preferences.

- **Managing the development environment**: Developers spend the majority of their time setting up their environment, and a well-designed environment has a significant impact on productivity and code quality.

  In this way, teams can ensure that the development environment is tailored to their needs and contains all the tools and integrations they need to accomplish their goals.

  There are different development environments as a service or product which provide us with a fully configured development environment, including the following:

  - **Coder** (`https://coder.com/`): This is a self-hosted remote development platform for shifting software development from local machines to on-premises and public cloud infrastructure. Build code on powerful servers and onboard new developers in minutes, all while keeping source code and data secure.

  - **GitHub Codespaces** (`https://github.com/features/codespaces`): This is a fully configured development environment in the cloud that starts in seconds from GitHub using Visual Studio Code, Jupyter, or JetBrains with the editor, terminal, debugger, version control, settings sync, and all of your extensions. Whether you are working in a browser or on your desktop, you can do it from any device. That's all there is to it.

  - **Gitpod** (`https://www.gitpod.io/`): This provides fully initialized, perfectly configured developer environments for any type of software project. Any team member can run code using Gitpod. By configuring environments once, PE teams enable developer self-service.

In my opinion, the team may face difficulties if it decides to move to a cloud-based development environment because mobile app development requires special environments, tools, and SDKs, but Uber's developer platform recently built a monorepo-based remote development platform using Kubernetes, which is a good example of that (`https://www.uber.com/en-DE/blog/devpod-improving-developer-productivity-at-uber/`).

- **Managing secrets**: Storing passwords, API keys, and other credentials securely and ensuring that they remain protected. By managing secrets effectively, sensitive data is protected from unauthorized access.

  There are different secret management tools and services that can be used, such as the following:

  - **HashiCorp Vault** (`https://www.vaultproject.io/`): Secure, store, and tightly control access to tokens, passwords, certificates, and encryption keys for protecting secrets and other sensitive data using a UI, CLI, or HTTP API.

  - **AWS Secrets Manager** (`https://aws.amazon.com/secrets-manager/`): Keeps track of database credentials, API keys, and other secrets throughout their life cycle, allowing you to retrieve, rotate, and store them as needed.

  - **Doppler** (`https://www.doppler.com/`): Allows developers and security teams to keep secrets and app configurations synchronized and secure across devices, environments, and team members.

As we discussed in the previous chapters, at scale, the responsibilities of all of the aforementioned points should be managed by a dedicated team, and this team can be the IDP and the DX teams.

The IDP optimizes the development process so that mobile apps can be developed and released much more efficiently.

This involves looking at the development environment, tools, and processes to find ways of improving overall productivity. This could include things such as automating processes, introducing new tools, or restructuring the mobile development team.

As a result of productivity engineering, mobile developers are able to spend more time on actual development work and less time on mundane tasks. By doing this, you will be able to improve your team's morale and speed up development cycles.

The Netflix **Mobile Productivity** (**MoPro**) team, for example, helps engineers worldwide create Netflix mobile applications quickly. In order to achieve this, it uses tools and infrastructure that optimize the DX. With sophisticated automated testing and productivity solutions, it supports a culture of experimentation, autonomy, and ownership.

To understand more about developer productivity, there is a framework called **SPACE** (`https://queue.acm.org/detail.cfm?id=3454124`) that captures some of the most important aspects, including the following:

- Satisfaction and well-being
- Performance
- Communication and collaboration
- Efficiency and flow

Organizations and teams can make better decisions by recognizing and measuring productivity with more than just one dimension.

There are a variety of tools and techniques that mobile developers can use to improve their productivity. This includes analytics and collaboration platforms such as the following:

- **Backstage** (`http://backstage.io`): This is an open platform for building developer portals. With Backstage's centralized software catalog, you can restore order to your microservices and infrastructure and enable your product team to ship high-quality code quickly.

- **LinearB** (`https://linearb.io/developer-experience/`): This is a platform for improving the DX with workflow automation and optimizing your delivery pipeline with tools your mobile developers love.

- **Compass** (`https://developer.atlassian.com/cloud/compass/`): This is a DX platform that brings your distributed software architecture and the teams collaborating on them together in a single, unified place.

- **Okay** (`https://www.okayhq.com/`): This is a platform to help you to build your own queries and dashboards on top of developer tools such as Jira, GitHub, PagerDuty, and many more.

By using these tools and techniques, mobile developers can streamline their workflow and eliminate time-consuming tasks.

Besides using productivity tools, mobile developers should also optimize their processes. The development process could be broken down into smaller tasks, or more efficient processes could be created for code reviews and bug fixes. Mobile developers can maximize their productivity by optimizing their processes systematically.

The benefits of IDP engineering

By employing an IDP, mobile developers can increase their productivity by improving their efficiency. It can also help them identify and fix errors faster, as well as save time by automating repetitive tasks. Additionally, an IDP can help to reduce costs associated with long development cycles, such as missed deadlines and delays.

The concept of developer productivity is fraught with misconceptions and myths, which can lead to poor decisions. Among them are the following:

- **A common myth is that working longer hours will result in higher productivity**. It is often the opposite that is true in reality. Burnout, as well as decreasing motivation and productivity, can result from working too many hours.

- There is no doubt that distractions can hinder productivity, but it is also important to recognize that breaks and downtime are equally important for preventing burnout and maintaining focus. **Work-life balance is crucial**.

- **People often assume that the best mobile developers work alone and don't require any help or collaboration from others**. In fact, collaboration and teamwork can lead to better results and increased productivity.

In light of DX and IDP teams, it is time to get to know more about the new era that is PE, and how it works with the IDP.

What is PE?

The concept of PE refers to the process of defining, building, and maintaining a platform that will serve as the foundation for the development, release, and expansion of the software.

This includes designing the infrastructure and **infrastructure as code** (**IaC**), setting up CI/CD pipelines, and automating the testing and release process.

PE plays an essential role in ensuring that Mobile DevOps platforms succeed.

In order to ensure that the platform is optimized for building and releasing mobile applications, PE works closely with the mobile development team. As part of this process, we set up the necessary tools and frameworks for building, testing, and deploying the application, as well as making sure that the platform is scalable and reliable.

The PE team is also responsible for monitoring and maintaining the platform. Among the tasks are monitoring the platform's performance and stability, identifying and fixing any problems, and implementing upgrades and updates as necessary.

The principles of PE include the following:

- The ability to handle increasing loads and usage
- Maintaining the platform's availability and functionality
- Keeping the platform and its users safe from malicious attacks and data breaches is the responsibility of security teams
- Keeping the platform up to date and easily maintained
- The platform should be reusable by multiple teams and applications

In many cases, platform engineers are part of larger engineering teams, so it's important to consider how the team communicates and how the process works. As a result, it becomes more like a centralized product team focusing on its internal platform customers, such as mobile developers, testers, and product managers.

In PE, common engineering resources are consolidated into one internal tool/platform to simplify the development of software.

Platform engineers' technical skills should also include cloud computing, containerization, IaC, automation, and monitoring expertise. Programming language and tool proficiency may also be required.

Nowadays, there is a large community of platform engineers (`https://platformengineering. org/`), but most of the topics seem to be mostly cloud-computing- and Kubernetes-related. However, I believe this will change over time as more topics related to mobile will be added and supported.

Benefits of PE

With PE, companies are able to develop and deploy software solutions that meet their needs more quickly and cost-effectively.

Furthermore, PE allows companies to update their software solutions quickly and easily, keeping them ahead of their competitors. Additionally, it reduces costs because it eliminates the need for manual coding, testing, and debugging.

For a good example of PE at scale, you can read about the history behind **Wise's PE** (`https:// www.wise.jobs/2021/03/25/introduction-to-the-wise-platform-team/`).

In order to ensure effective PE, it is essential to follow best practices. This includes ensuring that *the app's architecture is scalable and modular, making it easy to add new features and functionalities as the app grows*. Platform engineers should also ensure that *the database is properly designed and optimized for performance and that the app's data is stored securely*.

It is also important to regularly test the app's backend to identify and fix any issues before they affect the user experience.

Finally, platform engineers should stay up to date with the latest technologies and trends in mobile app development to ensure that their apps remain competitive and relevant.

Platform engineers will become even more critical as mobile app usage continues to grow. As mobile apps become more complex and feature-rich, new tools and frameworks will be needed to handle the increased workload. New technologies, including 5G, **artificial intelligence** (**AI**), cloud computing, **augmented reality** (**AR**), and **virtual reality** (**VR**), will provide platform engineers with new opportunities to innovate and create compelling mobile experiences.

The difference between platform engineers, Mobile DevOps engineers, and site reliability engineers for mobile

With more organizations adopting Mobile DevOps, it is becoming increasingly important to understand the differences between three related roles—Mobile DevOps engineer, site reliability engineer, and platform engineer.

Each of these roles requires automation and infrastructure to deploy, maintain, and monitor software. In spite of this, each role is unique in terms of responsibilities and focus.

Site reliability engineers, DevOps engineers, and platform engineers all play crucial roles in mobile app development. The specific focus of each role depends on the needs of the organization, and each role plays a crucial role in the success of a mobile app.

Platform engineers for mobile apps

Mobile app platform engineers build and maintain the platform that runs mobile apps, as we mentioned previously. Among their responsibilities are the following:

- Building and maintaining the platform services for running mobile apps, such as databases, caching systems, and message queues
- Developing tools to automate common mobile app development tasks
- Optimizing the performance of mobile app systems by fine-tuning platform services
- Designing and implementing the security and compliance features for mobile app systems
- Collaborating with mobile app mobile developers to ensure that the platform services are designed and built to meet the needs of mobile app development

The key metrics for platform engineers are uptime, scalability, developer satisfaction, time-to-market, security, infrastructure cost efficiency, and mobile app user satisfaction.

DevOps engineers for mobile apps

In mobile app DevOps, DevOps engineers streamline the process of developing and deploying mobile apps. To ensure that code is delivered to users as quickly and reliably as possible, they work closely with mobile app developers to automate the deployment and testing of mobile app systems.

DevOps engineers should be familiar with mobile app development frameworks such as React Native and Flutter. In addition, they should be familiar with CI/CD tools such as GitHub Actions, GitLab, and Bitrise.

In addition to automating, and managing configurations, Mobile DevOps engineers have expertise in security. They automate app delivery, set up CI/CD pipelines, and manage cloud infrastructure for mobile apps. Among their day-to-day responsibilities are the following:

- Delivering mobile apps through CI/CD pipelines

- Assuring code quality by building and maintaining systems for testing and integration

- Resolving incidents that arise from mobile apps

- Streamlining mobile app delivery by collaborating with mobile app developers

In addition to their technical skills, Mobile DevOps engineers must have excellent problem-solving skills to identify and resolve issues that arise during the release process.

The key metrics for DevOps are frequency, lead time, **Mean Time To Recovery (MTTR)**, and **Change Failure Rate (CFR)**.

Site reliability engineers for mobile apps

The mobile site reliability engineer is responsible for ensuring the reliability, availability, and performance of mobile applications. As part of their role, they collaborate closely with the development team to identify potential performance issues and optimize the application for maximum efficiency. Additionally, they must be familiar with monitoring and logging tools such as Prometheus, Grafana, and Elasticsearch.

Their expertise includes monitoring and managing mobile app performance, automating repetitive tasks, and troubleshooting problems. Among their responsibilities are the following:

- Establishing monitoring and alerting systems for detecting issues before they affect users

- Creating and maintaining mobile app data backup and **disaster recovery (DR)** systems

- Designing and building scalable, reliable, and fault-tolerant systems in collaboration with mobile app developers

The key metrics for site reliability engineers are app stability, crash rate, user engagement, response time, and server uptime.

While all three roles require collaboration with mobile app development teams, their specific focus varies. The goal of site reliability engineers for mobile apps is to ensure the reliability, scalability, and performance of mobile app systems in collaboration with mobile developers. To streamline mobile app delivery processes, DevOps engineers work with mobile developers. Platform engineers design and build the platform that runs mobile apps in collaboration with mobile developers.

Is my company in need of DX, an IDP, or PE?

In order to remain competitive in the digital age, businesses need DX, IDP, and PE teams. PE allows companies to create secure, scalable, and robust software solutions. With PE, companies can also develop and release software solutions more quickly and cost-effectively while having more control over the development process that meets their needs.

When companies take advantage of DX, IDP, and PE teams, they can reduce their costs. If you wish to remain competitive in the digital age, PE may be the answer for your business.

To invest in PE, the right tools must be chosen, a strong infrastructure must be built, and cross-team collaboration is required. To ensure success, Mobile DevOps teams should evaluate their PE strategy regularly.

Summary

Any organization that works with mobile developers should have a DX team. In addition to improving their morale and loyalty, it ensures mobile developers have the best experience with the company's products and services. In order to set up a DX team, meticulous planning and execution are necessary, and the team should be equipped with the necessary resources and tools.

Additionally, DX teams can take on a variety of projects, from creating new tools to providing support and guidance.

In this chapter, we covered the following topics:

- The concepts of DX and an IDP
- The importance of having a DX and IDP team
- The relation between Mobile DevOps and DX teams
- The concepts, benefits, and principles of PE
- The difference between DevOps engineering, site reliability engineering, and PE

For Mobile DevOps, it is important to ensure that you have the right tools and processes in place. This includes an automated testing framework, as well as a mobile device lab that allows mobile developers to quickly test and push out updates to their applications.

Ultimately, a DX team will help a company or organization become more successful in its development efforts by providing a better experience to mobile developers. Depending on how well a DX team is set up and executed, it can be a valuable asset to any organization. The DX team can be used for a variety of projects, from developing new tools and resources to responding to feature requests.

PE allows companies to create secure, scalable, and robust software platforms and solutions. With PE, companies can also develop and release software solutions more quickly and cost-effectively while having more control over the development process that meets their needs.

Finally, site reliability engineers for mobile apps are dedicated to ensuring that mobile app systems are reliable, scalable, and performant in collaboration with mobile developers. DevOps engineers work with mobile developers to streamline mobile app delivery processes. Platform engineers collaborate with mobile developers to design and build the platform used to run mobile apps.

In the next chapter, we will be discussing future trends in mobile app development and Mobile DevOps, and we will conclude with a summary of our book as well as our future predictions.

11

Predicting the Future of Mobile DevOps

In this book, we have discussed how mobile DevOps is a rapidly expanding field that is transforming the way mobile apps are developed, tested, and released. It is a disruptive form of technology that has revolutionized the way we approach mobile development, enabling teams to develop and release mobile applications at a much quicker pace than ever before.

In this chapter, we will cover the following topics:

- Future trends in mobile app development
- Future trends in mobile DevOps
- *Mobile DevOps Playbook* recap

Mobile DevOps provides organizations with the flexibility to adjust quickly to changing market conditions and customer demands, allowing them to develop and release mobile applications faster and more efficiently. Mobile DevOps solutions must be able to keep up with rapid changes in mobile technologies.

The next few years will be filled with mobile app development trends. Let's explore them together and look at how developers and businesses can stay ahead.

Mobile app development trends

Here we are in 2023; we're in the middle of another year, and the mobile app development industry is undergoing rapid changes. Let's take a closer look.

Cross-platform mobile development is on the rise

The mobile development industry has been on the rise in recent years, and this trend is expected to continue. In particular, more companies are realizing the potential of cross-platform mobile development.

Cross-platform mobile development also makes it easier to implement new features and updates by using a single code base; developers can quickly and easily add new features and updates to an app, as opposed to having to update multiple versions of the app for different operating systems.

Several factors will lead to the rise of cross-platform mobile development in the future, including cost-effectiveness, faster **time-to-market** (**TTM**), and consistency.

We discussed the various cross-platform frameworks in *Chapter 2, Understanding the Mobile Ecosystem*. But in my opinion, Flutter will gain traction in the next few years because it is not only cross-platform but is also an ecosystem that allows users to build six apps from a single code base, targeting different operating systems and devices.

Developing mobile apps with low code

The development of apps using low code is becoming increasingly popular since developers can create mobile applications with minimal or no coding skills. Low-code mobile applications are a great way to quickly and easily create mobile apps without writing much code. By using drag-and-drop components and pre-built functions, developers can quickly create a mobile app with lots of functionality without having to know much coding.

In my opinion, cloud services will be a significant part of the low-code era; for instance, **AWS Amplify** (`https://aws.amazon.com/amplify/`), with which you can create a full stack mobile app in hours and create an **Amazon Web Services** (**AWS**) backend for your iOS, Android, Flutter, or React Native app with authentication, data, storage, and more integration with other AWS services in minutes.

The advantages of low-code mobile app development include faster development, reduced development costs, and a simplified development process, but while there are advantages to low-code mobile app development, there are also some potential disadvantages that businesses should be aware of. Here are a few to consider:

- The customization potential of low-code platforms is limited due to pre-built templates and components. As a result, it may be difficult to create unique features or **user experiences** (**UXs**).

- It may be difficult for businesses to switch to a different low-code platform if they become locked into one.

- Due to their reliance on pre-built components that have not been thoroughly tested for security vulnerabilities, low-code platforms may be less secure than custom applications.

- For more complex applications, low-code platforms may still require some learning curve to use effectively, despite their ease of use.

Low-code mobile app development can indeed be a great way for businesses to create simple mobile apps quickly, but they should take into account the potential drawbacks before they decide which platform to use.

Security is getting more important

Mobile app development is becoming increasingly security-conscious as mobile apps grow in popularity. Developing secure apps is a must for developers.

In order to do this, developers must be up to date on the latest security tools, frameworks, processes, and technologies. To further secure their apps, developers should incorporate additional security measures such as encryption, session management, input validation to mitigate SQL injection, **cross-site scripting (XSS)**, and **two-factor authentication (2FA)**.

In *Chapter 8, Keeping Mobile Apps and DevOps Secure*, we discussed in detail how DevSecOps is used to keep mobile DevOps secure, how developers consider security at every stage of development, and how they integrate security into the mobile DevOps process. Since mobile apps are becoming increasingly complex, I believe that automation with security will become increasingly important.

Increase in the impact of AI and ML

Using **Artificial Intelligence (AI)** and **Machine Learning(ML)** is becoming increasingly popular, as we've noticed recently that most apps are now using AI in a range of different business domains in order to accomplish their goals.

With AI and ML, mobile developers can create apps that are more intuitive and user-friendly, as well as apps with enhanced functionality. AI and ML can also be used to create predictive analytics, which can provide personalized recommendations to users.

To stay competitive, developers should become familiar with AI and ML technologies, which have the potential to revolutionize mobile app development.

It is my prediction that AI will become more ingrained in businesses this year and in upcoming years and that tech companies will compete fiercely in the market. It is already evident in today's world that a wave of different tools, platforms, and apps is already incorporating AI.

Increase in the usage of cloud computing

Mobile app development increasingly relies on cloud computing to create apps that can run on multiple platforms and devices and improve mobile performance.

As a result of cloud computing's scalability and flexibility, mobile developers can adjust their apps to accommodate increased usage or new features as needed. Developers can use AWS to build, test, and deploy complex business apps on mobile devices using its cloud services.

As an example, AWS offers a variety of cloud services that can be integrated into mobile apps as backend services, such as the following:

- **AWS Amplify** (`https://aws.amazon.com/amplify/`) provides a serverless backend infrastructure that scales automatically, eliminating the need for developers to manage server infrastructure. It abstracts away the complexities of backend development, allowing developers to focus on building frontend experiences and delivering value to end users.

- **Amazon Cognito** (`https://aws.amazon.com/cognito/`) provides a secure and scalable user authentication and authorization service. It enables mobile app developers to easily add user sign-up, sign-in, and access control functionalities to their apps.

- **Amazon Pinpoint** (`https://aws.amazon.com/pinpoint/`) is a customer engagement and analytics service for mobile apps. It helps you send targeted, personalized messages to your app users via multiple channels, including push notifications, SMS, and email. These are only a few examples of cloud services for mobile apps.

The growing importance of UX

Mobile app development increasingly emphasizes UX. It is essential that developers create user-friendly and intuitive apps that are easy to navigate and understand by users. The UI should be well designed, clear, and concise, and incorporate voice commands, gestures, and animations.

UX includes factors such as how the app is designed, how it is used, how accessible it is, and how responsive it is. These factors all contribute to creating an app that people will remember.

By focusing on UX, developers can develop apps that are successful and popular worldwide with millions of users.

Therefore, it is imperative that developers focus on UX when developing their apps. The UX of an app can make it easier to use and more enjoyable, or it can lead to users abandoning it. AI and ML can play a significant role in UX, as we discussed previously in understanding user needs and expectations, as well as developing an app that is easy to use and aesthetically pleasing. UX practices should also be incorporated into the development process, as they can help to create an app that is both efficient and enjoyable.

The growing impact of AR and VR

In recent years, **virtual reality** (**VR**) and **augmented reality** (**AR**) have become increasingly popular in the gaming industry, as well as in commercial and consumer settings. Through mobile apps, businesses and developers can explore and take advantage of the endless possibilities this advanced technology offers.

As a result, AR and VR are becoming increasingly evident, and their potential for impact is becoming increasingly evident. AR and VR will continue to attract a great deal of attention and growth as these technologies have the potential to revolutionize how we interact with the world around us.

As we mentioned previously, AR and VR can enhance the UX of mobile apps. Mobile devices make it easy for developers and businesses to create immersive, interactive, and engaging applications. It is easier for users to interact with their environment, resulting in a more enjoyable and interactive experience.

Increasing use of voice apps

Voice apps are becoming increasingly popular in mobile app development. By creating voice-enabled apps, developers can provide users with a more intuitive and user-friendly experience. Voice apps can be used to provide users with voice-controlled access to features such as search, navigation, and scheduling.

Additionally, voice apps can be used to create interactive tutorials and simulations, which can be used to teach users how to use an app in a more efficient and effective way. Voice apps are an invaluable tool for mobile app development, and developers should take advantage of their many benefits.

The growth of IoT integration

There is no doubt that the **Internet of Things** (**IoT**) is becoming one of the most important parts of mobile application development. Through the integration of IoT devices into apps, developers can create apps that are more intelligent and provide a more personalized experience to consumers.

With IoT integration growing, smart home devices are becoming increasingly common, such as lighting systems, thermostats, and security cameras. With a smartphone app, for example, you can control your lights and security system remotely.

IoT integration looks very bright for the future, as IoT devices become more affordable and powerful. Consequently, more complex applications can be developed, such as predictive maintenance and autonomous vehicles. AI and ML will also be integrated into IoT.

As we discuss the future of mobile application development and how to prepare for mobile DevOps, organizations need to understand the needs and challenges of mobile application development, the potential solutions available, and the impact of emerging technologies. To implement the right mobile DevOps strategy, organizations must understand the needs of mobile developers, the challenges and complexity of mobile application development, and the impact of emerging technologies.

By leveraging the right tools and techniques, developers will be able to build powerful, reliable applications that satisfy their users' needs.

To take advantage of the opportunities presented by Mobile DevOps, developers need to be aware of trends and technologies that will shape their future.

Mobile DevOps trends

To stay ahead of the curve, organizations must begin planning for the future of mobile DevOps in order to remain competitive.

As we move forward, I believe the following will be the goal:

To achieve cost optimization, performance efficiency, increasing reliability, and speeding up releases, business teams and IT leaders must understand Mobile DevOps.

The following predictions are for mobile DevOps in 2023 and beyond.

Automating orchestrating of mobile releases will grow

Continuous delivery (CD) and release orchestration are important trends in mobile app development. In addition to maintaining quality and reliability, release management practices allow developers to build, test, and deploy mobile apps quickly and efficiently. In order to reduce costs, improve reliability, and speed up the release process, the automation of deployment and testing processes is expected to become increasingly important.

The rise in cloud-based infrastructure

In my opinion, this is the most important trend for mobile DevOps; as we discussed previously, mobile apps always need the latest hardware infrastructure operating systems and mobile devices.

As we all know, building iOS apps always require the use of the latest Apple chips, so I expect more companies to use cloud-based infrastructure so that they do not have to worry about maintaining the infrastructure and can focus on developing their apps instead. As a result, app development will be faster and more efficient, as well as scalability, performance, and testing being improved.

A growing need for automation

Automation is crucial in mobile DevOps, as it will help to speed up the development process, allowing developers to focus on the tasks that require more manual input. This will allow them to focus on more important tasks.

It is important for mobile developers to focus on tasks that matter and not waste their time on useless tasks.

The automation process can be used to release apps to app stores, conduct different types of testing, collect customer feedback, monitor performance, scan for security vulnerabilities, and so on.

In addition to saving time and money, automation also reduces the risk of errors, which can be costly and time-consuming. This increased use of automation can also contribute to better security of mobile applications as well as reduce the time required to complete certain tasks.

The shift-left will become more prevalent

As we discussed in *Chapter 5, Implementing a Robust Mobile App Testing Strategy*, **shifting left** refers to testing earlier in the development process. According to the shift-left or to that, testing should not be the final step of a development process, but rather an ongoing process that takes place throughout the entire development life cycle. Testing earlier allows any issues to be identified and corrected before the project has progressed further in development, reducing both cost and time.

It is obvious that shifting left will lead to cost savings. Team members can avoid having to rework projects if they discover bugs later on in the development cycle. Additionally, shifting left can also improve the customer experience, since software released with fewer bugs is more likely to be well received.

Shifting left can only be implemented if a robust testing process is built into the development process from the start. To ensure the accuracy of the software, automated tests should be conducted throughout the development process, as well as manual tests at various points. For any issues that may arise over time, teams should continue to monitor the software.

Increasing the importance of security and data protection

There can be no overstatement of the importance of security in mobile DevOps. Security and compliance with industry standards and regulations are increasingly important for increasingly complex and interconnected mobile applications.

In mobile DevOps, security and data protection are top priorities.

Mobile DevOps' future is also heavily dependent on security. In order to develop more robust and secure mobile applications, development processes will have to become more robust and secure. As part of this process, secure coding techniques will need to be used, as well as testing and validating applications.

Developers can ensure the security and reliability of their applications by following these processes.

Keeping an eye on the performance of mobile apps

Analyzing analytics will be essential for mobile DevOps teams to understand how users interact with their applications and identify improvement areas, monitor the performance of mobile apps, and diagnose and resolve any issues that arise.

In order to make informed decisions, teams will need tools to capture, analyze, and use data. In order to ensure applications remain reliable and meet user needs, it will be essential to monitor them in production and respond quickly to user feedback.

As a result, I believe AI and ML will also be part of the mobile DevOps strategy, and my dream is to be involved in app monitoring and performance because as we mentioned previously, organizations will consider these in their mobile apps. With AI and ML, tasks can be automated, predictions can be made more accurately, and mobile development costs and time can be reduced.

The rise of AI testing and codeless testing tools

Recent years have seen an increase in the use of AI for software testing. AI-driven codeless testing tools are now widely used to automate software testing and increase test coverage, such as Sofy.ai, Waldo, and Testsigma.

Using AI testing tools, we can automate the writing of test cases, increase test coverage, and reduce the need for manual testing, as we discussed in *Chapter 5, Implementing a Robust Mobile App Testing Strategy*.

Testers can create automated tests using codeless testing tools without having to write a single line of code. This makes testing much simpler and faster since testers do not need to spend time learning how to write code. As tests can be modified quickly when needed, codeless testing tools also allow for greater flexibility.

With AI-driven test automation tools, the software is analyzed, and automated test scripts are generated. Using these tools, testers can automate the testing process and find any problems quickly. In addition to simulating realistic user interactions, AI-driven test automation tools can also be used to test more accurately.

A rise in platform engineering and developer productivity

In 2023 and beyond, I believe that we'll see a shift from DevOps, **site reliability engineering** (**SRE**), and **platform engineering** (**PE**), which we discussed in *Chapter 10, Improving Productivity with Developer Experience and Platform Engineering*.

The term *DevOps* or *DevSecOps* has in the past tried to encompass too much in its job function, so we are now seeing an increasing number of DevOps and DevSecOps teams adopting platforms that streamline tasks such as writing rules and policies, creating pipelines, and coding to automate these tasks.

Rather than overburdening one group with certain tasks, the industry will adopt platforms that empower teams to perform at their best.

Through PE, developer teams can deliver more business value and achieve stronger outcomes.

In order to deliver changes to applications rapidly, mobile DevOps teams need to have a strong DevOps culture.

A future Mobile DevOps toolchain will maximize flow in IT value streams.

In order to meet customers' needs, mobile DevOps plays a critical role in ensuring that the app is developed, tested, and released in a timely manner.

Summary

We have reached the last station in this book and I hope that you have enjoyed it as much as I did and that it has added value to you personally and was able to teach you something that you can take back to your team or organization.

Taking a look at the book as a whole, let's recap what we learned.

From *Chapter 1*, we started addressing the challenges that we face with mobile app development and the concept of mobile DevOps, which entails integrating development and operations (mobile DevOps) practices to improve the efficiency and speed of mobile application development.

And we focus on that to *make sure you don't copy someone else's process* if you found it online. Develop a *strategy and plan that suits the needs of your stakeholders and team members*. Establish a standard process for your mobile DevOps best practices upfront.

Then, in *Chapter 2*, we understood the mobile ecosystem and explored together the various mobile platforms, frameworks, and unique functions of mobile devices to understand the challenges for mobile developers, QA engineers, release engineers, or anyone working in mobile development, since we need to think about how we will be able to tackle all of these challenges by utilizing automation to assist us in building, testing, releasing and monitoring great mobile apps.

Then, in *Chapter 3*, our journey toward mobile DevOps just began, and we discussed the mobile DevOps fundamentals including the concepts of **continuous integration (CI)**, **continuous testing (CT)**, **continuous delivery (CD)**, continuous deployment, and **continuous monitoring (CM)**. Also, we learned the difference between self-hosted and cloud-based CI/CD and the benefits of the cloud. After that, we learned about the checklist for mobile app releases and the concept behind the release train.

After that, in the next chapters, we started the actual implementation of mobile CI/CD and DevOps using different platforms, and we discussed the implementation of a robust testing strategy including different types of testing such as UI, snapshot, performance, and security.

Once the application has been successfully developed and tested, it is ready for release. This was when we discussed the releasing process of the mobile application to Beta testers, QA, or to the app stores and Google Play Store and make it available to users. This included the concept behind code signing, certificates, provisioning profiles, key stores, and more.

After releasing mobile apps, the next step was how to establish monitoring and observability for mobile apps and use that data to provide feedback to development teams. We discussed the different implementations of crash reporting and error monitoring with different options and platforms.

And because security is a crucial factor to take into account, we discussed how to inject security into mobile DevOps and CI/CD with the DevSecOps concept. This included how to train the team for security, which security tools are suitable for our team, and the difference between the security testing types. Also, we discussed the **Open Worldwide Application Security Project (OWASP)** guide for mobile app security.

In *Chapter 9*, we discussed a few mobile DevOps best practices such as ChatOps, upskilling the team, scaled Agile, and A/B testing to improve the speed and quality of mobile app development and deliver high-quality apps to users.

In *Chapter 10*, we discussed the concept of **internal developer platform (IDP)** teams, **developer experience (DX)** teams, the benefits of PE, and the difference between DevOps, SRE, and PE.

Our journey with mobile DevOps has finally reached its end; I hope you enjoyed it. As we discussed, mobile DevOps is expected to become increasingly popular in the coming years as businesses look to maximize the efficiency of their mobile development teams. It's likely that many organizations will have adopted mobile DevOps practices to streamline their mobile development processes. We discussed the trends of mobile app development and mobile DevOps that we should see this year and in the coming years.

There is no silver bullet; you should choose, build, and guide your process according to your needs and expectations.

Happy building!

Index

www.packtpub.com

Subscribe to our online digital library for full access to over 7,000 books and videos, as well as industry leading tools to help you plan your personal development and advance your career. For more information, please visit our website.

Why subscribe?

- Spend less time learning and more time coding with practical eBooks and Videos from over 4,000 industry professionals

- Improve your learning with Skill Plans built especially for you

- Get a free eBook or video every month

- Fully searchable for easy access to vital information

- Copy and paste, print, and bookmark content

Did you know that Packt offers eBook versions of every book published, with PDF and ePub files available? You can upgrade to the eBook version at packtpub.com and as a print book customer, you are entitled to a discount on the eBook copy. Get in touch with us at customercare@packtpub.com for more details.

At www.packtpub.com, you can also read a collection of free technical articles, sign up for a range of free newsletters, and receive exclusive discounts and offers on Packt books and eBooks.

Other Books You May Enjoy

If you enjoyed this book, you may be interested in these other books by Packt:

Azure DevOps Explained

Sjoukje Zaal, Stefano Demiliani, Amit Malik

ISBN: 978-1-80056-351-3

- Get to grips with Azure DevOps
- Find out about project management with Azure Boards
- Understand source code management with Azure Repos
- Build and release pipelines
- Run quality tests in build pipelines
- Use artifacts and integrate Azure DevOps in the GitHub flow
- Discover real-world CI/CD scenarios with Azure DevOps

Learning DevOps - Second Edition

Mikael Krief

ISBN: 978-1-80181-896-4

- Understand the basics of infrastructure as code patterns and practices
- Get an overview of Git command and Git flow
- Install and write Packer, Terraform, and Ansible code for provisioning and configuring cloud infrastructure based on Azure examples
- Use Vagrant to create a local development environment
- Containerize applications with Docker and Kubernetes
- Apply DevSecOps for testing compliance and securing DevOps infrastructure
- Build DevOps CI/CD pipelines with Jenkins, Azure Pipelines, and GitLab CI
- Explore blue-green deployment and DevOps practices for open sources projects

Packt is searching for authors like you

If you're interested in becoming an author for Packt, please visit `authors.packtpub.com` and apply today. We have worked with thousands of developers and tech professionals, just like you, to help them share their insight with the global tech community. You can make a general application, apply for a specific hot topic that we are recruiting an author for, or submit your own idea.

Share Your Thoughts

Now you've finished *Mobile DevOps Playbook*, we'd love to hear your thoughts! Scan the QR code below to go straight to the Amazon review page for this book and share your feedback or leave a review on the site that you purchased it from.

`https://packt.link/r/1803242558`

Your review is important to us and the tech community and will help us make sure we're delivering excellent quality content.

Download a free PDF copy of this book

Thanks for purchasing this book!

Do you like to read on the go but are unable to carry your print books everywhere? Is your eBook purchase not compatible with the device of your choice?

Don't worry, now with every Packt book you get a DRM-free PDF version of that book at no cost.

Read anywhere, any place, on any device. Search, copy, and paste code from your favorite technical books directly into your application.

The perks don't stop there, you can get exclusive access to discounts, newsletters, and great free content in your inbox daily

Follow these simple steps to get the benefits:

1. Scan the QR code or visit the link below

https://packt.link/free-ebook/9781803242552

2. Submit your proof of purchase
3. That's it! We'll send your free PDF and other benefits to your email directly

Made in the USA
Monee, IL
25 October 2023